PREFACE

In 1983 the Royal Society published a Study Group Report on Risk Assessment which has taken its place as a major work of reference. In the interim there have been some developments in the practices discussed in the 1983 report. Perhaps more important has been the increased concern and debate about the methods by which risks are identified and quantified and about organizational arrangements for managing risk. Also since the publication of the 1983 report, life expectancy has increased by two years in the UK (but by a greater amount in many other countries) and there is an
increased awareness of the fact that quality of life is important as well as duration.

Consequently, in 1991 the Council of the Royal Society thought it timely to institute an updated study in which public perception of risk and related considerations would receive greater attention. Council invited Sir Frederick Warner, who chaired the Study Group for the 1983 report, to undertake the organizing of the update.

For three of the main chapters in the 1983 Report a team was invited to contribute an update. They wrote chapters 2, 3 and 4, entitled respectively Estimating Engineering Risks; Toxicity, Toxicology and Nutrition; and Estimation of Risk from Observations on Man.

To fulfil the remit to pay increased attention to public perception of risks, the Study Group turned to two groups of social scientists, whose work has been supported by the Economic and Social Research Council. Their resultant contribution on this and related matters in the social context forms chapters 5 and 6: Risk Perception and Risk Management respectively. These two chapters draw attention to lines of thinking that are likely to be influential in the formation of public policy on many of the issues that surround risk and which deserve the attention of all who are concerned in these matters.

All the contributions were read by members of the Study Group and suggestions for improvement were made. It became apparent, however, that to edit the various contributions into a unified style and with full cross referencing would unduly delay the publication of the report, thereby missing occasions to which it should make a significant input. Moreover, to attempt to resolve all the issues raised, especially those in chapters 5 and 6, would pre-empt the very debate that Council and the contributors themselves wish to encourage.

The Council of the Society, therefore, decided that the Study Group's work should be issued, not as a report of the Society, but as six independent chapters attributed to those listed, as a contribution to the ongoing debate. Together they provide a comprehensive coverage of risk assessment and perception from a variety of points of view which will, it is hoped, give guidance on ways in which systems for risk identification, assessment and management can be improved in effectiveness and acceptability. The views expressed in the report are those of the authors alone, or of those quoted by them.

Chapters 5 and 6 differ somewhat, in style and in content, from the earlier chapters. In particular, chapter 6 sets up, as an expository device, a series of referenced points of view as opposed positions in the debate. Some of the contending positions will undoubtedly strike many practitioners as extreme and others as necessary complements rather than exclusively valid. As is said in Chapter 6, it is not intended to imply that all positions carry equal weight, that debates are always polarized or that combinations of points of view are impossible.

Council is grateful to all those who were involved in the preparation of this report – the Study Group and those who wrote or contributed to the various chapters – but especially to Sir Frederick Warner who led the Study Group through its work. The Study Group as a whole was served by a team housed at the University of Essex and funded by the Leverhulme Trust.

Sir Francis Graham-Smith
Vice-President and Physical Secretary
The Royal Society

RISK: ANALYSIS, PERCEPTION AND MANAGEMENT

Report of a Royal Society Study Group

Printed by Amber (Printwork) Ltd, Harpenden, Hertfordshire

ISBN 0 85403 467 6

British Library Cataloguing in Publication Data

A CIP catalogue record for this book is
available from the British Library

ISBN 0-85403-467-6

Published by the Royal Society
6 Carlton House Terrace, London SW1Y 5AG

CONTENTS

CONTENTS

Chapter 1

INTRODUCTION

Sir Frederick Warner, F.R.S.

1.1 ORIGINS OF THE STUDY GROUP AND TERMS OF REFERENCE

Since the Royal Society published a Study Group report on Risk Assessment in 1983, many developments have occurred, especially in the area of perception and communication of risk. These have led to the review of positions taken by those concerned with public policy and institutional arrangements. Consequently in July 1991, the Council of the Royal Society, following a suggestion from the author, invited him to set up a study group to review the 1983 Report on Risk Assessment with the following terms of reference:

(i) To up-date and advance the study on Risk Assessment published in 1983.

(ii) To consider and help bridge the gap between what is stated to be scientific, and capable of being measured, and the way in which public opinion gauges risks and makes decisions.

(iii) To compare the decisions taken on investment by society in the reduction of risks and the allocation of resources implied on risk–benefit criteria.

(iv) To report to Council with a view to a further publication by the Society.

1.2 MEMBERSHIP OF THE STUDY GROUP

The committee that agreed to conduct the study was:
Chairman: Professor Sir Frederick Warner, F.R.S.
Other members: Sir Donald Acheson, Dr John M. Ashworth, Sir David Cox, F.R.S.
Professor Sir Bernard Crossland, F.R.S., Professor Howard Newby, Reverend Professor John C. Polkinghorne, F.R.S. and Professor Charles W. Suckling, F.R.S.
Secretary: Dr Linda Appleby.

The Chairman made contact with several of the contributors to the original report of 1983 and found there was agreement on the objectives of the new study and for it to be done quickly. The detailed studies of the Health and Safety Commission of the United Kingdom had been paralleled by others conducted by professional bodies of scientists and engineers. These were given additional stimulus by the occurrence of major disasters such as the capsize of the ferry *Herald of Free Enterprise*, the Piper Alpha oil-rig fire, the Kings Cross Underground fire and the Clapham railway disaster. These were the subject of official inquiries and reports. Outside the United Kingdom, events such as the core-melt of the Three Mile Island nuclear reactor, the spectacular failure of Reactor No. 4 at Chernobyl, the oil spill from the *Exxon Valdez* tanker in Alaska, and the deaths at the Bhopal chemical plant illustrated that the organizational failures were widespread. At the same time, natural disasters occurred with great loss of life, the greatest from floods in Bangladesh and on a smaller scale from hurricanes and earthquakes. These led to the declaration by the United Nations of an International Decade of Natural Disaster Reduction from 1990.

Since 1983 the interests of social scientists had extended from the examination of risk perception based on psychology and the use of risk–benefit analysis in the management of risk and allocation of resources. In particular a series of seminars had been held at the London School of Economics to bring together anthropologists, economists, philosophers of science, students of government as well as psychologists to study in greater depth the perception and communication of risk.

The Chairman had discussions with the group responsible for the seminars, who agreed to be responsible for half the report with Dr John Ashworth providing overall coordination. It became clear that there would be examination of the role and conduct of government and official agencies on the local and international level.

The need of help, particularly on statistics, from official sources was recognized and the Chairman sought the cooperation of Sir John Cullen, Chairman Health and Safety Commission, and John Rimington, Director-General of the Executive. This was freely offered.

The group met first on 2 October 1991 following these discussions and decided to seek the help of bodies such as the Health and Safety Executive, the National Radiological Protection Board, the National Health Service, the Office of Population Census Survey and the Home Office, but not to invite them as members. Responsibility for the areas of work were accepted by:
Engineering risk: Professor Sir Bernard Crossland.
Toxicology: Professor Charles Suckling.
Epidemiology: Sir David Cox.
Perception: Dr John Ashworth.

The writing of chapters was by authors and collaborators identified in the text.

1.3 TERMINOLOGY

At its first meeting, the group decided to go ahead and use the definitions of terms set down in the 1983 report. In the course of the study, it has become clear that these have limitations but serve the purposes of the group of scientists and engineers concerned with putting numbers on risk. To do this, defined concepts are needed for embracing especially probabilities and consequences. Both of these are subject to uncertainties, related to lack of precision in models or random variations.

The systematic use of these concepts and the access to data on failures and reliability lies at the heart of quantitative risk assessment (QRA), a powerful tool for investigation and reduction of risk. It focuses on hazards that can be foreseen and placed in a conceptual framework for the design of a new system or the critique of one existing. It is an essential technique for use by those responsible for health and safety, particularly in the context of protection at work but more widely in public activities.

1.3.1 DEFINITIONS
These definitions begin with risk as the probability that a particular adverse event occurs during a stated period of time, or results from a particular challenge. As a probability in the sense of statistical theory risk obeys all the formal laws of combining probabilities. Explicitly or implicitly, it must always relate to the 'risk of (a specific event or set of

events)' and where appropriate must refer to an exposure to hazard specified in terms of its amount or intensity, time of starting or duration. The word 'risky' is undefined, and is not to be used as a synonym for 'dangerous'. All risks are conditional, although often the conditions are implied by context rather than explicitly stated. The risk of death while hang-gliding during a seven-day period is small for a randomly selected inhabitant of the UK, but its value will alter substantially according to age, season, weather and membership of a hang-gliding club.

An *adverse event* is an occurrence that produces harm (shortened to 'event' where unambiguous).

With risk defined as above, *hazard* is seen as the situation that in particular circumstances could lead to harm, where *harm* is the loss to a human being (or to a human population) consequent on damage and *damage* is the loss of inherent quality suffered by an entity (physical and biological).

Benefit is the gain to a human population. Expected benefit incorporates an estimate of the probability of achieving the gain.

Consider the existence of Nelson's Column as the hazard. It may be damaged by wind and lightning, and as a consequence, pieces may fall off and cause harm to people in Trafalgar Square. Risk would measure the probability of specified damage or harm in a given period.

Detriment is a numerical measure of the expected harm or loss associated with an adverse event, usually on a scale chosen to facilitate meaningful addition over different events. It is generally the integrated product of risk and harm and is often expressed in terms such as costs in pounds sterling, loss in expected years of life or loss in productivity, and is needed for numerical exercises such as

cost–benefit or risk–benefit analysis. Although detriment may represent the only numerical way of comparing different events associated with the same hazard, or the combined effects of events from different hazards, the fact that any such comparison is an arbitrarily weighted total of incommensurables must never be forgotten. Total detriment (per individual or per population) may be an aid to decision, especially when reasonable alternative systems of weighting lead to the same conclusion, but should not be regarded as a substitute for reasoned judgement.

The general term used to describe the study of decisions subject to uncertain consequences is *risk assessment*. It is conveniently sub-divided into *risk estimation* and *risk evaluation*. The former includes: (a) the identification of the outcomes; (b) the estimation of the magnitude of the associated consequences of these outcomes; and (c) the estimation of the probabilities of these outcomes.

Risk evaluation is the complex process of determining the significance or value of the identified hazards and estimated risks to those concerned with or affected by the decision. It therefore includes the study of risk perception and the trade-off between perceived risks and perceived benefits. *Risk management* is the making of decisions concerning risks and their subsequent implementation, and flows from risk estimation and risk evaluation.

1.3.2 OTHER DEFINITIONS
These definitions do not meet the whole requirements of engineers and scientists who specialize in risk studies, and British Standard 4778 1991 (Part 3, Section 3.2 = IEC 1990, 50 (191)) is used to define terms in availability, reliability and maintainability (ARM). It notes that in some areas of study the terms risk and hazard have a different more specialized interpretation, the latter meaning age-specific failure-rate. The section which

follows is set out as in the British Standard.

(a) RELATIONSHIP OF TERMS

The purpose of this section is to provide an understanding of the relation between hazard, risk and safety and ARM terms.

(b) HAZARD

(i) Concept
A general concept of a hazard as applied, for example, to an industrial process, or a commercial organization, is the potential for adverse consequences of some primary event, sequence of events or combination of circumstances.

Hazards can be classified according to the severity of their potential effects, either in terms of safety, economics or other consequences. Different industries use different classifications. Such classifications alone are purely subjective and usually require qualification and quantification, by definition of the precise form of the hazard and a quantified evaluation of the consequences.

(ii) Terms
Hazard: a situation that could occur during the lifetime of a product, system or plant that has the potential for human injury, damage to property, damage to the environment, or economic loss.

Major hazard: a large scale hazard which may have severe consequences.

Hazard analysis: the identification of hazards and the consequences of the credible accident sequences of each hazard.

(c) RISK

(i) Concept
A general concept of risk is the chance, in quantitative terms, of a defined hazard occurring. It therefore combines a probabilistic measure of the occurrence of the primary event(s) with a measure of the consequences of that/those event(s). Criteria for acceptability of some predicted risk or measured risk can be set voluntarily by the organization responsible and/or subjected to the hazard, or be set mandatorily by some regulatory organization.

(ii) Terms
Risk: a combination of the probability, or frequency, of occurrence of a defined hazard and the magnitude of the consequences of the occurrence.

Risk criteria: a qualitative and quantitative statement of the acceptable standard of risk with which the assessed risk needs to be compared.

Risk assessment: the integrated analysis of the risks inherent in a product, system or plant and their significance in an appropriate context.

Risk quantification: the estimation of a given risk by a statistical and/or analytical modelling process.

Note that this may be done by such logic tree-modelling methods as are employed in hazard analysis, or by statistical inferences from historical accident data derived from past circumstances similar to those of the product or system or planned operation of facitlities, i.e. by developing probabilities of future accidents from files of historical reports of such accidents.

Risk evaluation: the appraisal of the significance of a given quantitative (or, when acceptable, qualitative) measure of risk.

Individual risk: the frequency at which an individual may be expected to sustain a given level of harm from the realization of specified hazards.

Societal risk: the relation between frequency of occurrence and the number of people in a given population suffering from a specified level of harm from the realization of specified hazards.

(d) RISK MANAGEMENT

(i) Concept
The overall subject area concerned with hazard identification, risk analysis, risk criteria and risk acceptability, is generally known as risk management (see below) or loss prevention (see below). This includes the various techniques that have been developed for the assessment and control of risk. These techniques include the probabilistic assessment of reliability for the quantification of the chance of a hazard occurring.

(ii) Term
Risk management: The process whereby decisions are made to accept a known or assessed risk and/or the implementation of actions to reduce the consequences or probability of occurrence.

Note that a compromise is made considering increased cost, schedule requirements and effectiveness of redesign or retraining, installation of warning and safety devices and procedural changes. Risk management is also concerned with the mitigation of those risks deriving from unavoidable hazards through the optimum specification of warning and safety devices and risk control procedures, such as contingency plans and emergency actions.

(e) ECONOMIC RISK

(i) Concept
Economic risks are related to financial losses that represent the commercial consequences of a hazard. These consequences can include the loss of capital investment in a process plant or other commercial venture, together with the loss of the product of that process or venture. For example, the risk could be the damage caused by a fire in a production plant and the loss of expected future pro-

duction in that plant. The loss can be either partial or total, temporary or permanent.

(ii) Terms
Economic risk: the risk of financial loss associated with a product, system or plant due to potential hazards causing loss of production, damage or other financial consequence.

Note that risks to human safety can also have economic consequences.

Loss prevention: a systematic approach to preventing hazardous events or minimizing their effects.

Note that the activities may be associated with financial loss or safety issues. They are a form of risk management, but are not necessarily quantitative.

Capital cost: The total cost to the owner of acquiring an item and bringing it to the condition where it is capable of performing its intended function.

Operating cost: the total cost to the owner of the operation, maintenance and modification of a system or plant.

Maintenance cost: the total cost of retaining an item in, or restoring it to, a state in which it can perform its required function.

Life-cycle cost: the total cost of ownership of an item taking into account all the costs of acquisition, personnel training, operation, maintenance, modification and disposal.

Note that consideration of life-cycle cost may be important in making decisions on new or changed requirements and as a control mechanism in service for existing and future items.

(f) HAZARD AND RISK TO THE ENVIRONMENT

(i) Concept

The concepts of hazard and risk can also apply to the environment, either locally, nationally or worldwide. They include the consequences of some hazardous events that do not directly cause personnel harm or cause economic loss associated with the particular industrial plant, but do more generally affect the environment. The consequence of an event can therefore directly affect anything outside the boundary of the plant and only indirectly affect human safety or the economics of the plant at the source of the event. For example, atmospheric pollution affecting vegetation.

Note that risks affecting the environment should not be confused with risks caused by environmental effects, either natural or man-made.

(ii) Terms

Environmental hazard: an event, or continuing process, which, if realized, will lead to circumstances having the potential to degrade, directly or indirectly, the quality of the environment in the short or longer term.

Environmental risk: a measure of potential threats to the environment which combines the probability that events will cause or lead to degradation of the environment and the severity of that degradation.

(g) SAFETY

(i) Concept

Safety relates to the freedom from risks that are harmful to a person, or group of persons, either local to the hazard, nationally or even worldwide. It is implied that for the consequences of an event to be defined as a hazard, i.e. a potential for causing harm, there is some risk to the human population and therefore safety could not be guaranteed, even if the risk is accepted when judged against some criterion of acceptability.

(ii) Terms

Safety: the freedom from unacceptable risks of personal harm.

Note that safety is defined in the context of risk of personal harm. It is traceable quantitatively in decision making on acceptable risks.

Safety management: the application of organizational and management principles to achieve optimum safety with high confidence. This encompasses planning, organizing, controlling, coordinating all contributary development and operational activities.

These definitions are designed for use with all the standards related to BS 5750 (1987, 1991) on which is based the International Standards Organization ISO 9000. BS 5750 is concerned with quality assurance which has been increasingly used since the 1983 report. It forms the basis for avoidance of faults including those arising from human and group relations. These terms are identical with those adopted by the International Electrochemical Commission as IEC 50 (191) in German, French, Russian, Spanish and English. The importance of quality assurance in the management of risk became increasingly clear as the study progressed.

1.3.3 DEFINITIONS RELATED TO FINANCE

No attempt has been made to discuss the terms and methods used in the management of financial risk. The problems in respect of civil-engineering projects, associated with geotechnical uncertainties, have begun to be recognized and discussed (Peacock & Whyte 1992). The detailed information on insured risks has not been considered. It has been noted that the minimum insurance premiums per annum are not less than one in a thousand.

1.3.4 SOCIAL SCIENTISTS DEFINITIONS

The terms discussed above do not meet the needs of social scientists. Their views follow:

(a) There are serious difficulties in attempting to view risk as a one-dimensional objective concept. In particular, risk perception cannot be reduced to a single subjective correlate of a particular mathematical aspect of risk, such as the product of the probabilities and consequences of any event.

Risk perception is inherently multidimensional and personalistic, with a particular risk or hazard meaning different things to different people and different things in different contexts.

Given the essentially conditional nature of all risk assessment, one should accept that assessments of risk are derived from social and institutional assumptions and processes; that is, risk is socially constructed.

(b) Public attitudes favouring stricter regulation often go hand in hand with the desire to see a technology more widely developed. So calls for stricter regulation of a technology cannot be lightly brushed aside as solely representing an anti-technology bias.

(c) The ways in which information about risks is transmitted to various audiences have been extensively studied recently. However, much of the currently available advice on risk communication lacks direct empirical validation in terms of its effectiveness to meet set goals (e.g. to change beliefs and behaviour, or to distribute timely warning messages during an emergency), or in the capacity to avoid unintended consequences. The advice that 'One should no more release an untested communication than an untested product' is one to be recommended.

(d) Because all human activities involve some element of risk, the field of risk management is both wide-ranging and diverse. Traditionally, the broad spectrum of studies has been conveniently divided according to whether the hazards being managed are considered to emanate from the physical environment (natural hazards), from human-created technology (technological hazards) or from within human society (social hazards). This partitioning has been further exacerbated by specialization with respect to specific hazards within the three main groups, resulting in the creation of a much compartmentalized field of study with many variations in approach and terminology, which is here referred to as the 'risk archipelago'. The approach adopted in Chapter 6 is intended to produce some degree of integration into this fragmented field by focusing on the policy management aspects of risk management.

(e) The notion that risk assessment and risk management are overlapping, but separate, tasks is one scientists and technologists often find attractive, but in view of the observation that in the developed world today there is an established and ever-more densely institutionalized structure of multiple and competing risk-managing organizations, it is too simplistic and misleading.

Risk management cannot ordinarily be conceived as a single-seated goal-setting process. Indeed the nature of the appropriate management structures, their purposes and, especially, their design are the subject of a debate whose structure we have tried to elucidate.

These debates have as their significant underlying issue the need to bring together natural science expertise and knowledge about human behaviour and the operation of human institutions.

(f) As the human handling of risks is affected by a variety of institutions, it is important that attention be focused on the elements of institutional design for the public managment of risk. Analysis reveals that there are nine broad types of institutional 'players' at three territorial levels (supranational, national, subnational) whose operation is subject to a complex of underlying rules. In this study, a six-dimensional framework is proposed and elaborated which essentially encapsulates the 'rules of the game' with respect to public risk management.

(g) Risk management is also characterized by considerable diversity of opinion as to the principles that should be employed to govern the identification, measurement and regulation of risk. Seven contested areas are identified and examined involving such disputed topics as the degree of anticipation that should be adopted, the extent to which management systems should be 'blame oriented', the contribution of quantitative-assessment techniques, feasibility of institutional design, the cost of risk reduction, desirable level of participation and the regulatory target. These debates are exemplified with reference to six different types of hazard. The assessment presented here suggests that one thread running though these debated areas revolves around the emphasis placed on 'homeostatic' as against 'collibrational' regulatory processes. In the former, emphasis is placed on the use of feedback mechanisms to achieve pre-set goals, where as in the latter there is no pre-set goal, due to scientific uncertainties with regard to the future, and the system operates by means of 'opposed maximisers'.

1.4 OVERVIEW OF REPORT

1.4.1 CHAPTER 2, by Crossland *et al.*

In chapter 2 the authors up-date the earlier treatment of engineering risks and show the reduction in number of deaths, especially in areas such as road transport, from a combination of regulation such as compulsory wearing of seat belts, also improved road and vehicle design. It brings up to date the use of hazard and operability studies (HAZOP) to foresee problems at the design stage, mainly of complicated systems such as chemical plants. There is also the safeguard of audits, such as safety cases for North Sea oil rigs, recommended by the Cullen Inquiry into the Piper Alpha disaster.

It deals with the improved methods of inspection for faults and the philosophy of proof testing. Underlying these methods is the change brought about by quality assurance to British Standard 5750. The full implication of this is increasingly being seen in the improvement of communications between groups who are enabled to work in a framework designed to take advantages of the understanding deployed at every level.

The use of frequency–consequence curves has been reviewed and new material added on faults in software that can lead to disastrous failure of computer-controlled systems, of particular importance to aircraft. The use of finite-state machines parallels HAZOP studies for identification of problems at the design stage. Formal methods use logical arguments to detect inconsistency and time Petri nets are used to represent information and control flow.

The chapter ends with discussion of risk variation for different groups and uncertainty in risk estimation. The impossibility of testing some components is admitted, but many can be tested and the combination with judgement in risk analysis has practical utility.

1.4.2 CHAPTER 3, by Suckling *et al.*

The authors of chapter 3, on Toxicity, Toxicology and Nutrition, record the advances that have been made in evaluating toxicity by moving away from the estimation of dose required to kill half the animals used (LD$_{50}$ test) in favour of greater use of *in vitro* tests and a 'fixed dose procedure' which uses fewer animals. The advantages in reducing the use of animals and providing better models for humans, plus the use of human volunteers, are discussed. Current issues are in the field of immunotoxicity, largely because of public interest in the immune system from the side-effects of drugs and in development of AIDS.

The area of nutritional toxicology extends the earlier study on food additives to food itself in connection with disease. This is complicated by other human activites such as smoking (see chapter 4). The difficult area of dose–response relation, including length of exposure and intensity, becomes more important with increasing longevity and is fully discussed. (Ionizing radiation in this context appears in chapter 4).

Environmental concerns have stimulated interest in the area of ecotoxicology, in which institutional prescription begins to be increasingly important. The quantification of effects is still at an early stage.

1.4.3 CHAPTER 4, by Cox *et al.*

In chapter 4 the authors give new information from observations on human beings. It shows how epidemiology can add to the limited information obtainable by planned experiments on humans and shows its value in giving early signals of adverse effects not predicted. This is also important where harm, not resulting in death, is caused. The sources of data are listed and specific risks discussed. The contribution to risk made from natural sources of ionizing radiation, such as radon, and artificial such as medical procedures, is calculated to be about 1000 times that derived from nuclear bombs or power stations. This has not yet been publicly perceived, and at the same time, pre-occupation with risk from nuclear power and weapons has, in spite of Chernobyl, lessened. Ionizing radiation in the UV-B range is discussed with its effects on skin cancer through increased transmission by ozone holes. There is no clear evidence of adverse effects associated with radiation from electro-magnetic fields.

The development of AIDS is important, and problems in transmission are discussed. On broad trends in mortality, increase in life expectancy has taken the UK to a figure of 76 years compared with 69 years in 1950–55. (Compare infantile mortality rates of 8 per 1000 now with 28 per 1000 then.) An important factor is recognition of smoking, reckoned to cause one-third of all deaths in the UK in middle age. In spite of increased smoking by women, improvement in life expectancy continues and mortality decreases from cancer and respiratory or vascular diseases. Although there is some prospect of a large eventual increase from AIDS it is too early to estimate with confidence the ultimate scale of mortality. The earlier detailed tables on risk have been revised.

1.4.4 CHAPTERS 5 AND 6, INTRODUCTION

The authors of chapters 5 and 6 extend and replace the earlier 1983 treatment of risk perception and management, which was based on the ideas current then on psychology and risk–benefit analysis. Reference is made above to the critique of definitions used in the 1983 report as not sufficient for the purpose of risk management. This has to take account of Chapter 5 on the perception of risk, interest in which is demonstrated by the many publications, especially in the USA, to which reference is made. It acknowledges that the 1983 report had shown that scaling the magnitude of risk did not mean that acceptable levels could be established. It supported the consideration of the public's viewpoint as an essential datum in perception and showed that the differences presented administrators with a political choice in addition to accepting the scientific choices.

CHAPTER 5, by Pidgeon *et al.*

Since then, reports from the Health and Safety Executive on tolerability of risk followed the report of the Layfield Inquiry into Sizewell B nuclear power plant that 'the opinions of the public should underlie the evaluation of risk'. This led to the adoption of the ALARP (As Low As Reasonably Practicable) approach. This is not considered to take care of 'plural rationalists', stemming from different assumptions about human nature, distributive justice and the link between society and the physical environment. The conclusion of this line of thought is that perceived risk is socially constructed. In this, the psychology of individuals is important, reflecting their attitude to individual and societal risks, and their own positions in professional or other groups with different work relations. This has a large body of evidence from psychometric studies. It is worth recording the conclusion that the rank order of different hazards largely agrees with stated frequency.

By contrast (or development), the 'cultural theory' now claims some attention from social scientists. Anthropological studies illuminate how people value most the things they participate in or strongly identify with. Their 'groups' interact in social life according to rules or negotiations (the 'grid').

The linkage of the grid and group leads to four major cultural biases: hierarchists, sectarians/egalitarians, fatalists and individualists. From this it is argued that no common ground can be developed and that risk means just threat. This approach has generated great interest but has produced much less empirical evidence than that from psychologists. Only recently an attempt to unify psychological, social and cultural approaches has been made in the social amplification framework. This explains why certain hazards such as rail transport are a particular focus of concern whereas others, like road accidents, receive comparatively little attention. This arises from the amplification of signals filtered through the media, agencies, politicians and groups of activists. The reception accounts for secondary consequences in the form of sales resistance, regulatory constraints, litigation and investor flight. A third focus on social processes involves the process of judgement exercised by experts.

Arising from this, the process of risk communication has been studied in the US National Research Council arising from (1) desire by government to inform, (2) desire by government or industry to overcome opposition, (3) desire to share power between government and public and, (4) desire to develop alternatives to regulation. This becomes merged in a wider movement for democratic participation and for the 'right to know'. Ultimately the question of trust in experts and responsible authorities arises. These questions in risk communication are seen as an area for further research into the different viewpoints.

CHAPTER 6, by Hood *et al.*

The authors of chapter 6 return to risk management, characterized by diversity of opinion on identification, measurement and regulation of risk. Seven contested areas are identified and illustrated by six case studies. The discussion focuses on basic differences in terminology, saying that risk management has no single meaning. It opposes the view that assessment and management should be seen as separate tasks, the former concerned with establishment of probabilities and the latter with legal, political and administrative objectives.

This goes further, as already stated, in assigning to risk the meaning that the observer wishes to give it. There is an acknowledgement in the appendix to chapter 6 that risk–benefit analysis helps to produce decisions that are consistent over different areas of policy and a guide to the allocation of resources.

The use of risk management in insurance is discussed. (The financial and commercial aspects of insurance were not discussed in the first four chapters, if only on the grounds that these are a special area of high risk where the financial premiums are never less than 1 in 1000 a year, usually much more). It is clear that the stability of insurance has been affected by the claims that it should cover ambiguous risks like environmental pollution. The question of moral hazard also arises (in this connection the result of genetic information being held on individuals could arise but is not mentioned). 'Moral hazard' is a term specific to insurance and describes the situation where the 'protection' offered by insurance results in increased risk taking, i.e. behaviour change. It is a form of risk compensation.

The nine types of institutional player in public risk assessment involving supranational, subnational and national institutions are exemplified, and approaches to regulation by anticipatory or corrective measures. Information and communication have their part in this and an illustration of amplification found in the concentration of attention on global warming and ozone depletion, which in a short time led to the Montreal convention on CFCs and a measure of agreement at the Rio summit on the environment.

The growth of directives, enactments and funding in several areas is illustrated in diagrams. The establishment in the UK of integrated pollution control, the Environment Protection Act and the National Rivers Authority have extended the

coverage given by the Health and Safety Executive to hazards affecting the work force and general public. There has been a move to what is termed 'juridification' with a move away from experts and consensus towards processes which allow one side to win.

At this stage, the chapter comes back to the seven contested areas which cannot be summarized. Some of the considerations in respect of organizations and the contribution of total quality management have been referred to in chapter 2. Most of the terms are novel and not to be found in dictionaries, so close study is recommended. An example is anticipation as a principle to use in imposing controls before scientific evidence of damage is available of which the use in EC directives is giving rise to criticism.

In the section on blame the authors raise many questions on the allocation to individuals or corporate bodies and reflects the increasing tendency in the UK to litigate and to follow the example of the USA in class actions. (These raise many questions where basic regulation in the UK may be through EC directives, based more on continental civil law systems than on common law.) The discussion on strict liability shows the conflicts that arise.

The value of procedures such as HAZOP described in chapter 2 is conceded. The use of concepts like BPEO (Best Practicable Environmental Option) and BATNEEC (Best Available Technology Not Entailing Excessive Costs) is also discussed. Quantitative risk assessment is seen as having significant limitations and not to be regarded as a panacea.

On participation in risk management a case is made for extending the peer community with a wide group of stakeholders. The example of amateur ornithologists in identifying DDT with falling population of predators is quoted. Part of this argument for broader participation is linked with the challenge to scientific knowledge construed within a narrowly positivistic interpretation. There is an opposing view that risk-management decisions require the best available expertise and that extension would lead to this being over-ridden by ill-informed contributors and impoverished by whipped-up scares and over-politicization. The overall conclusion is in favour of further progress in examining decision procedures, their intellectual sustainablity and eventual utility. The alternatives are examined again in six case studies: natural hazards, public transport risks, safety critical software, crowd-related hazards, blood and 'sharps' hazards and global warming.

The chapter concludes with recommendations for further study of the changed conceptual and institutional framework since the 1983 report. The appendix on risk–benefit analysis concludes that reductions in risk can be valued and suggests a value of £200 to £300 for each change in risk of 1/10 000 (against the more conventional value of £2–3 million for a statistical life). This is higher than the figure of £0.5 million for the cost of one life allowed by the Department of Transport in 1988 values and prices and quoted in a Treasury Green Paper (1991). This also illustrates the problems in agreeing on a definition of risk by stating 'Risk is the possibility of more than one outcome occuring'.

1.5 CONCLUSIONS

The remit that was given to the study group by the Royal Society has on the whole been met. Chapters 2–4 have analysed data and brought up to date statistics relating to risk. They show the influence of discussions that have taken place and emphasize those uncertainties in risk estimation that arise from the models used and the judgements made.

Considerable progress has been made in mutual understanding as between the very different stances that tend to be adopted by natural scientists and by social scientists, although the bridge with social sciences has not been put in place. What has been achieved is an open discussion which needs to be continued in

public and also inside the groups concerned, which we hope will be aided by this report. Contacts have been maintained with other countries, especially the USA where the National Academy of Sciences has promoted the study of risk communication. The attitudes in other countries reflect the differences between and within the various cultures.

This report should contribute to the continuing discussion, which is important for the benefit of those who have finally to make decisions and regulations that satisfy the public conscience, having regard at all time to the effective use of resources in bettering the quality of life.

REFERENCES

British Standards Institution 1987 *Quality Systems. BS 5750.*

British Standards Institution 1991 *Quality vocabulary. BS4778.*

British Standards Institution 1991 *BS 5750.*

Institute of Chemical Engineers 1992 *Nomenclature for hazard and risk assessment.*

H.M. Treasury 1991 *Economic appraisal in Central Government.* London: HMSO.

Peacock, W.S. & Whyte I.L. 1992 Site investigation and risk analyses. *Proc. Instn civ. Engrs civ. Engng* **92**, 74–81.

Chapter 2

ESTIMATING ENGINEERING RISK

Sir Bernard Crossland, F.R.S. (Chairman), Dr P.A. Bennett, Dr A.F. Ellis,
Dr F.R. Farmer, Dr J. Gittus, P.S. Godfrey, Esq., Dr E.C. Hambly, Dr T.A. Kletz,
Professor F.P. Lees

2.1 THE APPROACH TO RISK ESTIMATION

Risks may be classified as falling into at least three classes, in a way similar to that suggested by Cohen and Pritchard (1980): (a) Risks for which statistics of identified casualties are available.

(b) Risks for which there may be some evidence, but where the connection between suspected cause and injury to any one individual cannot be traced (e.g. cancer long after exposure to radiation or a chemical).

(c) Experts' best estimates of probabilities of events that have not yet happened.

Additionally, there are risks that were not foreseen, for which causal connections are sought after new effects or casualties appear.

Many examples of substantial risk have an engineering content. Engineers are involved in the design and construction of systems and the components or sub-systems that form part of the systems. They additionally have professional responsibility for the safety of these systems. All systems have a probability of failure and the complete avoidance of all risk of calamitous failure is not possible, but the objective of engineers must be to reduce the probability to an acceptable individual and societal risk. Engineers attempt to quantify the risk by a physical appreciation of possible failure mechanisms or modes and their analysis. This requires quantification of the reliability of the components and the examination of the

systematic failure of software in Programmable Electronic Systems used, for instance, in the control of processes to establish the overall reliability of the complete system, based on experience verified by analysis, testing and inspection.

An example of the examination of past events in building up an understanding of failure modes is provided by the investigation of box-girder bridges (Merrison 1971). In contrast to this, individual engineering projects involving new techniques give rise to the problem of setting and achieving suitable target levels of risk. Flint (1981) discusses this in the context of civil engineering, pointing out that it has for some time been the practice to express design criteria in terms of events having a prescribed probability of occurrence in the lifetime of the structure, e.g. wave-loading for off-shore platforms, and flood level for the Thames barrier. In view of the potential for major consequences involved in engineering failures, it is not acceptable to wait for disasters to occur so as to build up a body of case histories as a basis for policy decisions. An anticipatory approach based on judgement and experience is required, and risk estimation attempts to provide this by methods based on the systematic analysis of complex plant into its component sub-systems, and the use of predictive techniques and modelling. Further analysis of failure mechanisms follows, and then the risk is synthesized by drawing together models of the individual sub-systems. This procedure requires access to a wide range of data on failures that have occurred in the past, a substantial body of scientific knowledge about the various processes that are intended to occur or that could occur in the system, and a similar breadth of knowledge concerning the behaviour in the environment of materials that could be released and the response of people, structures, etc. suffering exposure to those materials.

It is clear that the results of such a procedure will be subject to substantial uncertainties arising from inadequacies in the data and from insufficient depth or accuracy of the scientific knowledge applied. It is therefore important to recognize that there are other more traditional methods in wide-spread use which are essentially deterministic in nature.

The essentially deterministic approach can be illustrated by the factor of safety treatment in the design of a loaded structure. Such a structure will be deemed to have failed if the load or stress to which it is subjected exceeds the yield strength of the materials. Various factors such as wear, corrosion and misuse may increase the stress, and quality variations in manufacture, defects and fatigue may reduce the strength. Similarly the loadings will vary according to the use and environmental conditions that apply at the time. The traditional method of allowing for such variations is the application of a design safety margin, which is the difference between the design strength and design stress; the design safety factor being their ratio. This approach depends on estimation of mean values for strength and stress.

In practice there will be a distribution of stresses and of strengths, both having mean values with a spread about those means. On the reasonable assumption that the mean stress will be smaller than the mean strength it is clear that where the upper end of the stress distribution encounters the lower end of the strength distribution there will be structural failure. This leads to definitions of safety factors and safety margins in probabilistic terms (Lees 1980, pp. 114–116).

The deterministic approach incorporates the concept of variability of stress and strength, but implies that there is a level of probability of failure that is acceptable for design purposes, without quantifying that level. The probabilistic approach, in contrast, includes the low-probability events in the overall assessment. However, as an approach it is necessary for sufficient relevant data to be available, which is by no means always practical or economic.

In terms of decision making this means that the deterministic approach incorporates implicit value judgements as to what is an acceptable standard of practice, and is largely derived from an extension of past practice and experience, which may not be entirely adequate to deal with rapidly changing technology. In contrast, the probabilistic approach describes the hazard in terms of the risks of failure and their associated consequences, thereby enabling the decision as to acceptability to be externalized from the design process which assists in making the judgements needed.

The introduction of new technology has led to increasing use of computers that include software and which fulfil protection and/or control functions in safety-related or safety-critical systems. The term Programmable Electronic System (PES) is used to describe such systems (Health and Safety Executive 1987). The nature of software is such that it is not subject to random failure, but only to systematic failure. PESs, particularly their software, are therefore not readily amenable to the demonstration of risk reduction based on quantified reliability values. Wider, qualitative, arguments need to be applied, and this has led to the development of the concept of Safety Integrity Levels.

Software is a relatively new area of engineering which is still developing rapidly. Software has an immense potential to fulfil existing functions better or more cheaply or to fulfil otherwise impractical functions. Software is used for control and/or protection in a multitude of applications such as nuclear reactors (Health and Safety Executive 1992), oil production platforms, anti-lock braking systems, fly-by-wire aircraft, train control and central heating boilers.

The use of PESs in safety related systems and the risks associated with such use are introduced and discussed by the Institution of Electrical Engineers (1992) and by Bennett (1991), while Kletz (1991) notes the additional human problems posed by computer control in process plants.

During the life-time of systems the risk must be minimized by maintenance, inspection and re-appraisal, such as the regular inspection of bridges, dams, components of nuclear power plants, airframes and engines, and PESs and their associated transducers. In the estimation of risk it is necessary to examine the reproducibility and practicability of inspection systems. An example is the non-destructive examination of the components of the pressure circuits of nuclear power plant, where human access is greatly restricted or impossible so reliance must be placed on remotely operated inspection techniques. The validity and reliability of these procedures must be established. It should be recognized that excessively complex safety systems may be self defeating as they cannot be adequately validated and updated.

The risk of failure and the calamitous consequences that may result will be greatly influenced by management. The absence or lack of adequate management and auditing of safety were seen as an important contributory factor in several recent major disasters including the *Herald of Free Enterprise* (Steel 1987), the King's Cross Underground fire (Fennell 1988), the Clapham Junction railway accident (Hidden 1989) and the Piper Alpha disaster (Cullen 1990). Effective management and auditing of safety involves many of the principles of Total Quality Management (TQM) to ensure the maintenance of safe practices laid down in the safety case. Management of safety also involves the training of staff to observe, record and report, and as importantly to react to the onset of a potential disaster, and to organize evacuation and rescue procedures in the event of a disaster. The importance of effective management and auditing of safety in reducing risk cannot be too strongly emphasized.

One of the dilemmas for engineers in risk assessment is in defining what is an acceptable risk. As can be seen from Chapter 5, Risk Perception, and Chapter 6, Risk Management, there is a problem with this concept. For example, from the statistics in Chapter 4, it appears that the individuals involved in rock climbing or hang gliding or motor cycling accept a very high risk, whereas they would probably expect a much lower risk when travelling on public transport and yet an even lower risk for nuclear power plant. Though engineers involved in the assessment of risk are sensitive to the public perception of risk, it is necessary for them to quantify what is an acceptable risk in particular circumstances to have a target for their risk assessment exercise. This does not imply that the engineer will not try to reduce the risk further if this can be achieved at an acceptable cost. However, it is necessary to be realistic and allocate limited financial resources on the basis of cost–benefit assessment.

2.2 THE TECHNIQUES OF RISK ESTIMATION

2.2.1 HAZARD IDENTIFICATION

A vital component of risk estimation is the identification of hazards. The effectiveness of this requires a thorough understanding of the process or system which is clearly dependent on the knowledge, experience, engineering judgement and imagination of the study team to whom the task is assigned. It must include the human element – cultural, organizational, group and individual – which is frequently a contributing cause of disasters. A substantial body of experience has been accumulated and documented, for instance in codes of practice and procedures adopted. Reference to this literature reduces the likelihood of omitting significant hazards, and many of the techniques have been systematized to a useful degree. Lees (1980), and Kletz (1992) review hazard identification techniques, including safety audits, hazard survey, hazard indices and hazard and operability studies. These are briefly described in the annex to this chapter.

The exercise of hazard identification is a useful discipline in its own right in drawing attention to some areas of unacceptable risk, which can be eliminated or greatly reduced by modification of the design or the safety system. Hazard identification is a potential source of error as a consequence of a failure to identify all the potential hazards or the way in which they can arise. Having identified the hazards, it is necessary to quantify the risk; the process or quantification may be considered as falling into two phases, namely, reliability and failure analysis, and consequence modelling.

2.2.2 RELIABILITY AND FAILURE ANALYSIS

Reliability can be defined as the probability that a component will perform a required specified function. This may depend on the component's success in commencing to operate when required, continuing to operate subsequently, not operating before demand, and not continuing after the demand has ceased. The reliability of a multi-component system depends on the incidence of failures of its components. Data on such failures and their precursors may usefully be fitted to statistical distribution functions for use in reliability analysis. The choice of appropriate distribution functions is discussed by Lees (1980).

Availability of a system is related to its reliability, but differs in that it incorporates transition back to operation from the non-operational state through repair. Modelling of availability and reliability can be achieved in various ways as reviewed by Lees (1980). The level of complexity required depends on the type of study. Very useful results can be achieved through simple analysis without resorting to the more sophisticated techniques.

2.2.3 EVENT AND FAULT-TREE ANALYSIS

One of the most important developments in system-failure analysis is the application of various forms of logic diagrams that represent the sequences of failures that may propagate through a complex system. Of the several types of logic diagram that have been used, those known as event trees and fault trees are now the most widely used.

An event tree specifies a range of possible outcomes, so that for a given frequency of occurrence of an initiating event, the frequency of a particular outcome is given by the product of the initial frequency with all the probabilities at each of the intervening steps. Such a chain is referred to as an accident sequence; a recent example of an event tree is shown in figure 1, from Carter (1991) which considers pipeline risks.

tion, qualitative evaluation and tree quantification.

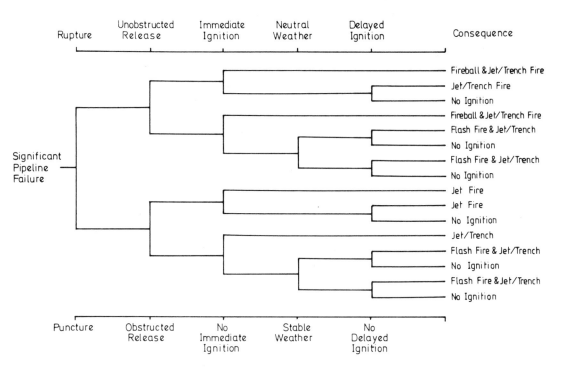

Figure 1. Pipeline Risk Assessment Method: Event Tree. (Source: Carter 1991.)

A fault tree attempts the reverse process, working back from a particular event (known as the top event) through all the chains of events that are the precursors of the top event. The key components of a fault tree are thus event specifications and logic gates ('and/or' gates).

The engineering application of fault trees dates back to the 1960s in the aerospace industry (Boeing Company 1965), but wider use is evident, particularly in risk estimation studies (United States Nuclear Regulatory Commission 1975 Health and Safety Executive 1978 and 1981, Vesely *et al.* 1981), and logic trees are widely used outside engineering, for example in business decision trees. The basis of the technique as applied to reliability engineering, and developments in the methodology are discussed by Vesely (1970) and Barlow *et al.* (1975). The basic steps in the use of event and fault trees are system definition, tree construc-

The quality of the result depends very much on the ability of the analysis team, and the technique is by no means foolproof. Particular problems that are of concern include:

(a) how to treat common-cause failures, that is, those multiple failures arising from a single event or failure;

(b) how to allow for the propagation of uncertainties in the primary inputs;

(c) how to ensure a sufficient degree of comprehensiveness of the systems definition;

(d) how to specify bounds to the fault tree so that the problem is numerically tractable;

(e) what form and parameters of probability distributions to incorporate in the failure-data inputs.

Okrent (1977) discusses technical aspects of several of these points. The Lewis report (1978) criticizes the Rasmussen study (United States Nuclear Regulatory Commission 1975) on several grounds, including (e) above, but supports the general approach and comments on the various techniques described:

There are many things one can do to carve out tractable methodologies – event trees, fault trees, failure modes and effects analysis. In particular it is incorrect to say that the event tree/fault tree analysis is fundamentally flawed, since it is just an implementation of logic. On the other hand, the successful implementation of such a methodology rests heavily upon the availability of an adequate data base, effective computing tools, a sufficiently deep understanding of the detailed engineering of the system to permit construction of the logic trees, and some logically sound procedure for limiting the universe of discourse.

The translation of event trees into several discrete events for the purposes of consequence modelling invariably involves the adoption of simplifying assumptions; for example, for the purposes of gas dispersion calculations the prevailing weather may be described by a limited set of windspeed, stability and directional probabilities. The sensitivity of the results of the analysis to these assumptions needs to be tested and where necessary the depth of the analysis increased to ensure that the finite set of events modelled is sufficiently representative.

More widespread discussion includes the criticism that the technique does not give adequate allowance for human failure, such as operator error, and some external hazards to the system, such as terrorism. Layfield (1987) in the public planning inquiry into Sizewell B nuclear power station recognized the importance of human error, and he arbitrarily increased the predicted risk tenfold to allow for it. However, techniques are now being developed for providing estimates of the probability of human-error through procedures known as human-reliability assessment (HRA). The use of HRA is recommended in the nuclear industry (Health and Safety Commission 1991 *a*) although, because of its limitations, it needs to be used intelligently and with discretion. HRA may also be appropriate in other industries such as transport and chemical.

There is no doubt that many of these criticisms are irrefutable in the absolute sense, but they do not necessarily detract from the usefulness of the methods. In addition to the contribution they make to the quantification of reliability, and therefore of risk, they constitute a highly effective means of providing genuine insight into the requirements of sound engineering. Thus the methods can provide an excellent basis for the qualitative assessment of risk even though it may not be practical to extend the process to numerical evaluation. This is necessary regardless of the existence of potential threats from outside the engineered system. Although these methods vary in their particulars, they are all attempts to define and render tractable a significant sub-set of an enormously complex labyrinth of potential sequences and interactions that the real systems represents.

2.2.4 EVENT AND RELIABILITY DATA BANKS

The techniques described above have created a demand for the data on the occurrence of events and failures. There are now numerous data banks in existence, developed within various industries and covering a wide range of components, systems and instruments (Lees 1980, Hecht & Fragola 1977). The European Safety and Reliability Data Association (ESREDA) has brought together about 50 data-bank owners and users (European Industry Reliability Databank Handbook 1991). Another source of data is provided by the American Institute of Chemical Engineers (Guideline for Process Equipment Reliability Data, with Data Tables, 1989). The purpose of using such data is to incorporate in a clear manner statistically based measures of reliability in the analysis, derived from many instances, rather than estimates based on models of the sub-system. Greater accuracy is thus achieved, but it is important not to waste effort in seeking greater accuracy than the problem demands. For example, some branches of a fault tree may be relatively insensitive to the failure rate used, and would not require accurate inputs of those data.

Failure data may be classified according to various characteristics, for example, overall rates, distributions of failures in different modes, variation with time, and repair times.

In spite of the advances brought about by the establishment of these data banks their use is not without considerable problems. The way in which the data are categorized and allocated to categories is crucial in determining the effectiveness of their use. The amount of data held in the various banks is very large, but the requirements that motivated their being established vary, and in consequence there is a great variety of practice in categorization and allocation, so that caution must be exercised in the use of data from different banks, The problems involved in defining groups and determining their response under various exposures have much in common with those encountered in epidemiology.

Further difficulties arise because of the proprietary nature of the data. It may also be the case that the information is of commercial use, and it may be sensitive, i.e. pertaining to controversial issues in safety of particular industries, devices, etc. However, it should be recognized that safety is not enhanced by secrecy. It is expected that this whole area will move much more into the public arena as organizations realize the advantages of pooling data classified according to

agreed definitions. Industry-specific and component-specific databases can be produced such as that developed in the offshore industry through the OREDA project (Offshore Reliability Data Handbook 1984) or the European Industry Reliability Handbook (1991).

Although there is considerable uncertainty about the confidence to be attributed to rare-event analysis, it is important to recognize the difference between a singular rare event (e.g. pressure-vessel failure, or meteorite impact) and a rare consequence resulting from a chain of more frequent events.

2.2.5 THE ROLE OF TESTS

Failure data as incorporated in reliability data banks are principally derived from experience gained in service, that is to say the acquisition of the data is not the prime purpose of building the system, but is a by-product. For some types of failure there is no prospect of establishing an adequate data base in this way, because the events are rare, and some other means of estimating failure probability is required if the systematic analysis of chain events is inapplicable.

In such cases it is usually not economically feasible to do a sufficient number of tests either at full or reduced scale, and it is then necessary to gain understanding of the mechanisms of failure, to develop a model of the mechanisms, and to do tests to establish whether or not the model is valid. An example would be the failure of pressure vessels for nuclear reactors, the models required involve fracture mechanics and crack propagation. Carefully designed controlled tests, constituting a scientific programme of experimental research, are required in such cases. There are many areas where reduced-scale physical modelling is being used extensively (e.g. estuary flow, wind-tunnel models of sites and design engineering features). In work of this type one of the crucial aspects is the selection of appropriate scaling factors.

The combination of mathematical models verified by a limited set of tests has provided an economical means of extending benefits to be gained from testing. Where the model is proven, it may with due care be used to examine a far wider range of parameters than is practical physically. Where anomalies are exposed their investigation may reveal an issue or failure mechanism that had been overlooked.

The recent worldwide effort to investigate the dispersion of dense gases is a good example of developing a programme of tests, at small and field scale, and the mathematical models that complement each other (see for example, McQuaid & Roebuck 1985, Britter & McQuaid 1988, Puttock *et al.* 1991). The international collaboration in such programmes has an important bearing on the effectiveness and acceptability of the work. Such collaboration is a feature of the recent and on-going programmes of work that are being supported by CEC under their Major Technological Hazards, Science and Technology for Environmental Protection Programme.

It is important to recognize the new identity of purpose between risk assessment and quality management as laid out in BS5750/ISO 9000 (1987). Methods of quality control play an important role in the manufacture, commissioning and operation stages. For example, various techniques are available for non-destructive testing of metal components such as radiography, ultrasonics scanning, eddy-current and magnetic methods, dye penetration, vacuum and pressure tests, and leak detection. Proof testing is frequently a requirement laid down in the specification or made by the inspection authority. This involves overloading the component, such as a crane sling or pressure vessel, before it is put into service to ensure that there is an adequate safety margin above the maximum working load or pressure. Testing to failure using the mode for which the component is de-

signed is often done to show that an adequate margin against failure has been achieved, and also to examine how failure is likely to occur. Corresponding quality control methods and proof testing are applied in other areas such as with electronic and electrical components and systems, and in the validation of computer software, particularly in safety-critical systems.

The primary purpose of these methods of quality control is to demonstrate compliance with standards or specifications. Consequently it is important to establish the validity of these methods when performed by various organizations worldwide. One example is provided by PISC (Plate Inspection Steering Committee) which was set up in 1974 to assess the capability and reliability of non-destructive inspection procedures for structural components, and in particular those for nuclear power plant (Crutzen *et al.* 1992). PISC-I involved 33 institutions from ten European Countries in a round robin involving the application of manual ultrasonic examination of welds and their associated heat affected zones according to appendix 1 of section XI of the ASME Boiler and Pressure Vessel Code (1971). Three test plates containing flaws deliberately implanted during the welding process were examined, followed by destructive examination of the plates.

The unsatisfactory nature of the results of PISC-I (1979–80) led to PISC-II (Nichols & Crutzen 1988) in which there was an examination of alternative test methods and procedures and of parameters that influence flaw detection and sizing. PISC-III (Crutzen *et al.* 1991) demands a capability demonstration of non-destructive testing with assemblies of real geometry containing realistic flaws, and it includes tests in hot cell facilities and on a full scale vessel. Many other aspects have been or will be covered, including not least human reliability studies in relation to NDT.

An approach that has been encouraged by PISC is that of performance demonstration rather than adherence to procedures and techniques laid down in codes and standards. This concept has been examined for some years by the USA (ASME section XI, appendix 8, 1989–90), and it is similar to the concept of inspection validation recommended in the UK by the Marshall Committee (Spanner *et al.* 1991).

PISC provides an example of the efforts of engineers to better establish the reliability of sub-systems and to improve their technology. This is essential to achieve credibility of their risk estimation.

2.2.6 CONSEQUENCE MODELLING

The output of the hazard identification and the reliability and failure analysis is a compilation of possible failures, each with a quantitative set of parameters that characterize it for purposes of consequence modelling. These will include, for example, inventories of materials in the release, their physical and chemical status, the duration of the release, how much energy is released at the same time, as sensible or latent heat, and any other characteristic having a bearing on the behaviour. A similar range of variables must be taken into account in the consequence modelling, as suggested in the second report of the Advisory Committee on Major Hazards (Health and Safety Commission 1979, paras 22–25).

The common feature in these various quantitative descriptors is the inclusion of a figure for the expected frequency of occurrence for each release. The number of possible items in such a compilation of failures is clearly very large, being derived from the outputs of event- and fault-tree analysis. It is usual to group together the releases where their degree of similarity permits, so making the number of inputs to the consequence model more manageable. Thus, in the Rasmussen study (United States Nuclear Regulatory Commission 1975), the number of release categories finally specified was 14.

The type and level of damage will depend on the particular damage mechanism involved and on the degree of exposure. The effect will be related to the type of dose-effect relation that applies, whether there are thresholds below which no significant harm is suffered, and the scope and effectiveness of remedial measures. The form of the dose-effect relation is also probabilistic, usually expressing the severity or the probability of occurrence of harm as a function of dose.

The nature of the dose-effect relationship also impinges on the suitability of the dispersion models used, and places additional constraints on their validity. For example, although the total dosage is a sufficient measure for cases where there is a linear relation between dose and effect, it is inadequate in dealing with the effects of irritant gases (chlorine, ammonia, etc.). For these materials the fatal damage level is related to the duration of exposure (t) and to the concentrations (c) possibly in some non-linear manner such as $c^m t^n$ (Eisenberg 1975). Exposure needs then to be expressed in terms of these two variables separately, and not as total dosage.

It is evident from the above that one can consider consequence modelling as a continuation of the systematic analysis of chains of causes and effects that started with the in-plant analysis of failures. The behaviour outside the plant is just as much a part of the overall accident sequence as the failure leading to release, with the same probabilistic character in respect of the various effects that may follow from the previous event. Inherent safety depends on the success of engineering design or the addition of various protective devices. It is important to recognize that though the tasks of the design engineer and the consequence modeller are distinct they are not separate, and there is a need for a very close interaction both at the specification and design stage and as experience accumulates during the operation.

It is important that the results of the programme of work noted in the previous paragraphs should be disseminated to the 'user'. This includes, in addition to the plant designer the plant safety engineers, the plant operators, the safety consultants and assessors, the government regulators and policy makers.

The principal method by which this technology transfer takes place is through the use of consequence models (i.e. mathematical models of varying degrees of sophistication ranging from source models through dispersion models to those for estimating the impact on man and on the environment). More attention is now being given to the evaluation of model quality and to methods by which model quality might be improved. Hanna (1991 *a*, 1991 *b*) describes the evaluation of a number of dense-gas dispersion models against results from field trials on the dispersion of ammonia and anhydrous hydrogen fluoride. Further work along these research lines is needed and the CEC is supporting research aimed at developing procedures which should ensure that technical models used in major hazard assessment are correctly evaluated.

2.3 RISK ESTIMATION FOR SYSTEMS INVOLVING COMPUTERS

2.3.1 GENERAL

There are several techniques, many of more general use, that are particularly suitable as aids to risk estimation for systems that include computers. Some of these are directed specifically at software, others at the wider system. The selection of techniques introduced below is by no means complete, and all the techniques have a place both as risk estimation tools for existing or proposed systems and as design aids. More extensive description and references are provided by the International Electrotechnical Commission (1991) and British Standards Institution (1991).

2.3.2 COMMON CAUSE FAILURE ANALYSIS

Common cause failure analysis aims to identify potential failures in redundant systems or sub-systems that would undermine the benefits of redundancy because of the appearance of the same failure in the redundant parts at the same time.

Systems intended to take care of the safety of a plant often use redundancy in hardware and majority voting. This technique is used to avoid random component failures, which would tend to prevent the correct processing of data in a computer system. Such failures may be associated with external events, for example, if a computer system is installed in one single room then shortcomings in the air conditioning might reduce the benefits of redundancy.

Internal effects are also major contributors to Common Cause Failures (CCF). They can stem from design errors in common or identical components and their interfacing, as well as ageing of components. The scope of the analysis, however, goes beyond hardware. Even if 'diverse software' is used in different chains of a redundant computer system, there might be some commonality in the software approaches that could give rise to CCF, such as in the common specification.

2.3.3 CHECKLISTS

Checklists aim to provide a stimulus to critical appraisal of all aspects of the system rather than to lay down specific requirements. Many checklist questions are of a general nature and the assessor must interpret them as seems most appropriate to the particular system being assessed. As a result there may be questions in the checklist being used that are not relevant to the system being dealt with which should be ignored. Equally there may be a need, for a particular system, to supplement the standard checklist with questions specifically directed at the system being dealt with.

It should be clear that the use of checklists depends critically on the expertise and judgement of the engineer selecting and applying the checklist and it should be fully documented and justified. The objective is to ensure that the application of the checklists can be reviewed and that the same results will be achieved unless different criteria are used.

2.3.4 FAILURE MODES, EFFECTS AND CRITICALITY ANALYSIS

Failure modes, effects and criticality analysis aim to rank the criticality of components that could result in injury, damage or system degradation through single-point failures so as to identify those components that might need special attention and control measures during design or operation. A very simple method for criticality determination is to multiply the probability of component failure by the damage that could be generated; this method is similar to simple risk-factor analysis.

2.3.5 FINITE STATE MACHINES OR STATE TRANSITION DIAGRAMS

Finite state machines or state transition diagrams aim to implement the control structure of a system, and thus to identify potential design shortcomings. A specification or design expressed as an FSM can be checked for completeness (the system must have an action and new

state for every input in every state), for consistency (only one state change is defined for each state–input pair) and reachability (whether or not it is possible to get from one state to another by any sequence of inputs). These are important properties for critical systems and they can be checked.

2.3.6 FORMAL METHODS

Formal methods (Institution of Electrical Engineers 1991) aim to base the development of software on mathematics. This includes formal design and formal coding techniques which provide a means of developing a description of a system. The resulting description can be subjected to mathematical analysis to detect various classes of inconsistency or incorrectness. Moreover, the description can in some cases be analysed by machine, or animated to display various aspects of the behaviour of the system. Animation can give extra confidence that the system meets the real requirement and does not embody undesired failure modes.

A formal method will usually offer a notation (generally some form of discrete mathematics being used), a technique for deriving a description in that notation, and various forms of analysis for checking a description for different correctness properties.

2.3.7 TIME PETRI NETS

Time Petri nets (Bologna 1992) aim to model relevant aspects of the system behaviour and to assess, and possibly improve, safety and operational requirements through analysis and re-design. Petri nets belong to a class of graph theoretic models that are suitable for representing information and control flow in systems exhibiting concurrency and asynchronous behaviour.

A Petri net is a network of places and transitions. The places may be 'marked' or 'unmarked'. A transition is 'enabled' when all the input places to it are marked. When enabled, it is permitted (but not obliged) to 'fire'. If it fires, the input marks are removed, and each output place from the transition is marked instead. The potential hazards can be represented by particular states in the model. This can help identify otherwise unexpected ways in which failure can occur and it may help identify unexpected hazards.

2.4 EXPRESSION OF RISK

As can be readily appreciated from Chapters 5 and 6 there are considerable difficulties in determining and quantifying the public and political understanding of risk, and particularly what is an acceptable societal risk. Engineers involved in risk assessment would do well to read Chapters 5 and 6, but ultimately they must face up to quantifying what is an acceptable societal risk so that they have an objective to satisfy. Experience may indicate that this level of risk will have to be further reduced as the subject of risk assessment is better understood, and as a result of public and political pressure.

2.4.1 INDIVIDUAL RISK

This is one of the most widely used expressions. Usually it is expressed as a mortality rate as this is more readily measured and quantified. However, fates worse than death, such as the seriously injured road casualties, may be considered by some as a more serious risk. Mortality data may be defined as the fraction of the population at risk that suffer death per unit time. In this form it may be calculated simply as the annual number of deaths divided by the total population at risk (Grist 1978). It is also possible to calculate the risk borne by an individual located in the vicinity of an installation from which a harmful substance might be released in an accident. Although these two calculations will yield numbers having the same units, their composition is quite different.

2.4.2 DEATH PER UNIT MEASURE OF ACTIVITY

There are many risks for which it is possible to relate the detriment to any one of a variety of measures of activity rather than to a simple unit of time. For example, passenger transport deaths may be expressed relative to, *inter alia*, the total number of passenger-hours, or passenger-miles, or the number of operations. It is well known that the rank order and apparent relative risks are very much dependent on the choice of the measure of activity.

Clearly there are many possible measures of activity for any given undertaking, and wherever risks are related to just one such measure one may sensibly ask how the risk would look relative to other relevant measures. A measure that has been used for occupational risks, originally for the chemical industry, is the Fatal Accident Rate (FAR), originally referred to as the Fatal Accident Frequency Rate. This is defined as the number of deaths per 100 million man-hours of exposure, though this can be interpreted for workers as the number of deaths per 1000 people involved in an activity during the working lifetime of 10^5 hours (Kletz 1992). Hambly (1992) has extended FAR to provide a perspective of every day risk in domestic, work, transport and social situations. Though FAR is useful in comparing average risk in different occupations and activities, it is not easy to establish the time spent at risk for part-time activities such as sport or the sub-population at risk.

2.4.3 Loss of life expectancy

Various authors have used loss of life-expectancy as an expression of risk. This is discussed in Chapter 4, and elsewhere (International Commission on Radiological Protection 1977, Bowen 1976, Martin & ApSimon 1974, Reissland & Harries 1979, Griffiths 1971).

However, the essential conceptual problem remains defining what is an acceptable risk. The HSE (1988) described a conceptual framework for risk to members of the public. Above a certain level, which it is proposed should be one in ten thousand per year, the risks should be considered intolerable and call for immediate action to reduce them irrespective of cost. Barnes (1990) in the Hinkley Point Inquiry, suggested a lower level of tolerability. A risk of one in a million is suggested as being broadly acceptable to the public. Between these two levels the risk is considered tolerable but not negligible, and there is a need to reduce it further as far as is reasonably practical. Below the broadly acceptable level the risk is negligible and the employer should not be required to seek further improvement.

Different questions can arise in land-use planning in the vicinity of major industrial hazards. For this the HSE (1989) has introduced the concept of a 'dangerous dose' which may cause severe distress or serious injury, but is unlikely to cause death unless the recipients are highly susceptible to the effects. HSE would normally recommend against even a few new houses if the predicted individual risk of a dangerous dose was ten per million per year or greater, or an even less risk for a larger development.

2.4.4 Frequency against consequence

In cases where the magnitude of the consequences of an accident may vary over a wide range it has been found useful to present a graph of frequency vs consequence (fc). For instance Farmer (1967) used fc lines in relation to the release of I-131 from thermal nuclear reactors. More usually the consequence referred to is the number of fatalities, n (fn). However, the values actually experienced are very irregular and it is more useful and usual to plot cumulative frequency of n or more fatalities vs number of fatalities (Fn). Such graphs have been used to express the results of risk estimation studies as, for instance, in the transport of dangerous substances (Health and Safety Commission, 1991a) and the historical records of incidents involving multiple fatalities (United States Nuclear Regulatory Commission, 1975, Health and Safety Executive, 1978, Fryer & Griffiths, 1979).

Figure 2 reproduces the Fn curves from Coppola & Hall (1981) for various man-made hazards to which some supplementary data has been added. Data are given for early deaths and early plus delayed deaths for 100 commercial reactors. Rasmussen (United States Nuclear Regulatory Commission, 1975) was criticized for multiplying-up his risk estimates for IPWR and IBWR and labelling the resulting line 100 nuclear reactors, because of significant differences in risk from one reactor site to the next. However, in the 1970s this was probably not unreasonable in setting targets for the then perceived nuclear reactor programme. For comparison data are given on a similar basis for 100 PWRs based on the degraded core analysis for the Sizewell B PWR (Gittus, 1986). The United States Nuclear Regulatory Commission (1986) has investigated the risk to nuclear power plants from external events such as earthquakes, fire, flood, etc., and the Fn curve for early fatalities for the Surry PWR caused by seismic initiation is also given in figure 2.

Several authors have proposed that risk criteria should include some discount for delayed vs early deaths (Griffiths, 1981, Kinchin, 1978, Litai, 1980, Levine, 1980, Okrent, 1981), such as can occur due to

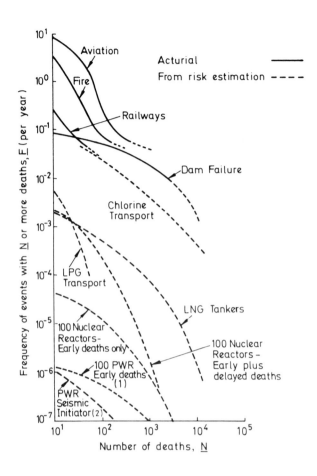

Figure 2. Examples of *F* vs. *N* lines for various man-made hazards. The risk esti-mates the frequencies are potential events, whereas the actuarial lines are based on actual events. The actuarial lines have extended on the basis of risk as-sessment. (Sources: Coppola and Hall 1981, (1) Gittas 1986, (2) United States Nu-clear Regulatory Commission 1986*a*.)

the release of radioactive materials. How-ever, this may be too simplified as with some man-made hazards, such as the 1984 Bhopial Disaster, fates worse than death should be taken into account.

The view has often been stated that the risk can be represented by the 'expected value' (i.e. the sum or integral of the pro-duct *f* times *c*) of the *fc* curves. The prob-lem with the expected value approach is that it implicitly presumes a linear trade-off between frequency and consequence size as a basis for the social evaluation of risk, which amounts to reducing risk to a single scale. However, as a concept this is too simplistic; risk to a particular indi-vidual cannot be equated with risk to the society as a whole or societal risk

(Health and Safety Executive 1992). So-ciety appears to consider a single event which causes many deaths to be more serious than many individual accident deaths.

In the Health and Safety Commission Re-port (1991 *b*) on Major Hazard Aspects of Transport of Dangerous Materials (appen-dix 6) two lines on the *Fn* graph are used to define the limits of what are deemed as an intolerable societal risk and a negli-gible societal risk (figure 3). The upper line is based on a risk of 2 in 1000 per year of an accident with 500 deaths, which for the Canvey Island complex was deemed to be just tolerable, whereas the lower line is set three orders of mag-nitude lower. A third line, referred to as

26

a local-scrutiny line, is assessed for the particular locality associated with road, rail and marine transport risks. Risk assessments that fall between the top two lines are considered as possibly unjustifiable risks, whereas risks that fall between the two lower lines are subject to improvement according to the 'as low as reasonably practicable' (ALARP) principle.

2.5 FORMS OF UNCERTAINTY IN RISK ESTIMATION

The uncertainties in risk assessment cover a wide range of types; some are quantifiable by established techniques, but others are less tractable.

Considering first the engineering of an installation, one may proceed with some confidence in analysing systems composed of items or sub-systems for which there exist models validated by tests and a substantial body of in-service data. Associated uncertainties arise from the data and can be treated by well-established methods. Uncertainty of a less quantifiable nature may arise through the need to exercise judgement when the data are insufficient.

An essentially unquantifiable uncertainty concerns the question of whether or not all significant accident sequences have been considered. As more risk analyses are completed the likelihood of such an omission should be reduced, assuming that there is good exchange of information. Much depends on the quality of the team doing the analysis, and the credibility of the results may be conditioned by the confidence one has in their professional ability. Similar categories of uncertainty can be identified in the modelling of consequences. Whereas some of these uncertainties are amenable to investigation by tests, given the resources, there are some that for various reasons are not investigable by direct tests. It is apparent that the overall uncertainty may vary over a considerable range, depending on the particular components of the estimate. Dunster & Vinck (1979) made the following observations:

"Uncertainties in estimates of probabilities of events by factors of less than two or three can hardly be expected, and uncertainties by a factor of ten or more may well occur, even in carefully conducted studies. The estimation of the magnitude of the consequences in human terms almost always involves environmental modelling and similar factors of uncertainty are to be expected."

Uncertainties of this magnitude might be thought at first sight to throw serious doubts on the usefulness of risk estimation. These doubts are not justified, because the significance of a given factor will depend on the level of risk involved.

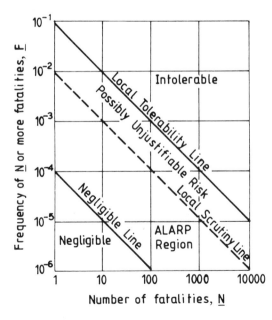

Figure 3. Societal Risk Tolerability. (Source: Health and Safety Commission Report 1991b.)

Thus, a factor of two on an individual risk of 10^{-3} per year will be important, but applied to a lower level, say 10^{-6} per year, it will be much less significant.

It is thus very important to be able to judge what is significant and what is negligible in dealing with uncertainty in risk, as the blind pursuit of accuracy for its own sake may squander resources better spent in a more selective manner. As suggested by Kletz (1992) a selective strategy might be based on a cost–benefit calculation. This has brought about an improvement in resource allocation within limited areas, but not on a broad national basis. The lack of a better understanding and quantification of cost benefit is a further reason why the uncertainties of estimates of probability should not cause too much concern at this stage of development of the subject.

It is a reasonable generalization to say that the accuracy of the consequence modelling should match that achieved in the frequency of occurrence estimates. However, there may be special considerations of siting that would place a premium on the accuracy of hazard-range estimation for a particular installation.

Although such observations may seem obvious enough, there are numerous examples of risk estimation in which the practitioners have been carried away by the methodology, producing quite extraordinary results. In the Comptroller-General's report to the US Congress (1978) attention is drawn to one study on liquefied natural gas risks that includes an estimate of 5×10^{-50} per year for the probability of a particular event in which about 100 000 people might be killed. The report goes on to comment that the organization doing these calculations apparently considers the probability that its dispersion estimates are wrong to be less than 10^{-40}. This is a good example of the deficiency referred to in the aphorism usually attributed to Gauss; namely, that the lack of mathematical culture is re-

vealed nowhere so conspicuously as in meaningless precision in numerical computations.

Coupled with the question of uncertainty is the problem of validation. Critics of risk estimation argue that the procedure is flawed because it yields results that are untestable. This is related to the view that a scientific theory should be examined in terms of its falsifiability. Although it is true that some of the overall results of risk estimation are not amenable to tests, for a variety of reasons, many of its components are testable, and are being tested. The criticism fails to recognize that risk estimation is a synthesis of science and engineering knowledge that has been brought about because it has a practical utility, and not as an attempt to establish a new branch of science.

It is sometimes asserted that estimates of risk are shown to be unrealistic and pessimistic by comparison with the accident record. For example, the 1978 Canvey Report (Health and Safety Executive 1978, appendixes 14 and 15) contains an estimate that up to 6000 deaths could result from the rapid release of 1000 tonnes of ammonia in an urban area, whereas in the accident record given in the second report of the Advisory Committee on Major Hazards (Health and Safety Commission 1979) the largest number of deaths is 18 resulting from a 38 tonne release, and another release of 600 tonnes resulted in no deaths at all. However, the Canvey Report does not seem so unrealistic in the light of the 1984 Bhopal Disaster, when an escape of methyl isocyanate caused over 2000 deaths in the shanty town which had grown up around the plant.

This difference does not demonstrate any discrepancy between experience and estimates, but rather illustrates the point that a given toxic release may result in consequences ranging from no casualties of any kind to many deaths, depending on the particular circumstances. That such a range exists is the essential point of the probabilistic description, and it is to be expected that our experience will be predominantly at the high probability/low consequence end of the *fc* curve (see figure 2).

The accident record states the facts of experience, from which important conclusions may be drawn concerning the phenomena that need to be considered, but for rare events it cannot on its own be used to show whether or not a risk has been reasonably estimated. This depends on the proper use of adequate models, especially for cases outside of our experience.

The accuracy of estimates of risk is being progressively improved by selective attention to important areas of uncertainty. The realistic goal is adequacy in relation to the needs of the engineer and to enable effective mitigation of consequences.

2.6 CONCLUSIONS

A sufficient number of studies estimating risks have now been done for there to be an adequate appreciation of the techniques involved. Although it is clear that studies vary in quality, and that there are points of contention over technical matters, there is consensus concerning the overall approach described here. There is now a background against which the reasonableness of a study can be judged, through open discussion, and this provides the basis for the emergence of risk estimation as a useful predictive technique. The process of peer review is important not only as a means of crucial examination of the techniques used, but also in identifying competent people and organizations.

Risk estimation is not a precise technique, and comparisons of risks associated with different systems can only be approximate. However, no matter how precise estimates of risk might be, they would not provide the sole key to decision making. The main benefit of estimating risk lies in the achievement of detailed understanding of the engineered system and the implications of various siting and technical options. This understanding is needed to ensure that no matter what decision is made the implementation is carried through in a competent fashion.

Techniques for estimating risks can be usefully applied to simple as well as complex systems. Reliability analysis has proved to be cost-effective in numerous studies on items such as ventilation systems and colliery winding gear. The individual engineer can make use of these techniques in his contribution to the overall task. In a broader context, risk estimation is proving to be very influential in such fields as regulatory requirements, planning and siting. This places a high degree of responsibility on those who practise the techniques. Ill-founded estimates or over-zealous reduction of risk ultimately constitute a burden on society, either through the sacrifice of safety or through the imposition of unreasonable constraints on the operator. It has to be recognized that it is impossible to completely eliminate risk.

For progress to be made, the following are necessary conditions: (a) There should be continuing attempts to improve the data relevant to the identification and estimation of risk.

(b) There should be continuing attempts to improve design, control procedures and protective measures, with the object of preventing hazards from arising.

(c) Effective arrangements should be established to learn from accidents and to feed the lessons back into the design process.

(d) There should be better understanding of quantified risk, both by the public and by those professionally involved.

(e) Quantified-risk assessment should be treated as a serious academic subject; but care must be taken not to make the treatment artificially rigid, thereby losing the flexible approach needed to fit best the needs of real situations.

REFERENCES

AICE 1987 *Dow's fire and explosion index: hazard classification guide.* American Institute of Chemical Engineers.

ASME Boiler and Pressure Vessel Code 1974 *Section XI: Rules for inservice inspection of nuclear power plant components. New York: ASME.*

Barlow, R.E., Fussel, J.B. & Singpurwalla, N.D. (eds) 1975 *Reliability and fault tree analysis.* Philadelphia, Pennsylvania: Society for Industrial and Applied Mathematics.

Barnes, M. 1990 *Hinkley Point Public Inquiries.* London: HMSO.

Bennett, P.A. 1991 Safety. In: *Software engineers reference book* (J.A. Mc Dermid, ed.) Oxford: Butterworth Heinemann.

Boeing Company 1965 *Systems safety symposium.* Seattle.

Bologna, S. 1992 Real-time software requirements, specification and animation using extended Petri-nets. In *Theory and application in safety aspects of computer control* (P.A. Bennett, ed.). Butterworth Heinemann. (In the press.)

Bowen, J.H. 1976 Individual risk vs public risk criteria. *Chem. Engng. Prog.* **72**, (2), 63–67.

British Standards Institution 1987 *Quality systems. BS5750.*

British Standards Institution. 1991 *Guide to the assessment of reliability of systems containing software. London: DD198.*

Britter, R.E. & McQuaid, J. 1988 *Workbook on the dispersion of dense gases. Health and Safety Executive Control Research Report No. 17.*

Carter, D.A. 1991 Aspects of risk assessment for hazardous pipeline containing flammable substances. *J. Loss Prev. Process Ind.* **4**, 68.

Comptroller General's Report to Congress of the United States 1978 *Liquefied energy gases safety.* US General Accounting Office EMD-78-28.

Coppola, A. & Hall, R.E. 1981 *A risk comparison. United States Nuclear Regulatory Commission Report (NUREG/CR–1916, BNL–NUREG–51338, R7, RG).*

Crutzen, S., Jehenson, P., Nichols, R.W., Herkenrath, H. & Strosnide, J. 1992 *Summary of the three phases of the PISC programme.* PISC Report No. 17, CEC JRC Ispra and OECD/NEA, Paris.

Crutzen, S., Jehenson, P., Nichols, R.W. & Strosnide, J. 1991 *The PISC III programme – status report.* SMIRT II Trans. Vol. G.

Cullen, The Hon. Lord. 1990 *The public inquiry into the Piper Alpha disaster.* London: HMSO.

Dunster, H. J. & Vinck, W. 1979 The assessment of risk - its value and limitations. *European nuclear conference – foratom VII congress, Hamburg,* pp. 162–166. Essen: Vulkan-Verlag.

Eisenberg, N.A. 1975 *Vulnerability model – a simulation system for assessing damage resulting from marine spills.* National Technical Information Service AD–A015–245.

EUROSTAT 1991 European industry reliability handbook, 1991, vol. 1, *Electrical power plants. Paris: EUROSTAT.*

Farmer, F.R. 1967 Siting criteria – a new approach. *Atom* **128**, 152–170.

Fennell, D. 1988 *Investigation into the King's Cross Underground fire. London: HMSO.*

Fernandez-Russell, D. 1987 Individual risk statistics for Great Britain. Research Report No. 2. Environmental Risk Assessment Unit, University of East Anglia, Norwich.

Fernandez-Russell, D. 1987 Societal risk estimates from historical data for U.K. and world-wide Events. Research Report No. 3. Environmental Risk Assessment Unit, University of East Anglia, Norwich.

Flint, A.R. 1981 Risks and their control in civil engineering. *Proc. R. Soc. Lond.* A **376**, 167–179.

Fryer L.S. & Griffiths, R.F. 1979 *World-wide data on the incidence of multiple fatality accidents. United Kingdom Atomic Energy Authority report SRD R149.*

Gittus, J.H. 1986 Degraded core analysis for the pressurized water reactor. *Sci. publ. Affairs* **2**, 121.

Griffiths, R.F. 1977 *Critical review of the USCG report by Raj et al. on spills of anhydrous ammonia on to water, with an alternative assessment of the experimental results.* United Kingdom Atomic Energy Authority report SRD R67.

Grist, D.R. 1978 *Individual risk – a compilation of recent British data.* United Kingdom Atomic Energy Authority report SRD R125.

Hambly, E.C. 1992 *Preventing disaster. Proc. R. Instn* (In the press.)

Hanna, S.R. *et al.* 1991 *a* Evaluation of fourteen hazardous gas models with ammonia and hydrogen fluoride field data. *J. Haz. Matls* **26**, 127–158.

Hanna, S.R. *et al.* 1991 *b* Uncertainties in the hazardous gas model predictions. Proc. Int. Conf. and Workshop on Modelling and Mitigating the Consequences of Accidental Releases of Hazardous Materials, New Orleans. *Am. I. Chem. Engrs.*

Health and Safety Commission 1979 Advisory *Committee on major hazards – second report.* London: HMSO.

Health and Safety Commission 1991 *a Second report on human reliability assessment – a critical review. Advisory Committee on the Safety of Nuclear Installations Study Group on Human Factors.* London: HMSO.

Health and Safety Commission 1991 *b Major hazard aspects of the transport of dangerous substances.* London: HMSO.

Health and Safety Executive 1978 *Canvey: an investigation of potential hazards from operations in the Canvey Island/Thurrock area.* London: HMSO.

Health and Safety Executive 1981. *Canvey, a second report.* London: HMSO.

Health and Safety Executive 1987 *Programmable electronic systems in safety related applications.* London: HMSO.

Health and Safety Executive 1989 Risk *Criteria for land-use planning in the vicinity of major industrial hazards.* London: HMSO.

Health and Safety Executive 1992 *The tolerability of risk from nuclear power stations.* London: HMSO. (In the press.)

Hecht, L.O. & Fragola, J.R. 1977 Reliability data bases, a review. *8th Product Liability Prevention Conference, Hasbrouck Heights, New Jersey*, pp. 137–146. New York: IEEE.

Hidden, A. 1989 *Investigation into the Clapham Junction railway accident. London: HMSO.*

International Commission on Radiological Protection 1977 Problems involved in developing an index of harm. *Ann. ICRP* **1**,(4), 1–24. (ICRP publication No. 27) Oxford: Pergamon Press.

International Electrochemical Commission. 1991 *Software for computers in the application of industrially related systems.* Geneva: IEC.

Institution of Electrical Engineers 1991 *Formal methods in safety critical systems.* London: IEE.

Institution of Electrical Engineers 1992 *Safety related systems: a professional brief for the engineer.* London: IEE.

Kinchin, G.H. 1978 Assessment of hazards in engineering work. *Proc. Inst. Civ. Engrs* **64** part 1, 64, 431–438.

Kletz, T.A. 1991 Human problems with computer control in process plants. *J. Proc. Cont.* **1**, 111–115.

Kletz, T.A. 1992 HAZOP and HAZAN. *Inst. Chem. Engrs.*

Layfield, Sir Frank 1987 *Sizewell B public inquiry. London: HMSO.*

Lees, F.P. 1980 *Loss prevention in the process industries.* London: Butterworth & Co.

Levine, S. 1980 *TMI and the future of reactor safety.* Stockholm: Atomic Industrial Forum (International Public Affairs Workshop).

Lewis, H.W. 1978 *Risk Assessment Review Group report to the United States Nuclear Regulatory Commission.* (NUREG CR 0400). US Nuclear Regulatory Commission.

Litai, D. 1980 A risk comparison methodology for the assessment of acceptable risk. Ph.D. thesis, Massachusetts Institute of Technology, Department of Nuclear Engineering.

Martin, A. & ApSimon H. 1974 *Population exposure and the interpretation of its significance* (IAEA SM 184/9). pp. 15-26. International Atomic Energy Agency.

McQuaid, J. & Roebuck, B. 1985 *Large scale field trials on dense vapour dispersion,* rep. No. 10029. Brussels: Commission of the European Communities.

Merrison, A.W. 1971 *Inquiry into the basis of design and method of erection of steel box girder bridges.* London: HMSO.

Nichols, R.W. & Crutzen, S. (ed) 1988 *Ultrasonic inspection of heavy steel components: PISC II final report*. Elsevier Applied Science Publications Ltd.

1984 Offshore reliability data handbook. Hovik: OREDA, P.O. Box 370, N–122.

Okrent, D. 1977 *A general evaluation approach to risk–benefit for large technological systems and its application to nuclear power (UCLA–ENG–7777)*. University of California.

Okrent, D. 1981 Industrial risks. *Proc. R. Soc. Lond.* A **376**, 133–149.

1979–80 *PISC I results,* vol. 1–6. EUR 6371 EN.

Parfitt, J.P. 1992 Societal risk estimates from historical data for U.K. and world-wide Events. Report SRD AR5. SRD Association, Culcheth, Warrington.

Puttock, J.S. *et al.* 1991 Dispersion models and hydrogen fluoride predictions. *J. Loss Prevention*, **4**.

Reissland, J. & Harries, V. 1979 A scale for measuring risks. *New Scient.* **72**, 809–811.

Spanner, J.C., Doctor R.S., Taylor, T.T. & Muscara, J. 1991 *Qualifications process for ultrasonic testing in nuclear inservice inspection applications*. NUREG/CR–4882 PNL–6179.

Steel, D. 1987 *Formal investigation into the MV Herald of Free Enterprise ferry Disaster. London: HMSO.*

United States Nuclear Regulatory Commission 1975 *Reactor safety study (USNRC, WASH 1400). Washington, D.C.*

United States Nuclear Regulatory Commission 1990 a *Analysis of core damage frequency surry power station, unit 1 – external events,* vol. 1, rev. 1. NUREG/CR–4550 Sand 86–2084.

United States Nuclear Regulatory Commission 1990 b *Evaluation of severe accident risks – Surry unit 1,* vol. 3. rev. 1. NUREG/CR–4551, Sand 86–1309.

Vesely, W.E. 1970 A time-dependent methodology for fault-tree evaluation. *Nuclear Engineering and Design* **13**, 337–360.

Vesely, W.E. *et al.* 1981. *Fault tree handbook.* United States Nuclear Regulatory Commission. Rep. NUREG–0492.

ANNEX: HAZARD IDENTIFICATION TECHNIQUES

Safety audit: this is essentially an attempt to subject an existing or specified system to a systematic, critical and comprehensive review of activities with a view to minimizing accident and loss. The result of such an audit is a plan of proposed measures for improvement, and a monitoring exercise to assess results (British Chemical Industry Safety Council 1969).

Hazard survey: this may be regarded as a component of the safety-audit procedure, but may also be extended to cover not only the identification of hazards associated with a particular installation, but also the management and emergency arrangements. Such a survey does not necessarily result in any proposal for modification to practice, but would be expected to be updated periodically. The draft Regulations on Hazardous Installations include guidance notes on hazard surveys (Health and Safety Commission, 1978).

Hazard indices: these are essentially inventories of materials and plant related to the potential for harm based on such parameters as heats of combustion, toxic limits, etc. Very many of such indices is evident in the literature, based, for example, on maximum permissible concentrations or intakes for radioactive materials, and on air-quality standards for pollutants. Perhaps the most widely used is the Dow Index (Dow Chemical Company 1987) for fire and explosion. Hazard indices are essentially design and practice guides based on the potential for harm, and usefully supplement other techniques of hazard identification and control.

Hazard and operability studies: these constitute an important technique in the field of hazard control, and consist of a systematic examination of operations in terms of design intention of every part of the process, and the causes and consequences of deviations from normal operation. The analysis is based on a check list of guide words that specify the intentions (e.g. transfer, circulated, pressures) and deviations (e.g. more of or than, part of, as well as). The study team must then assess the possible consequences of these deviations. The technique has proved fruitful in overcoming operability problems and in hazard identification and is described by several authors (Chemical Industry Safety and Health Council 1977, Lawley 1974, Knowlton 1981).

REFERENCES

British Chemical Industry Safety Council 1969 *Safe and Sound*. London.

Chemical Industry Safety and Health Council 1977 *Guide to hazard and operability Studies*. London.

Health and Safety Commission 1978 *Hazardous installations (notification and survey) regulations*. London: HMSO.

Knowlton, R.E. 1981 *An introduction to hazard and operability studies*. Vancouver: Chemetics International Ltd.

Lawley, H.G. 1974 Operability studies and hazard analysis. *Chem. Engng Prog.* **70**(4), 45–66.

Chapter 3

TOXICITY, TOXICOLOGY AND NUTRITION

Dr Susan M. Barlow, Professor J. W. Bridges, Professor P. Calow, Dr D. M. Conning, Professor R. N. Curnow, Professor A. D. Dayan, Dr I. F. H. Purchase, Professor C. W. Suckling, F. R. S.

3.1 INTRODUCTION

This chapter examines the potential risks to people and to other living organisms from exposure to substances at concentrations that may cause harm, whether found in nature or not, and including substances in food; how these risks may be identified and assessed, and measures that may be taken to minimize them. Potential toxicity to humans, including nutritional problems, and toxicity to other organisms in the environment are discussed. There is considerable overlap across these fields in matters of toxic risk. Subjects are discussed under whichever heading is the most informative, for example monitoring under ecotoxicology, with an indication of its wider relevance.

A discussion of the identification and avoidance of risks, as is the subject of this chapter, will inevitably concentrate on potential harm rather than on concurrent benefits. However, decisions on what risks are tolerable and what are not should be taken with consideration of the consequent benefits gained or foregone and the risks of alternative courses of action. The belief that regulation or other actions can exclude all risk, leaving pure benefit, is a delusion.

Modern society is critically dependent on the use of a wide variety of chemicals. Technological development has resulted in prolonged and more intense and widespread contact with naturally occurring toxic materials (e.g. lead, arsenic, antimony, asbestos) than was the case before the industrial revolution. Moreover

there has been, over recent decades, greatly increased inadvertent contact with many thousands of synthetic compounds not previously present on Earth, some of which have spread widely throughout the environment. In addition, many chemicals are deliberately administered to people and to domesticated animals both prophylactically and therapeutically, and in food.

The number of chemicals to which mankind is exposed through natural processes is enormous, for example combustion of wood gives rise to many thousands of chemicals some of which, such as dioxins, are toxic. Many plants, some regularly used as foods, contain potentially toxic substances. A variety of fungi, both microscopic and macroscopic some of which can grow on food, produce potent toxins, and many animals secrete poisons. Some inorganic materials, e.g. some metals and minerals, are toxic.

Experience will have provided protection against acute responses to noxious substances (i.e. the immediate effects of a relatively large dose) whether from food or from contact with plants or animals. However, over most of mankind's history, given the short lifespan and the multiplicity of immediate problems of existence, the causes of chronic effects (i.e. those delayed in onset and resulting from repeated or prolonged exposure to relatively low doses) were not often recognized. Only in recent times has the way been cleared, by the great reduction in deaths from many infectious diseases and from malnutrition, for recognition of the less immediate but nevertheless potentially serious effects that some natural and manufactured chemicals may cause.

Harm to the health of oneself and one's family and of children in general is among the risks reported to be uppermost in the mind of the public. Consequently, concerns have increased about the possible risks to health from chemicals, whether man-made or of natural origin. These have led to a massive growth in toxicological investigation, directed towards identifying and quantifying the effects of possibly harmful substances, assessing the implications and devising appropriate precautions. Needless to say, toxicology also plays an essential role in the development of therapeutic compounds.

The inclusion of nutrition in a chapter on toxicology may, at first sight, seem strange but there are good reasons for doing so. There is considerable public concern about chemicals that may be present in food as contaminants, for example as residues of chemical treatment (e.g. pesticides) or as products of microbial contamination, and also about additives deliberately introduced during processing, for example as preservatives. Moreover, it is now widely recognized that both inadequate and excessively high consumption of some nutrients may be dangerous.

Much of the risk management considered in this report arises from situations in which a given event is likely to cause injury or death, for example an explosion in a mine or a factory, collapse of a bridge, collision between vehicles or contact with a live electrical wire. The task is then to identify and prevent or minimize the occurrence of circumstances in which the event might occur and secondarily to minimize the degree of injury likely to be caused should the precautions fail to prevent the event.

In contradistinction, the first task of the toxicologist is not to investigate how substances may come into contact with organisms, but to find out what may happen if they do. The second task is to estimate what dose and hence what exposure an organism is likely to withstand without harm. The third, of interest to the ecotoxicologist in particular, is to identify pathways by which a substance may reach a susceptible organism. On the basis of all this and of other information, protective measures can be prescribed.

For most physical hazards the consequences of an accident will include instant trauma, that is to say physical damage to the body, which is usually readily diagnosable. Toxic hazards, on the other hand, may result in a wide range of immediate, delayed or cumulative effects. These may manifest themselves in many ways, for example in disturbance of functions of the body's systems or of behaviour, or in abnormalities of structure. Some effects may be quickly apparent but others may be slow in onset and difficult to recognize and diagnose, at least in their early stages. As with physical trauma, the consequences will range from the trivial to the fatal but with the added possibility of harm to future generations if genes are affected. Many toxic hazards differ from the physical also in that the causal agent is not localized but widespread and invisible and this increases the concern.

The first line of defence against harm to the environment from toxic substances, keeping them out, is not the subject of this chapter. However, we include in section 4 a brief discussion of some important procedures for project management, which have been developed for the avoidance or minimization of pollution, and for avoiding harm from the release of genetically modified organisms (GMOs). Pollutants and GMOs are, of course, both potential contributors of toxicants in the environment. These approaches are particular relevant to this report because they show how some of the issues raised in Chapters 5 and 6 are being addressed in practice.

Considerable importance is attached in this chapter to the scientific understanding of mechanisms. By 'mechanism' is meant the processes that gives rise to a particular phenomenon, for example the changes in behaviour of systems in the body that are produced by a given toxicant and lead to its clinical effects. A knowledge of mechanisms, expressed in scientific terms, is important in toxicology for several reasons. It may suggest means of early diagnosis and treatment, possibilities of *in vitro* testing to reduce tests with animals and give guidance on the extent to which the response of one organism may be extrapolated to others. The significance of a response of a system that diverges from that of others may be explained, so that it may be possible to infer reasonable implications for species at risk.

A scientific understanding of mechanisms will make any technology more flexible and more robust. For example, it will assist in predicting what will happen

if the operation or the operating environment move outside the range envisaged in the design. The basis will have been laid for the deployment of a variety of scientific investigational techniques to deal with problems when something unforeseen does occur.

The matters addressed in this chapter are relevant across the globe but, in considering the allocation of resources, we should not lose sight of the fact that the amelioration of the human lot afforded by the increase in scientific understanding is by no means evenly spread across the world's population. Millions do not benefit fully from the advances in the sciences of toxicology and nutrition that have led to a substantial increase in life expectancy and improvement in quality of life for many. Malnutrition still accounts for millions of preventable deaths.

Much useful information on matters dealt with in this chapter is given in two books by the British Medical Association: *The BMA guide to living with risk* (Penguin 1990) and *Hazardous waste and human health* (OUP 1991).

3.2 ASSESSMENT OF TOXIC HAZARDS TO HUMANS

3.2.1 EXPOSURE AND DOSE
In the previous report (The Royal Society, 1983) the principles of toxicity testing were described. There are now many guidelines from regulatory authorities and reviews which set out the detail of requirements for toxicity testing of new and existing chemicals. There is a considerable degree of agreement internationally about these methods, which have not changed substantially in recent years, and hence it is not appropriate to provide detailed descriptions of toxicity testing methods here.

The principal purpose of toxicity testing is to provide data about the types of adverse effect produced by chemicals, their incidence and relation to dose. The occurrence and extent of a toxic effect is dependent on the dose of toxicant, though factors such as the species and the state of health of the threatened organism and other stresses may also affect the outcome. The basic concept of dose is simple, as in the amount of a medicine taken. (In clinical practice selection of the dose is complex and depends on many factors such as age, sex and body weight.) It will often be the case that the available information on substances in the environment relates to ambient concentrations, that is to say to concentrations in an organism's surroundings to which it may be exposed. Dose will then have to be estimated from exposure. Dosage over time may be important, in which case duration and frequency of exposure will need to be taken into account as well as concentration. The toxicologist is often faced, therefore, with the difficult task of estimating not only toxic and tolerable dose, but also what patterns of exposure are likely to result in an intake that would exceed the tolerable dose.

As is well known, some substances that are at some level of intake beneficial, indeed essential to life, may be toxic at too high a dose. For example, in some parts of China excessive intake of selenium (itself an essential nutrient), consequent on a high level in the soil, leads to liver and heart damage which kills many young people. The death of a child who has taken iron tablets prescribed for its mother's anaemia is another example.

Many factors complicate the prediction of potential toxicological effects and tolerable doses. The extent to which toxicology, epidemiology apart, can be studied in people is very properly limited. Toxicologists thus have recourse to laboratory experiments in which various organisms or *in vitro* preparations serve as models for the human being. All these experiments are inevitably, to a greater or lesser extent, abstractions from reality that serve as models of the actual organism of interest.

The effects of exposure to some toxicants may not become apparent for a long time. For example, those cancers for which the initial insult is exposure to radiation or to a chemical but which may not develop until after some subsequent events, as yet poorly understood, which may occur several decades later.

An additional difficulty is the fact that exposure is likely to vary widely across a population. Moreover, response to a given exposure may be affected by the physiological status of the individual (e.g. according to age, sex, health, pregnancy, genotypic differences). A very few individuals may respond to certain chemicals in one or other of a wide variety of idiosyncratic and unpredictable ways, for which tests have not yet been devised.

Organisms, including people, are rarely exposed to just one potentially toxic substance at a time. Exposure to mixtures is more common. It has been estimated that there are some 4000 different chemicals in tobacco smoke and 500 or more in coffee. Toxicity may be exacerbated by additive or even synergistic effects. Conversely, there is now considerable evidence of the existence in foods of a wide range of substances that are antagonistic to the toxic effects of compounds, for example by binding them in innocuous forms.

3.2.2 CURRENT PRACTICE IN TOXICITY TESTING

The most frequent method of assessing safety-in-use is to assess the dose that produces no adverse effects (the No Observed Effect Level, NOEL) and to apply an appropriate but arbitrary, empirically chosen safety factor to it. The determination of a NOEL is therefore critical, being required for the safety assessment of new chemicals being placed on the market and, in recent years, to fulfil regulatory requirements to update the toxicological information available on existing chemicals in a process of re-registration. There is, however, some criticism of the commonly use direct method of estimating NOEL in that smaller studies tend to produce higher values. Here, as in other studies, careful statistical analysis is important, including the fitting of an assumed dose response curve to the data. From time to time animal and other studies are also done to follow up observations made from epidemiological studies so as to confirm their relation to chemical exposure and explore the mechanisms by which the toxic effects are caused.

The experimental design for toxicity studies is in principle fairly straightforward. Experiments compare observations made on two groups of animals. Both groups are maintained under precisely the same conditions, except that one is divided into smaller groups, each of which is exposed to a different level of the substance under test while the other, the control group, is not exposed at all. The size of the experiment and the frequency and nature of the observations made is determined by statistical and biological considerations of the endpoint. Interpretation of the results often requires careful statistical analysis, which may, for example, include age adjustment to account for natural mortality during the experiment.

Observation of adverse effects relies on laboratory examination of tissues or body fluids and careful observation of functional changes in the animals. It is usual to classify toxicity tests according to the length of dosing, route of administration and specific endpoint being studied. Thus the length of dosing is described as acute (1–14 days), subchronic (1–6 months), chronic (6–24 months) and life-time (18–30 months in rodents). Typical routes of administration include, intravenous, oral, dermal, ocular and inhalation. Specific endpoints that are frequently studied include carcinogenicity, reproductive and developmental endpoints, sensitization and neurotoxicity and behaviourial endpoints.

Many chemicals are metabolized in the liver and elsewhere in the body, with the result that target organs potentially receive doses both of the parent chemical and its metabolites. In assessing the toxicity of a compound, for the purposes of

human hazard and risk assessment, the critical relation is between the concentration over time of the proximate toxicant (be it the original chemical or its metabolite) and the adverse effects it causes in the target tissue. The information on target tissue dose is obtained from studies of the metabolism and kinetics of the chemical and its metabolites, a task which is complex and difficult to do and often requires the use of radioactive tracer techniques. As metabolism and kinetics often differ between species, it is this information that can explain the differences in species response. For medicines, such data are an essential input in determining the appropriate dose and frequency of administration.

By and large, testing methods used in industry have become more standardized. The Organisation for Economic Co-operation and Development (OECD) and other organisations have facilitated this process as a means towards reducing barriers to international trade. There remain some differences between the requirements of various regulatory authorities and these are gradually being resolved either through the OECD or by bilateral discussions between industry and the principal regulatory authorities of the pharmaceutical industry. However, there is increasing attention to the detailed conduct of toxicity studies spurred on by improvements in science and by the application of Good Laboratory Practices (GLP). In general, selected parameters are studied more carefully using methods with greater sensitivity.

The conduct of a comprehensive set of toxicity tests is a time-and resource consuming activity. The largest studies, such as life-time carcinogenicity studies in rodents, take three to four years to complete and may cost in excess of £500 000. The testing strategy for a new chemical requires careful sequencing. Thus acute studies are carried out initially in order to provide both hazard information for safety assessment and information for the design of subsequent sub-chronic studies. Information from the 28 and 90 day studies is an essential prerequisite for the design of chronic and life-time studies. Hence, the provision of comprehensive toxic hazard data on a chemical can take from 3–5 years.

3.2.3 RECENT ISSUES IN TOXICITY TESTING

At first almost all toxicological testing was focused on determining the acute effects of substances on laboratory animals, usually rats or mice, with death as the adverse outcome. However, it gradually became apparent that the range of potential adverse effects that must be explored is much wider in two respects: first, chronic as well as acute effects, and second, a range of consequences other than death, for example harm to the fetus (teratological effects), the causation of tumours, the production of allergies and, in effect, any cause of diminution of the quality of life.

Development of toxicological science, as already noted, has extended from conventional testing for regulatory purposes to detailed exploration of mechanisms and to a realization of the importance of extending the range of toxic actions that are studied. Examples of the extended range are given in the following paragraphs and the approach to mechanisms of toxic action is briefly discussed in the next section.

Interest has recently grown in the field of immunotoxicity, which includes both the production of sensitization and of immunosuppression. This interest has been driven by the enormous developments in the science of immunology, the observation that side effects of medicines and other substances can often involve immunological effects, and possibly by raised public awareness of the importance of the immune system arising from publicity of the AIDS epidemic. The developments in immunology have provided a range of specific measurements of the function of

the immune system which in turn have led to suggestions that these methods should be used in the identification of chemicals that damage the immune system. The major problem faced is that measurements of specific endpoints within the complex immune system frequently show changes whose significance it is impossible to deduce.

The strategy that is evolving is to enhance the observations made in standard sub-acute and chronic toxicity studies (for example by histopathology of organs in the immune system) in order to identify any adverse effects on the immune system. If adverse effects are seen in these standard studies, then specific observations on components of the immune system may help to provide an understanding of the mechanism of production of them. In sensitization testing, the greater understanding of cellular mechanisms of contact allergy has allowed the development of improved, more quantitative methods of identifying both contact and respiratory allergens.

Concerns about possible neurological effects of those exposed to chemicals has resulted in great interest in neurotoxicology. The current methods of assessing neurotoxicity are considered by many to be inadequate and the developments in neuroscience provide many opportunities of improving methods and understanding mechanisms of toxicity. Current methods of assessing neurotoxicity in standard toxicity tests depend on general observation of behaviour and on histopathology of the central and peripheral nervous system. Definitive evidence from histopathology may require special techniques and hence the conduct of special studies. More recently, specific behavourial tests have been suggested by some to be necessary for the proper assessment of the neurotoxicity of chemicals.

This in turn presents real problems of interpretation. Functional changes may be seen, but as behaviour is a very-high-level function, what is the relevance of observations of behavioural changes in rodents to the assessment of hazard in man? How is this information to be incorporated into hazard and risk assessment? The simple application of the no-effect level and safety factor method of risk assessment seems far too crude to deal with the uncertainties of neurotoxicity. Once again, the pragmatic approach is to rely on specific observations of clinical and histopathological changes made in standard studies. If any effects are observed, appropriate behavioural and other functional tests may be applied.

In both immunotoxicity and neurotoxicity testing, there has been a tendency to develop techniques that rely on sophisticated measurement or estimation of changes in a few of the vast number of biochemical, cellular or physiological variables. These results may be misleading or difficult to interpret when knowledge of their significance and of how to extrapolate from animal to man is inadequate. As a general guideline, new methods should rely on well-understood biological processes, changes in which provide data relevant to hazard assessment.

There is a growing criticism of the standard animal carcinogenicity study as a means for identifying chemical carcinogens and assessing human carcinogenic risk. In the course of the past decade it has become apparent that chemical carcinogens can be divided into two broad classes on the basis of their mechanism of action: genotoxic and non-genotoxic carcinogens. Genotoxic carcinogens are defined as those that produce demonstrable damage to the DNA which, it is assumed, is the critical event in the induction of carcinogenesis, though, as has been mentioned, the actual onset may be delayed for many decades. However, there are now many carcinogens – up to a third of those tested in the National Toxicology Programme of the USA – which do not show any evidence of

genotoxicity in a variety of test systems. Non-genotoxic carcinogens tend to produce cancer in a single organ in a single sex and/or species of rodent. As virtually all proven human chemical carcinogens are genotoxic, there is growing concern that non-genotoxic carcinogens identified in current rodent carcinogenicity studies may be the result of inappropriate design of these studies and hence that the information provided may not be of value in human risk assessment. Much of the concern revolves around the extremely high doses administered in some long-term carcinogenicity studies, because of the insistence that a 'maximum tolerated dose' should be selected as the top dose in an experiment. For chemicals with low toxicity, this may result in extraordinarily high doses being given which are far in excess of those to which man is exposed. Thus, doses of saccharin up to 5% by weight of the diet were required to produce the carcinogenic effect in the bladder of experimental animals.

As an understanding of the mechanism of action of non-genotoxic carcinogens develops, it becomes possible to use more appropriate risk assessments. For example, several chemicals (e.g. trimethylpentane, which occurs in petrol, and d-limonene, which occurs in citrus fruits) produce cancer in male rat kidneys but not in females and not in mice. The mechanism is now known to be associated with binding of these chemicals to alpha-2u-globulin which is specific to male rats. Hence it is concluded that there is no human hazard from exposure to these chemicals.

The reliability of the results of long-term studies is of great concern to regulators and to industry. Ultimately it may be possible to achieve the major aims of toxicity testing – namely to provide accurate information for human hazard assessment – by using a combination of genotoxicity assays with modified sub-acute and chronic toxicity studies. This may allow, at the same time, a reduction in the number of animals and in the amount of distress to which these animals are exposed.

3.2.4 MECHANISMS OF TOXIC AC- TION

Regulatory toxicity testing provides comprehensive data on the potential toxic effects of a chemical. It is usual to provide information from tests in several species (e.g. acute toxicity in the rat, guinea pig and mouse, chronic toxicity in the dog and rat, reproduction in the rat and rabbit and carcinogenicity in the rat and mouse) which may indicate species differences in response. One reason for these may be that the kinetics of the compound's uptake, metabolism and excretion differs with resulting differences in tissue levels of the proximate toxicant. There may be other physiological (e.g. differing receptors) or anatomical reasons why information from animal studies, particularly of a quantitative nature, may not be totally relevant to human hazard assessment. It is for these reasons that studies of the mechanisms of toxic action, which may resolve the uncertainties, are becoming increasingly important. The methods used are research-based and cannot be standardized, because the problems tackled are so varied. Studies of mechanisms, in addition to refining human hazard assessment, provide valuable information on the underlying reasons for particular toxic responses and may reveal new insights into normal physiology.

3.2.5 RESPONSES TO CONCERN ON THE USE OF ANIMALS

Public concern about ethical issues associated with experimentation with animals has provided an incentive to reduce the use of animals in toxicity testing, and to use them more humanely. As part of this overall movement considerable attention has been placed on the development of alternatives to animal studies in toxicity testing.

There is no shortage of proposals for *in vitro* test systems for toxicity assessment. A considerable amount of work is being done to validate *in vitro* tests against known toxicity of chemicals. In spite of all this activity, no new *in vitro* test systems have been definitively introduced into the regulatory framework for testing of chemicals since the introduction of *in vitro* mutagenicity studies in the late 1970s. To many toxicologists this is not surprising, as screening tests in toxicity aim at finding as wide a variety of potential toxic effects as possible in dozens of organs, thousands of enzymes, millions of cells or combinations of them. Thus toxicological evaluation for hazard assessment needs data from the integrated systems of whole organisms. This cannot be provided by tests *in vitro*, highly specific, reproducible and informative though they may be. Nevertheless, *in vitro* tests are increasingly being used as a method of screening during the development of new chemicals for specific toxicological endpoints, for example skin corrosivity or eye irritation. When used as screening methods these tests help to identify the highly toxic materials, which may allow the selection of less toxic analogues or, if toxicity testing is still required, a modification of the subsequent *in vivo* tests to take account of the chemical's toxicity and to reduce the severity of effects.

This ethically motivated development has been accompanied by an increasing awareness of the scientific value of employing *in vitro* or limited *in vivo* procedures to screen out substances without recourse to a full conventional testing in animals. For example, in the development of pharmaceuticals, chemicals are tested on isolated enzymes or receptors to select the most promising candidates for development as medicines, and industrial and agrochemicals can be examined for severe acute toxicity on isolated skin before milder but still important actions are studied in tests on animals.

In one method, developed by ICI in the early 1980s to test the corrosive effect of chemicals on the skin, chemicals are applied to slices of rat skin in the laboratory. Their effect is assessed by measuring the change in electrical impedance of the skin, which corrosive chemicals lower to below a certain threshold value. This test has given no false negatives (that is 100% of all corrosives are predicted) but there is a false positive prediction rate of about 10%. For several years some laboratories have used this method as a pre-screen. The approach is now formally recognized by the OECD, which states, in its 1992 update of the test guideline on skin irritation/corrosion, that it may not be necessary to test *in vivo* materials for which the corrosive properties are predicted on the basis of *in vitro* tests. But the OECD concluded that it was highly unlikely that *in vitro* tests would be able totally to replace *in vivo* tests for at least ten years.

It is not possible to reproduce *in vitro* the complex pattern of effects that maintains whole living organisms. Extrapolation from *in vivo* observations in a given species to an entire free-living population with its range of ages, sexes, health, nutrition, concurrent exposure to a variety of chemicals and through the whole life cycle, is itself complex and difficult. To attempt to do so from the further abstraction from reality that is inevitable in *in vitro tests*, in the current state of knowledge, could not establish a basis for safe usage.

The role and need for *in vitro* and *in vivo* testing remains under intense debate. For the present, it seems that both are essential: *in vitro* for possible initial screening and for the precise analysis of specific actions, and possibly to indicate certain simple direct effects, and *in vivo* for the study of complex actions and interactions in physiological systems that cannot be studied except in whole animals.

It follows that, although the risk of rejecting a potentially beneficial substance because of an adverse effect *in vitro* may be acceptable, such tests cannot be accepted as evidence for safety in the current state of knowledge.

Alternatives are also being developed for the LD_{50} (lethal dose for 50%) test which has been a mainstay of toxicity testing for decades. In this test the dose required to kill 50% of the exposed animals, usually rodents, is determined using enough animals, usually between 80 and 100, to give a statistically acceptable result. The past ten years has seen a move away from this type of test to a 'fixed dose procedure' which uses many fewer animals and causes less distress. This test, developed initially by the British Toxicology Society, has been welcomed by the European Community and fully ratified by OECD. It should now begin to replace the oral LD_{50} test for the majority of regulatory acute-toxicity tests. There is an analogous interest in Germany (Spielmann 1992). The validation of a new test (establishing its predictive reliability and reproductility across laboratories) and subsequent acceptance by international agencies is a lengthy process. For example the fixed-dose procedure took more than ten years to be accepted and it still requires animals. The encouraging message, however, is that it has been possible to find an alternative that is both ethically and scientifically superior to current methods. The search for further improvements continues.

3.2.6 TESTING IN HUMAN VOLUNTEERS
The limitations of tests in biological and physical models and the consequent need for observation of man are discussed in detail in the first section of the next Chapter, in the context of epidemiology. In the narrower context of the laboratory, there is a tradition extending over many centuries of scientists experimenting on themselves and on willing

colleagues and students, to explore normal physiological mechanisms and the causes and abnormal processes of disease. Much important knowledge and many valuable techniques have been obtained in this way. Examples include Lavoisier's study of human metabolism, Ross's discovery of the malaria parasite, Forssman and cardiac catheterization and the Haldanes and the effects of anoxia.

The motivation for doing studies on humans and its special value arises from the opportunity to study the species of interest, thus avoiding the assumptions that underlie the extrapolation from one species to another. Moreover, experiments with humans offer the possibility of exploring subjective as well as objective responses, including higher intellectual functions.

There are, of course, ethical obligations not to harm a fellow human, to respect the autonomy of the individual and to preserve confidentiality. These ethical considerations, together with legal concepts of obligations and liabilities, have led to the development of complex and comprehensive codes of conduct that govern what experiments physicians and others may consider doing in healthy subjects and with patients. Overshadowing all is the memory of the abuse of medical skills brought to light in the Nuremberg trials and elsewhere.

In the development of pharmaceuticals it is often the practice to investigate the effects of promising candidate compounds in healthy volunteers before proceeding to clinical trials. The objective is usually to investigate the administration, absorption, metabolism and excretion of the substance, to begin to measure its pharmacodynamic effects and to seek evidence of unwanted effects. The knowledge thus obtained can give advance warning of undesirable side effects, increase confidence in efficacy and help define the nature and protocols for clinical trials, thus improving their safety and efficiency and reducing risk.

Given a satisfactory outcome of the initial experiments, others may follow to explore the effects of physiological state (age, nutrition, etc.), sometimes to examine interactions between co-administered drugs or between genotypic variants and a drug, and to quantify the effectiveness and tolerability of different preparations of a pharmaceutical.

For non-pharmaceuticals also there is potential value in studies on people, to define acceptable exposures, and to identify metabolites that can be used as a basis for monitoring so as to identify untoward exposures at an early stage. Of courses it will always be the hope that, as a result of good working practice, no effects will be observed during the normal use of a chemical. The corollary is that unless there were considerable confidence that any effects in a study in volunteers would be minimal and transitory, it would be ethically, legally and professionally unacceptable deliberately to administer that substance to volunteers.

Even the administration of a new and promising pharmaceutical to a patient is not acceptable unless the departure from normal practice offers a significant possibility of benefit to the individual concerned in relation to any additional risk. For example, there would need to be evidence of therapeutic value from a model system, or other basis for a reasonable expectation of benefit. Then, one would need to consider the adequacy of knowledge about the therapeutic effects and any potential toxic actions of the proposed treatment as they might be affected by the condition of the individual patient. Professional judgment would be exercised, with consideration of the nature of the condition to be treated (the likely incidence, severity and reversibility of its harmful effects) and of the expected benefits of the proposed treatment in comparison with conventional therapy and with leaving the condition untreated.

3.3 NUTRITIONAL TOXICOLOGY

This section discusses some issues of potential harm from substances in food that are currently the subject of public concern. It provides insights in the context of risk reduction on, among other things, the importance of dose, the value of an understanding of the effects of specific nutrients and not merely of food as a whole, and of the interaction of laboratory and epidemiological evidence.

Although there is an understandable reluctance among nutritionists and the purveyors of food to acknowledge that food can be poisonous, there has been, throughout human history, a conflict generated by fear of hunger on the one hand and fear of poisoning on the other. This conflict has been resolved to some extent by the recognition of the guiding principle of toxicology that the dose–response relation determines whether a given substance can induce an adverse effect.

That this relation holds true for some nutrients is well illustrated, for example, by vitamin A (retinol). Excessive doses are associated with adverse hepatic effects and in pregnant women an intake of around five times the desirable amount could cause adverse effects in the fetus. For most xenobiotics (biologically active substances not normally found in the organism under consideration), a safety factor of at least 100 is commonly set between the maximum amount that should be consumed and the amount expected to be harmful. Retinol is thus an example of a natural and vital nutrient that may be acutely toxic at dosages that are easily reached if supplements are consumed without care. Adequate intake of vitamin A can be attained through the consumption of beta carotene, which is not associated with adverse effects except at enormous dosage.

The essential metal zinc provides another example. The nutritional requirement is 9.5 mg per day for adult males. Doses as low as 75 mg per day have been associated with adverse effects. (CMAFP 1991)

That the dose–response principle also holds true for chronic toxicity provides the gateway to an understanding of current interest in the relation between diet and health. Thus, the recognition that the long-term ingestion of small amounts of a xenobiotic may increase the incidence of age-related degenerative disease or of neoplasms, and that this phenomenon also exhibits a dose–response relation, makes it easier to conceive that nutrients may conform to the same principle, albeit at higher rates of consumption.

3.3.1 CORONARY HEART DISEASE (CHD)

Arterial disease (arteriosclerosis; atherosclerosis) is a degenerative change in arteries that progresses with age. It occurs predominantly in males, though there is an increased incidence in post-menopausal females. It is characterized by the accumulation in the arterial wall of lipid, cholesterol and cellular detritus with the consequent deposition of fibrous tissue and proliferation of smooth-muscle cells. The consequence is localized thickening of the wall with encroachment on the arterial lumen (the space enclosed by the walls of the artery) and damage to the endothelial lining of the artery. This in turn may provoke thrombus (blood clot) formation, which itself may be incorporated into the lesion, at that stage known as an atheromatous plaque. With time, the condition progresses around the artery and along its length, resulting in considerable narrowing and loss of elasticity. In smaller vessels, the damaged endothelium and narrowed lumen may provoke further thrombus formation that may block the lumen entirely, causing acute ischaemia (reduction in the flow of blood) in the tissues supplied by the artery.

The coronary arteries which supply the muscle of the heart with blood and oxygen are vulnerable to the disease. The gradual impairment of blood flow deprives the cardiac muscle of oxygen, causing the condition known as angina pectoris, chest pain on exertion, initially relieved by rest but increasingly persistent. Should a thrombosis occur in a coronary artery, the cardiac muscle supplied by that artery dies and this may be fatal, an event known colloquially as a 'heart attack'.

Several risk factors are known to predispose to the disease. These include age, high blood pressure, cigarette smoking, genetic factors, lack of exercise and an elevated serum cholesterol concentration. The last mentioned is also under genetic control but, in addition, comparative studies of national populations have shown that the serum cholesterol level is directly related to the level of consumption of saturated fatty acids in the diet. More precisely, serum cholesterol correlates with the relative excess of saturated fatty acids over polyunsaturated fatty acids.

Not all saturated fatty acids are equally culpable. Current information suggests that the acids primarily responsible are C12 and C14 (lauric and myristic), C16 (palmitic) to a lesser extent and possibly not at all, whereas C18 (stearic) is without adverse effect. (CMAFP 1991)

The picture is further complicated by the finding that individuals who consume relatively more anti-oxidant vitamins, such as C, E and beta-carotene, are to some extent protected against the adverse consequences of high intakes of saturated fatty acids and high serum cholesterol. The major source of vitamin E in the diet is vegetable oil (seed oil) which is rich in polyunsaturated fatty acids, themselves believed to be protective against the adverse effects of saturated fatty acids.

A further finding of interest is the recent recognition that death from coronary heart disease is more common among males who were of low birth weight or who had low weight gain during the first year of life. The mechanism of this effect is unknown. It may relate to an adverse socio-economic environment, itself a risk factor for coronary heart disease, or it may represent some kind of nutritional programming *in utero* or during the neonatal period, which perhaps establishes a degree of insulin resistance, another risk factor. It is not easy to postulate a mechanism whereby the interaction of these many factors results in arterial disease. An hypothesis under investigation suggests that the uptake of low-density lipoprotein (LDL) cholesterol by the liver (and its subsequent excretion in bile) is impeded by excessive consumption of shorter-chain fatty acids, an effect abetted by a high circulating insulin level. In the absence of adequate amounts of antioxidant vitamins, the increased amounts of LDL cholesterol are vulnerable to oxidation, with the formation of peroxy radicals and cholesterol oxides. These are toxic to endothelium and to macrophages (scavenging cells) resulting in the accumulation of lipid and cholesterol in the sub-endothelial regions of the arteries. The consequently obstructed arteries are more vulnerable to thrombosis when the consumption of an essential fatty acid, alpha-linolenic acid, is inadequate to counteract the synthesis of certain prostaglandins which stimulate arterial construction and platelet aggregation. A good dietary source of linolenic acid and its derivatives is fish oil; Inuits living on their traditional diet of fish and seal meat suffer relatively little from heart disease. (BNF 1992, Gey *et al.* 1991, Steinberg *et al.* 1989)

Much work is required to test this hypothesis, but its confirmation would go some way to explain why an increased consumption of seed oils, fruit and fish appear to offer some protection against arterial degeneration and the thrombotic complication. If, on the other hand, the hypothesis is not supported, then an alternative must be sought.

3.3.2 CANCER (CMAFP 1991)

It has long been known that some types of cancer have different incidences in different parts of the world. Although these have been attributed to varying genetic susceptibilities, the possible influence of environmental factors cannot be discounted. More recently, studies of migrant populations have shown that where the immigrants adopt the life-style (including diet) of the host nation, they also exhibit after one or two generations similar disease patterns, particularly in respect of age-related degenerative diseases and cancer. This has resulted in many investigations that have attempted to identify the responsible dietary components; so far without success.

The human diet is known to contain many components that, experimentally, can be shown to be mutagenic or carcinogenic and many substances that inhibit such activity. In addition, in some parts of the world, food is contaminated by fungi which produce carcinogenic mycotoxins. One such mycotoxin, aflatoxin produced by *Aspergillus flavus* which grows on ground nuts, can cause cancer of the liver. It is also known that some methods of cooking, especially roasting and grilling, cause the formation of carcinogenic heterocyclic amines, albeit in very small amounts. None of these

amines has been shown to be directly associated with the human cancers observed, but any or all could play a part in initiating the disease and it is feasible that other components of the diet are instrumental in enhancing the development of tumours.

Experimental work has shown that the burden of naturally occurring tumours is decreased (and longevity increased) if animals are restricted in energy consumption. Experiments have shown that fat consumption accounts for only part of this effect, though other studies have suggested that a minimum intake of linoleic acid is necessary before tumours are induced; but once that level is achieved, increasing levels of consumption of other fatty acids provoke an increased response. However, studies of human populations have not produced consistent findings, indeed, many studies have been contradictory. Most studies have been concerned with cancers of the breast and colon, and the possible role of fat consumption and, in the colon, with the consumption of insufficient non-starch polysaccharides (dietary fibre). Internationally, the incidence of breast and colorectal cancer are highly correlated.

Cancer of the breast is a major cause of death in developed countries but there is no clear evidence that this is related to fat consumption. It is possible that the levels of consumption are above that at which a discriminatory effect would be observed. More recent studies have suggested that, as with arterial disease, population groups with an increased consumption of anti-oxidant vitamins tend to show a reduced cancer burden.

Although more work is needed to elucidate the mechanisms involved, it is clear that components of the diet interact with the many biological processes involved in degenerative and neoplastic diseases to increase the incidence (or shorten the latent period) in ways akin to those observed in chronic toxicity experiments.

3.3.3 NATURAL TOXICANTS

There are several substances present in plant foodstuffs that are known to be toxic in some circumstances (usually failure of adequate processing or excessive consumption due to lack of other foodstuffs). In general, adequate cooking and access to a variety of foodstuffs reduces the toxic entity to negligible proportions in the diet and therefore to a non-toxic dose. These safeguards may be reduced by excessive consumption of a limited range of raw vegetables, or if plant-breeding programmes, designed to increase the natural pest-resistance of crops, result in increased concentrations of toxic substances naturally present as a defence against predators. Suitable safeguards are now incorporated into such programmes. Occasionally cultivated crops, with reduced natural pesticide production, have been contaminated with wild pollen resulting in hybrids high in natural toxicants. Usually, the bitter taste that results prevents hazardous consumption. The possibility, remote though it may be, of the presence of a natural toxicant demands caution in introducing a novel type of plant into the diet.

3.3.4 ANTICANCER AGENTS

There are many substances, mainly of plant origin, that are known to inhibit experimental carcinogenesis. Many different mechanisms may be involved. There is epidemiological evidence that the prevalence of cancer is reduced in people with higher concentrations of anti-oxidant vitamins in their blood or tissues. It seems likely, therefore, that the human burden of cancer is reduced by many such substances in the human diet. Some of these substances act by stimulating the enzyme systems that promote the destruction or excretion of cancer-causing chemicals. One such system is involved also with the metabolism of foreign substances, such as medicines, raising the possibility that dietary constituents may influence the efficacy or toxicity of drugs.

It is established in experimental animals that the ability to metabolize phenobarbitone requires adequate dietary protein, but whether such effects occur in man in the absence of marked over- or under-nutrition is uncertain. Similar findings have been established with fat; that is, fat deprivation reduces drug metabolizing activity. This effect may be related to the integrity of the membranes on which the enzyme systems are located, in that deprivation of polyunsaturated fatty acids decreases enzyme activity, whereas excess of polyunsaturated fatty acids results in further increased activity in the presence of an inducer. Dietary carbohydrate has the opposite effect, in that drug metabolizing activity is reduced when serum glucose concentration is raised. Diabetic animals, for example, show reduced drug metabolizing activity. These effects vary between species.

Although it is known that stimulation of some activities can be achieved with some dietary constituents in man, the amount of available information is small. It seems likely, however, that metabolic activity in humans can be influenced by dietary constituents but in the normal course of events, to an extent that is unlikely to be of clinical significance.

3.3.5 RISK ASSESSMENT

It is clear that normal human diet contains many thousands of substances that influence human physiology and biochemistry and that there is the potential for adverse effects. It is also the case that mankind is equipped with potent mechanisms to protect against and repair such damage and that many dietary constituents also possess protective properties. At present, it is not possible to characterize the interactions involved in a way that will enable quantitative risk assessments to be undertaken: the system is too complicated and the available information too sparse.

Several studies in Western countries have estimated proportions of deaths from

48

cancer associated with dietary factors. The estimates range from 10% to 70%, with a preferred estimate of 35–40%, but there is agreement that the 'guesstimates' on which these conclusions are based are uncertain in the extreme.

For coronary heart disease (CHD), multi-factorial analysis of several risk factors has allowed good prediction of the relative risk of death from CHD when comparing male populations in northern and southern Europe. The combination of risk factors allowed fairly accurate identification of the men who sub-sequently developed the disease, but did not predict accurately the number of deaths from CHD (i.e. the absolute risk). Predictions made for northern European men using southern European data underestimated the number of deaths, whereas the prediction for southern Europeans using northern data overestimated the number of deaths. This suggests that other unidentified factors were involved (assuming correct classification of the men on entry to the study). Until these are identified, risk assessment must be incomplete.

The death rates observed in northern Europe were accurately predicted on the basis of experience in North America where, presumably, the unidentified factors were comparable in impact. It is possible, therefore, on the basis of population studies, to identify risk factors that predispose to the development of CHD in comparable populations, but it is not possible to predict the outcome within a population or to allocate, with precision, a risk to individuals within a population on the basis of risk factors that are not extreme values (Key 1980).

For the moment, therefore, there are many promising lines of investigation but at present insufficient consistent information to assess risks and to develop public-health guidelines beyond currently accepted broad principles. These are similar for the prevention of cancer and of arterial disease, namely, restriction of fat consumption, especially of saturated fatty acids, maintenance of the consumption of anti-oxidant vitamins, increased consumption of non-starch polysaccharides and adequate physical exercise.

3.4 ECOTOXICOLOGY

(Some of the material in this section is adapted from a Royal Society study group report on pollution control priorities, not yet published, which deals in greater detail with some of the issues raised.)

3.4.1 THE NATURE OF THE ENVIRONMENT

Ecotoxicology is concerned with the adverse impact of chemicals on ecosystems. By 'ecosystem' is meant an interdependent body of living organisms, usually of diverse species, together with the physical environment in which they live. Within an ecosystem there may be

several communities of interacting organisms which occupy more or less precisely distinguishable physical environments. Within communities there will be populations of species. Whereas in human toxicology attention usually focuses on the health of the individual, in ecotoxicology it is populations and communities that are critical.

An ecosystem includes many organisms, animal and vegetable, that interact dynamically in complex ways among themselves and with their physical environment. Many factors affect the dynamics of an ecosystem and hence the dynamic balance within it. Among them are light, temperature, energy and nutrient supplies, competition, predation (including harvesting by humans), pollution and disease. An important attribute of an ecosystem, of much concern to ecologists, is robustness (the extent to which a system can withstand or adapt to the stress imposed by a change in one or more of the factors that drive the dynamic processes). The converse of robustness is sensitivity.

The term 'ecotoxicology' is regrettably increasingly being used to refer to the study of how chemicals reach man through the environment. The tracing of the potential routes for toxicants through the environment to the human population is, of course, important. To some extent it overlaps the tracking that is necessary to establish the potential for harm to the wider environment, for example transmission of toxicants up the food chain, of which the identification of mercury in fish as the cause of Minamata disease is the best known example in humans, and, in the wild, the effect of DDT on raptors. This section concentrates on potential for harm to organisms other than humans.

The conventional dichotomy of humans and their environment, like most demarkations of disciplines, is essentially a matter of convenience and can be a, dangerous oversimplification in practical contexts.

3.4.2 THE NATURE OF THE RISKS

Harm to the living environment may be caused by the accidental or deliberate release of toxic substances into the environment for example in effluents or for pest control. Acute damage from high concentrations is likely to be local and, though serious, less long-lasting than continued influx of toxic substances that are not degraded in the environment but persist. Risks will be the greater if their physical properties are such as to lead to their accumulating in particular tissues and, perhaps, being passed up the food chain. For example, mercury is itself toxic and persistent and, in the form of some of its organic derivatives, it also bioaccumulates.

Potentially toxic materials in the environment are, of course, classed as pollutants. There are, however, also pollutants that are not directly toxic, for example, grit carried down from road works on to a spawning bed.

As subsequent paragraphs will make clear, it is not easy to specify what damage will have serious consequences, or indeed to identify damage when it has occurred. With humans, the death of, or serious harm to, an individual will be a matter of acute concern to many, though its wider impact may be greatly attenuated under the cloak of statistical anonymity. In ecosystems, however, the level of concern is the population or even the community. Reduction of species variety and of habitat are rightly deplored, but in a given situation the long-term global or local significance is often a matter of dispute.

This complex and difficult situation is being confronted essentially in three ways: by research designed to establish any adverse effects that specific substances and mixtures may have in the environment; by monitoring to assist in obtaining a better understanding of processes in the living environment and of the effectiveness of strategies that are adopted to protect it; through organizational arrangements, project selection and project-design strategies that are conducive to the wellbeing of the environment. The first two strategies are discussed in the remainder of this section and the third in section 3.5.

The scope of the subject is very wide. To contain the discussion within reasonable bounds examples relate mainly to the aqueous environment. However, the principles are equally applicable to toxic effects on terrestrial and aerial populations and communities.

3.4.3 CRITERIA OF NORMALITY

Communities, populations and ecosystems can undergo large changes, usually cyclical but sometimes irreversible, without human intervention. It is often difficult or impossible to attribute such observed effects reliably to causes, for example to pollution. Moreover, given the natural variability in the environment over time, it may be difficult to identify indicators of a healthy ecosystem or of its sensitivity. The difficulty becomes clear when one attempts to define a 'healthy' ecosystem, for example as one in which all species show active, normal behaviour, including reproduction.

The nature of the perceived risk from pollutants will be influenced by conclusions as to what are critical structural attributes (biodiversity) or functional attributes (e.g. energy flows).

3.4.4 EXPERIMENTAL AP-PROACHES

Two observational approaches are necessary to get to grips with these issues, a predictive mode in which tests are devised that predict adverse impacts and enable them to be anticipated, and a retrospective mode, that is to say, monitoring to assess the impact of pollutants and the effectiveness of measures taken to control them. Monitoring is also necessary to detect changes, sometimes unforeseen, which may be caused by human activity.

3.4.5 PREDICTIVE TESTS

The principles of testing in ecotoxicity have much in common with those undertaken for the protection of people. There are, however, some special considerations in ecotoxicology.

As in human toxicology, experiments can be done on systems from the biochemical to the whole organism, but extension through to ecosystem level is possible and is now sometimes obligatory. Tests at the biochemical level are usually simple and of short duration (and hence cheap), precise and general. Tests on ecosystems, on the other hand, are long-term and labour intensive (and hence expensive), often imprecise and producing results that are valid only for the particular ecosystem that has been studied.

Most current laboratory tests for potential ecotoxicity are, in fact, acute tests of the LD50-type on single species.

How should tests be designed? Ideally, tests for ecotoxicology should:

(a) provide a satisfactory basis for predicting hazards in the environment;

(b) be well understood in that all critical parameters have been recognized and can be controlled in the laboratory;

(c) be open to monitoring for accuracy and consistency: procedures and observations should be clearly recorded (as required by Good Laboratory Practice) and should be demonstrably reproducible between laboratories by comparing the results of specified tests done in different laboratories.

(d) be as simple and as cost effective as possible consistent with effective prediction, and;

(e) not subject living organisms to undue suffering.

Requirements (c) and (d) place considerable weight on using species that can be easily and reproducibly cultured. The treatment of organisms before a test may have a significant effect on the outcome. A detailed analysis of the application of bio-assays in the resolution of environmental problems will be found in Maltby & Calow (1989).

Tests designed to explore ecological risks should either be at population level or produce output that can be related to population/community responses. In addition to acute responses they should cover chronic, sublethal effects, because these impacts on reproduction and development are as likely as mortality to affect population, community and ecosystem dynamics. Chronic toxicity levels are sometimes deduced from acute tests. The reliability of this procedure is uncertain and further research is needed.

It is often argued that if tests are to be confined to a single species then it should be a 'key' species. However, 'key' can be interpreted in several ways. For example one might specify the species most sensitive to stress, most important in the structure of a community (keystone), most important in the functional economy of the ecosystem, most important to man economically or aesthetically, as representative of particular taxonomic groups or as representative of a particular trophic group. (A trophic group of species is one that feeds on organisms at a particular level; for example, in an aqueous environment: detritus, protozoans, vegetation, small crustaceans or fish.)

Although there has been some success in identifying key species, especially in respect of their importance in the functional economy of an ecosystem, generally sensitive species have proved to be hard to find. In any case, species used in laboratory tests are almost always chosen on grounds of convenience and cost and are rarely key species in any sense.

There is promising work on relating the sensitivity of the test species to the distribution of sensitivities to a threatened ecosystem and thus to predicting the range of susceptibility of species within the ecosystem from the response of the test organism. However, this approach is complicated by the fact that not enough

is known about relative sensitivities of species to different toxicants. It has been found that the No Observable Effect Concentration (NOEC) can vary by more than 100-fold across different species exposed to the same chemical. There is evidence to suggest that general mechanisms dominate in chronic responses whereas specific mechanisms dominate in acute toxicity.

There may be potentially useful interactions between laboratory studies and field monitoring programmes that have focused on indicator species/assemblages (e.g. the Freshwater Biological Association's River Community Programme.) Comparisons should give clues about which species/groups can be expected to drop out under particular pollution conditions, and draw attention to sensitive species for further consideration. It would not be acceptable, even if practicable, to attempt to evaluate predictions of toxicity on a scale beyond that of the small enclosed ecosystem. It is therefore necessary to monitor natural, open systems to ascertain whether the regulatory procedures in force are protecting the environment.

As has been mentioned, this section is exemplified mainly from the aquatic environment. Toxicity testing for effects on land is very similar to that for water, both in the laboratory and in ecosystems. With some compounds, especially pesticides, there may be even greater emphasis on persistence and on products that could be formed by chemical reaction in soil or through metabolism by various organisms. The possible effects of residues on humans will also be considered. There is the added complication on land that the outcome will often depend on the soil and many soil types may have to be considered. Moreover, the number of different organisms permanently present in a given locality may be very high and increased from time to time by mobile species notably birds and insects. The extent of testing required for chemicals that may be applied on land, especially for those used for their biological activity, is therefore very great indeed.

3.4.6 MONITORING

In the management of risk, monitoring is a tool for investigating how things stand and a contributor to precautionary action in the face of our uncertainty and ignorance. We cannot be sure that things will turn out as we predict because we may be uncertain about the implications of those factors that we have recognized or suspected, and we may be ignorant of the importance of other, unrecognized factors. Monitoring shares with epidemiology at least two important tasks: that of observing patterns that indicate that unrecognized risks are being expressed, and that of exploring hypotheses about causal relation in populations. (Epidemiology has other tasks also, such as estimating probabilities for particular events.)

The prediction of the fate (as persistence and bio-accumulation) and the biological effects (as toxicity) of contaminants that may enter the environment is essential for the avoidance of toxic stress on the environment. However, as we have noted, such predictions carry a high level of uncertainty, owing to difficulties in extrapolating results of laboratory tests to the natural environment, to the complexity of many ecosystems and to the impossibility of direct validation. In these circumstances monitoring becomes an essential component of risk control measures, with the objective of identifying and measuring significant changes within the natural environment caused by man's activities, and relating them so far as is possible to specific pollution.

Protection of the environment, be it land, air or water, increasingly demands management, in the sense of requiring or encouraging some activities and discouraging or prohibiting others. No system can be effectively managed without information on its state and the changes that

are taking place within it. Many of the uncertainties that inhibit decisions on current environmental problems stem from inadequate historical records. To assist in taking wise and timely action in the future, an ongoing database on both animate and inanimate elements of the environment must be maintained. What data to collect need very careful consideration. The six activities set out below may indicate the types of data that should be sought.

Monitoring that merely collects data in the expectation that they may be useful, but without a protocol for ongoing review, has no place in a scientific programme. Useful ongoing review is best ensured by designing the monitoring to challenge hypotheses. The formulation of hypotheses will often be part of a research programme with the objective of establishing a better understanding of the effects of toxicants on the environment and the mechanisms involved. Such understanding will contribute greatly to the devising and implementation of effective and efficient precautionary measures, and to the avoidance or minimization of risk.

Monitoring for environmental purposes thus encompasses the following six activities. The first three, which can conveniently be called biological monitoring, seek information on the state of the living environment itself, whereas the others, chemical monitoring, are essentially concerned with concentrations of pollutants and are relevant to the establishing of causal links and the enforcement of regulations.

(1) Establishing the status of individuals, populations, communities or ecosystems, especially in unpolluted locations, so as to establish a base-line, and also the extent of natural variability and any observable patterns thereof.

(2) Assembling a background pathology database in non-polluted sites for senti-

nel species representing a community, that can serve as indicators of its health, to make comparisons with polluted sites.

(3) Detection of changes over time in individuals, populations, communities or ecosystems, which may or may not be due to pollution, and general surveillance of environmental quality.

(4) Establishing a relation between observed changes in the biota (at the individual level and at higher levels) and pollution.

(5) Analysis of the quantity and composition of flows of pollutants into the environment and of their subsequent distribution.

(6) Detection of changes in the environment of concentrations of pollutants or of classes of pollutants (e.g. those imposing a biological oxygen demand in aqueous environments).

3.4.7 MODELS

All models are abstractions and the conclusions drawn from them are valid only insofar as all the factors and interactions that are relevant to the matter under investigation have been appropriately included. Models retain their validity under sufferance of what they have left out.

Any experiment that is designed to throw light on what is happening outside the laboratory is a model. Single-species toxicity tests used in isolation as predictors of the compound's effect in the environment are highly simplified models, but are by no means devoid of predictive power. Despite these reservations, several types of model have proved to be useful in ecotoxicology. Some of the most important are as follows.

(a) Models that relate responses observed at the individual level and below (physiological, cellular and biochemical) to population effects.

Energy budget models have proved particularly useful because, to some extent, they integrate physiological processes and have obvious links with population processes. Thus any factors that cause reductions in the energy available for production will slow growth, and hence potentially increase the time it takes to become reproductive and ultimately reduce reproductive output. There are expectations that the models can be made transparent, open to discussion and experimental analysis, and hence a way of guiding research and better understanding.

(b) Models that relate physico-chemical properties of chemicals to their biological effects, known as Quantitative Structure Activity Relationships (QSARs).

QSARs are mathematical relations between the observed effect of a particular chemical and its structure which permit prediction of the behaviour (usually but not exclusively biological) of similar untested chemicals with a specified reliability. The most widely used QSAR approach is based on that developed by Hansch, in which it is assumed that the levels of biological activity in a set of compounds are a function of their free energies, as they interact with biomolecules, and that their free energy is adequately represented by the algebraic sum of, in particular, their hydrophobic, electronic, and steric properties (though other properties, such as molecular connectivity, may also be invoked).

In general, prerequisites for confident prediction from QSAR techniques (whether Hansch or other) are that the set of chemicals all have the same parent skeleton as the compound of known toxicity with which the comparison will be made, and the substituents on the skeleton differ only in so far as they do not affect physico-chemical features that are not taken into account in the predictive model. When these conditions are satisfied, predictions are often good.

However, predictions of biological activity can sometimes be made even across different series of compounds, but never across series with radically different mechanisms of biological activity as, for example, chlorinated compared with organophosphorus pesticides, the latter having their effect through highly specific enzyme inhibition. In general, the pattern of QSARs is specific for each given mode of action.

As long as the limitations as to structure and mode of action are borne in mind, the potential of QSAR for identifying substances as potentially dangerous to the environment is considerable. It may suggest mechanistic links between chemical structure and toxicity, but these should not be accepted unless confirmed experimentally. The technique can be used as a powerful guide but it should not replace standard ecotoxicity testing.

(c) Models that predict normal states of ecosystems to use as comparators against observed states.

There is considerable public concern as to the quality of rivers and lakes and of the seas. We may all have our personal, subjective way of estimating quality, but for purposes of public policy an objective procedure needs to be established and accepted. However, it is clear that no one definition and measure of quality will satisfy all purposes.

One approach has been to define quality in terms of pollutant content, either directly as concentrations of particular chemicals, or in terms of a consequence of pollution, such as Biological Oxygen Demand (BOD). This parameter measures the amount of oxygen that will be consumed by bacterial degradation of dead organic material present in the water, either from death of organisms naturally present or from sewage or other pollutants. If BOD is high then the concentration of dissolved oxygen may fall below that necessary to support life.

Such measures of quality are essential inputs into decisions as to the technology that should be deployed to reduce toxic risk from pollution.

A complementary way of defining quality is in ecological terms and this has the advantage of using as criterion a measure of the attribute that is the overall objective, namely a healthy, sustainable environment.

A promising model, developed in the UK for fresh waters, is RIVPACS (RCEP 1992). (RIVPACS is the acronym for the River Invertebrate Prediction and Classification System, which was developed by the Institute of Freshwater Ecology in collaboration with the U.K. water industry). In RIVPACS the ecological quality of unpolluted stretches of water, in various biological and physical environments, is established through a survey of the species of small invertebrates present. Species differ in their sensitivity to pollutants and their presence or absence can thus provide the basis for a scale of pollution. The same survey undertaken in any given location will then enable its biological quality to be compared with that of a similar but unpolluted environment, and given a rating according to the extent of the divergence.

There are, nevertheless, some problems with this approach that counsel caution in the interpretation of results. Chief among them is that the model is based on correlation analysis, so that divergences from the norm cannot be attributed with confidence to any particular causation. Clearly, this invites further work on the mechanisms of links between physical and chemical predictors and community structures within the model.

There appears to be no similar model developed for seas. Surveys of lesions on fish in polluted and unpolluted sites, as suggested under monitoring, could provide a basis for defining marine-water quality. An encouraging development is the obtaining of evidence of incipient effects of pollutants by detection, even in apparently unaffected fish, of the DNA coding for enzymes that detoxify specific pollutants.

Many species surveys of plants and of animals are conducted on land, and for some a relation with pollution is explored. However, the relative inhomogeneity of land compared with stretches of water and the potentially greater variety of habitats on land may militate against a RIVPACS type of approach.

(d) Models that predict the distribution of poiiutants, released from point sources, across the environment.

Such models incorporate patterns of emissions and factors that will affect their dilution and movement, such as local topography and weather. They have had some success in predicting concentrations of pollutants in water courses. Models of the spread and deposition over thousands of miles of gaseous effluents from the combustion of fossil fuels have, of course, contributed greatly to understanding the damage to the environment caused by 'acid rain'.

3.4.8 Is ecotoxicity testing effective?

The task in ecotoxicology is essentially the same as that in human toxicology, namely to predict safe exposures to potentially toxic chemicals. The vastly increased number and variety of species at risk and of habitats involved obviously increases the difficulties. Some regulatory authorities seek to cope with the variety by requiring results from tests on several species, each from a different taxon. All apply safety factors to the empirically determined no-effect levels.

In general, the extrapolation from laboratory to field often invites making assumptions about the following:

(a) a relation between short-term (often acute) and long-term (often chronic) levels;

(b) the relation between the responses of one or a few species and that of the many present in the ecosystem of interest;

(c) the relation between simple laboratory conditions and the complex conditions in the field.

All these require further detailed exploration. Some work has already been done on the relation between acute and chronic responses and more, through ECETOC, is in the pipeline. Mention has already been made of the relation of sensitivities within and between species and more work needs to be done on their elucidations. Finally, there is still much need for research that looks at predictions from simple laboratory tests and from models in more complex microcosms and mesocosms.

Given the uncertainties in testing for ecotoxicity and of extrapolating laboratory data to the wild, procedures have been devised to identify those compounds that, by reason of toxicity, bio-accumulation and persistence, appear to have greatest potential for harm (e.g. the E.C. Black and the U.K. Red List), and to apply especially strict control measures to them. In the UK the control on manufacturing sites is Best Available Technique not Entailing Excessive Cost (BATNEEC).

The effectiveness of the measures taken to protect the environment depends on the timeliness and quality of the information on which regulatory requirements are based, the appropriateness of the regulations to the need and the efficacy of enforcement of compliance.

There is little if any evidence to suggest that, in recent years, the contribution made by toxicity tests to regulatory decisions has failed to provide warnings of the potential for harming the environment. Moreover, uncertainties have been addressed by the application of stringent safety factors and by procedures such as BATNEEC.

Ideally, decisions under BATNEEC and similar procedures would be informed by quantitative estimates of the relevant costs (including opportunity costs, ie. the costs of benefits foregone) and benefits. Many of these are, however, difficult to estimate. This problem is examined in the Royal Commission on Environmental

Pollution (RCEP) report on *Freshwater quality* (RCEP 1992). Estimating costs that should be attributed to environmental damage presents a major challenge to ecotoxicologists.

Continued research and development along the lines suggested in this section should lead to a better understanding of potential for harm and thus to procedures that are both more effective and more efficient in protecting the environment, and that, as is an objective in testing for human toxicology, reduce distress to test organisms to a minimum.

3.5 THE MANAGEMENT OF ECOTOXICOLOGICAL RISKS

Section 3.4 is mainly concerned with establishing the likely consequences of the entry of toxic substances into the environment, that is to say, with the major impact of pollution. However, it may be helpful to discuss briefly an approach that has been proposed for the management of projects to minimise pollution and its effects, and which demonstrates how some of the contentious issues raised in Chapters 5 and 6 are being addressed in practice, and that some are in fact not antithetical but complementary.

The detailed procedure developed by RCEP in its 12th report, *Best practicable environmental option* (RCEP 1988) calls for a diligent and timely search for and consideration of all relevant information combined with a recognition of inevitable uncertainty, and action that can be taken to reduce it.

It may be rightly objected that it is impossible to define 'best' unequivocally when conflicting values come into play, and that one can never be sure that the full set of feasible options has been considered. If, however, a set of project options that is acceptable overall can be identified then the final choice will be

relatively unimportant. This is the procedure recommended as 'satisficing' by Herbert Simon when, as is usually the case, it is impossible to identify an optimum (Simon 1969).

The BPEO procedure emphasizes the importance of not prejudging issues. Thus the objective should initially be stated without the limitations imposed by specifying the means, and then alternative options for achieving the objective should be sought diligently and imaginatively so as to identify as complete a set as possible. Environmental considerations should be introduced into the planning at the earliest possible stage, so that environmentally advantageous possibilities are not excluded by the prior application of other criteria. The information used in the evaluation of the options, its analysis and the conclusions drawn should be presented in concise but not unduly condensed form to those who have to decide which option to select (see section 3.7).

The BPEO procedure recommends that the design of the selected option be critically reviewed. It will have been guided by professional experience in the relevant industry, usually structured into codes of practice. However, as the Hazard and Operability Study (HAZOP) handbook published by the Chemical Industries Association (CIA) (CIA 1987) makes clear, the scope of application of such codes is limited by the extent of established experience that underpins them. This may not, however, be adequate to identify and deal with all hazards that may arise from new technology or even from known technology in new circumstances. It was the recognition of these limitations that led to the development of HAZOP to challenge the design as an additional step in the pursuit of the minimization of risk.

A HAZOP study forces an imaginative and comprehensive consideration of the consequences of a manufacturing process running under conditions or performing in ways that were not envisaged in the design. If the consequences are judged to be unacceptable and a credible mechanism can be proposed, then action must be taken to deal with the revealed risk. If some of the possibilities that are envisaged do not prove incredible on examination, then the challenging has not gone far enough. In this way hindsight, in the form of experience-based codes of practice, is reinforced by a procedure that encourages maximum foresight.

The BPEO procedure recommends, wherever possible, intermediate stages of scale-up (e.g. field trials in the release of genetically modified organisms (GMOs)) between laboratory and full scale. In most situations pilot-scale experience brings a greater degree of realism compared with laboratory experimentation, allowing evaluation under conditions that are closer to full-scale practice. Application of such techniques as HAZOP and pilot trials are responses to the recognition of the inevitability of uncertainty and ignorance, which is of primary importance in the management of risk.

HAZOP has been adapted, under the name GENHAZ, to testing proposals for the release of genetically modified organisms (RCEP 1991). The connection with toxicity is that one of the concerns relating to the release of GMOs is that toxic chemicals (for example pesticides), coded for by genes introduced in the modification, will be transferred to other organisms or expressed in tissues not desired (e.g. in potato tubers instead of in leaves).

The 13th report of the RCEP on the release of genetically engineered organisms to the environment (RCEP 1989) exemplifies the detailed examination of a complex and developing technology and the recommendation of measures to reduce risk. It would provide another informative case study through which to examine the issues raised in Chapter 6.

As will be clear from the foregoing, the procedure proposed by the RCEP for identifying a BPEO requires an integrated approach to risk management at all levels of an organization and at all stages of a project, from conception, through evaluation, design and scale-up to implementation and, when necessary, to subsequent disposal of product or (as is illustrated in GENHAZ) clean-up of site. It recommends the full use of experience in the design process but also the taking of all reasonable measures to deal with inevitable uncertainty and ignorance. It also calls for the minimum of secrecy and appropriate consultation and participation.

The basis for the choices and decisions at all stages of the project selection (e.g. the origins and reliability of data, the assumptions adopted and details of the evaluation procedures) should be recorded as an 'audit trail' that can both serve as a record and facilitate consultation, participation and review.

3.6 THE DEVELOPMENT OF SAFETY REGULATIONS INVOLVING TOXICOLOGY

Early recorded concerns about safety focused on the adulteration of food, with comments by Cato (234–149 BC) and Pliny The Elder (23–79 AD) on adulteration and how to identify it. However, in England, it was not until 1266 that Parliament enacted the prohibition of the sale of any 'corrupted wine' or of any meat, fish, bread or water that was 'not wholesome for man's body' or 'that was kept so long that it loseth its natural wholesomeness'. These statutes continued in force until repealed in 1844.

Chemical analytical methods for assessment of the purity of food developed slowly, but by the beginning of the 19th century a variety of qualitative methods had become available. Frederick Accum published his treatise on *Adulterations of food and culinary poisons* in 1820 in which he described various types of adulteration and methods available to detect them. His treatise received immediate publicity and stimulated the debate on this problem. It was not, however, until 1860 that parliament in the U.K. enacted the Food and Drug Adulteration Act with the purpose of protecting the integrity of the food supply. Subsequent statutes in 1872 and 1875 prohibited adulteration of food, so that it would reach the market place in its natural and most nutritious state. Adulteration of food still remained a problem in many countries and various methods have been adopted to prevent it. In the USA for example, Dr Harvey Wiley who was the Chief Chemist of the US Department of Agriculture documented the widespread adulteration of food found in the market place. In the early part of the 20th century he used a 'poison squad' of volunteers to assess the toxicity of commonly used adulterants (benzoic, boric, salicylic and sulphurous acids, borax and formaldehyde). In 1906 the US Congress

enacted the Food and Drugs Act which prohibited the mis-branding and adulteration of food.

Over the next decade the emphasis of public interest and regulatory control everywhere moved from the purity of the food supply to safety. Animal experiments started in the early part of the century as part of the methodology for assessing the safety of food and other products.

By 1940 it was recognized that chronic studies of toxicity were a necessary requirement for the assessment of safety of chemicals, to identify harmful effects that might be delayed due to accumulated physical damage or as a consequence of accumulation of chemicals in storage depots within the body. These studies were much more complex than the acute studies used over the previous decades and their conduct was codified by the introduction of guidelines.

It was also realized that the results of toxicity and other experiments would require careful evaluation and skilled judgment before they could be extrapolated to man. Much of the subsequent history of regulatory toxicology has been concerned with deciding on appropriate and relevant types of experimentation for different types of product and use, and with how to interpret the results in predicting 'safe' use by man and animals, and latterly the safety of the environment.

In 1949, the US Food and Drug Administration (FDA) published a monograph entitled *Procedures for the appraisal of the toxicity of chemicals in foods*. The procedures included the use of the 100 times safety factor, which had been developed earlier by various FDA scientists, notably Arnold Lehman. It was also recognized

59

that the interpretation of studies in animals and the relevance of the findings to human health presented particular technical and scientific problems. However, the development of toxicology and of the chemical industry had reached the stage where more widespread testing of chemicals was required by statute.

UN agencies and other international bodies became involved in the early 1950s in suggesting guidelines for the safe use of food additives and pesticides. Development by FAO and WHO of the concepts of Acceptable Daily Intake (ADI) of food additives and (Provisional) Tolerable Weekly Intake (PTWI), etc. rapidly popularized the idea of a 'safety factor', which could be used to suggest the probable safe level to the human population based on the No-Effect Level (NEL) in animal experiments. It was widely argued that the 'safe' level for man could be arbitrarily but effectively set at 1/100th of the NEL in animal toxicity tests, assuming a ten-fold difference in sensitivity between species and a ten-fold inter-individual variation in sensitivity.

Attempts have been made to extend this approach to reproduction toxicity (1/500 of the NEL, incorporating a further factor of 5 as an arbitrary allowance for the type of effects), and carcinogenicity (1/1000 of the NEL). The latter has not been generally accepted, because neither it nor the subsequent attempts to derive risk levels from mathematically ingenious but biological remote manipulations of experimental results have gained general confirmation or acceptance. The safety factor approach has probably served us well over the years by suggesting tolerable doses or exposures below the level at which harmful action could be detected.

In recent decades the publications of the Joint Expert Committee on Food Additives (JEFCA) and the Joint Meeting on Pesticide Residues (JMPR) of the United

Nations Organization have influenced methods of testing food additives and contaminants. Their risk assessments have been very influential in national decisions about the acceptability and permissable concentrations of such chemicals in food. Similarly, over the past decade, the conclusions of various expert Scientific Committees of the European Commission have become increasingly important.

In England and Wales the food adulteration laws of the 19th and early 20th centuries were eventually replaced by the Food and Drugs Act 1955. This set out the two basic criteria of food law which have been followed ever since: first, that food should not be injurious to health and second, that food should be of the nature, quality and substance demanded by the purchaser. It provided the main framework for control of food additives and contaminants. The Food Act 1984 consolidated the 1955 Act, with its main provisions largely unchanged, with other pieces of food legislation. A bigger change occurred with the introduction of the Food Safety Act 1990, which replaced most of the 1984 Act. It gave Ministers new or additional powers to make regulations in a number of areas relevant to safety, such as novel foods, irradiated foods and food contaminants. It also set out enabling provisions to make regulations stemming from the European Community Directives, which are having an ever increasing influence on food safety regulations in Community Member States. In addition to the Food Safety Act, the Medicines Act of 1968 and the Food and Environmental Protection Act of 1985 cover aspects of regulation of veterinary drug and pesticide residues respectively in food.

Over the 40 years since the early 1950s legislative measures on pesticides, occupational health exposures, clean air, cosmetics, veterinary products and medicines were introduced. Some of these were triggered by particular events that caught the public interest. For example, Rachel Carson's book *Silent Spring* was published in 1962 and generated increased public concern about the use of pesticides, and considerable tightening of the regulations regarding their assessment and safety.

Since 1960 there have been two major impulses to the development of scientific toxicology affecting pharmaceuticals and other types of chemicals. One was the tragic discovery of the teratogenic effect of thalidomide in pregnant women in the early 1960s. The changes that followed were comprehensive, encompassing both a wider range of required testing and far more stringent conduct of studies and of their interpretation. The other, in the mid-1970s was the realization that many carcinogens were also mutagens, which resulted in widespread official demands for genetic toxicity testing and increasing pressure to undertake carcinogenicity testing of pharmaceuticals and many other types of chemical, because many appeared unexpectedly to be mutagenic under some circumstance or other.

For pharmaceuticals, animal toxicity experiments extending from a single dose to many months of daily treatment were originally regarded as a simple extension of the tests done to detect and explore the pharmacological effects of candidate medicines. As understanding of the mechanisms of chemical toxicity grew, the experiments became more complex and lengthier, and increasing attention was paid to functional and biochemical disturbances, and to investigations of the mechanisms underlying toxicity.

The legislation introduced over this period required a wide range of toxicity tests, which had much in common irrespective of the product area being tested. Nevertheless, the guidelines for testing were developed around product areas and on a national basis, and considerable divergence occurred in the details of the testing requirements. By the 1970s there was a reasonably clear idea of the test requirements for individual chemicals, depending on their use, and it was recognized that differences in national regulations presented a potential barrier to international trade. The OECD set out to harmonize the guidelines for toxicity testing and this has gone some way towards ameliorating the problem of differences in national regulations. Among the OECD regulations, those involving Good Laboratory Practices (GLP) were most influential, and now all laboratories providing toxicity data to regulatory authorities in OECD countries are required to perform to those exacting standards.

There have been several trends during the past decade that have had an impact on regulation and toxicity testing. Possibly the most influential has been the growing public concern for environmental pollution. Although much of this concern has been about the reduction in diversity of species and habitats, to a large extent regulatory activity has focused on potential effects on human health as a surrogate for the whole environment. However, more attention is now being given to ecotoxicology and to regulation designed specifically to protect the environment.

Legislation has been introduced requiring the control of dispersion of chemicals and a significant increase in the amount of knowledge required to assess the safety of such chemicals. Developments in the regulation of chemicals have to balance the socio-political demands for improvements in the economic well-being of society with concern for safety and the scientific developments that underpin regulatory provisions. Early regulations involving toxicology testing were based on pragmatic observations in experimental animals using testing systems based on simple principles (e.g. using the route and duration of exposure expected in people). More recently, there have been examples of regulations built on new scientific developments, notably the introduction of mutagenicity testing in the late 1970s with the development of bacterial mutation test systems (such as the Ames test). Improvements in analytical methodology have allowed the introduction of methods to assess the metabolism and disposition of chemicals. Developments in the biological sciences have encouraged the development of toxicology into functional areas not previously considered (such as immunotoxicology). The regulations are generally conservative, in that they develop on the basis of well accepted scientific principles. The overall impact has been a significant increase in the attention paid to the safety of chemicals by increasing the range of toxicity studies and the chemicals that require testing.

Over the next few years public concern about the environment will inevitably lead to substantial increases in data requirements for existing chemicals, whether they be industrial chemicals, pesticides or other chemicals to which people are exposed. The issues being tackled are of formidable complexity and it will be some time before the full impact of regulations is known.

3.7 MECHANISMS FOR REGULATORY DECISION MAKING

Regulatory decision making in toxicology usually represents an uneasy blend of experience and skilled judgment applied to information from a range of *in vivo* and *in vitro* experiments. The skills lie in devising investigations appropriate to materials as different as, say, a new herbicide or a motor fuel to which workers may be exposed, a new cleansing agent for the home, and a pollutant dispersed in the environment. Judgment must be exercised in deciding how applicable the results of experiments on a given species in the laboratory are to different species and in differing circumstances. Judgment is also called for in evaluating the possible importance of divergent and unexpected results, for example, whether they are the consequence of biological variation or of a hitherto unforeseen biological action. The uneasy blend results from the need for decisions to be consistent and for the reasoning behind them to be stated, while accepting that most can only be based on an empirical approach to many complex factors. There are many important precedents but few toxicological 'laws' and very few mathematical models for valid prediction other than limited extrapolation based on unusually extensive toxicological investigation.

Advice to decision takers on scientific evidence in regulatory toxicology is probably best provided by a group of experts, because of the diversity of the information to be evaluated. Decision takers or their advisers have to decide first whether the data available are appropriate and come from properly performed experiments. Then they must consider the nature and magnitude of the benefits arising from the exposure. The ultimate decision about the acceptability of that risk (cost–benefit analysis) will require judgments beyond the scope of science alone involving, for example and according to the case, ecology, clinical medicine, sociology, economics and even concepts of public good against individual detriment. (For a discussion of cost–benefit in relation to pollution see RCEP 1992).

Lazy decision takers may find it convenient to rely soley on options graded in order of merit according to an overall score arrived at by combining scores for various factors, usually after differential weighting. This practice is harmful in that it discards information on which the decision takers should be expected to base their judgments, and it may obscure the controversial nature of value judgments that have already been applied (for example by the weighting). The cautionary observation 'We shall find many devices for enabling ignorance to masquerade as knowledge so that decisions may be made' (Loasby 1976) is highly relevant in this context. Scoring of individual factors may be helpful but will convey greater meaning if each level is defined by a descriptive statement. A profile of about half a dozen salient attributes for each option, if clearly presented, is readily understood and far more informative than a combined score.

In many national and international agencies, the types of toxicity testing required in any given circumstance and evaluation of the evidence will be done by a group of scientifically trained officials and experienced academics, who together should apply pragmatism and prudence. In other countries the legal process places more overt power in decision making with the authorities, which is likely to produce greater consistency but may risk increasing detachment of the responsible bodies from new developments in science and from changing popular perceptions of the acceptable and the intolerable.

That regulations should be prescribed for the testing of compounds, and for controlling the use of those that can reasonably be considered to pose a risk to health, is obviously essential. It is likewise necessary that regulations be unambiguously written and firmly enforced. There is, however, a risk that rigid regulation may impede the development of the very understanding that is necessary for improving the protection of the health of people and of the environment. Standardization of testing, if not accompanied by the funding of exploratory research into the underlying science, could re-

duce toxicology to a repetitive technology, merely the applying of a fixed and unchanging pattern of tests, without adequate discrimination according to the problem in hand. Similarly, questioning of the appropriateness of routine tests could be inhibited; for example, questioning the relevance of testing human proteins in animals and the use of the results as a basis for deciding whether the proteins can safely be used in humans.

Moreover, it appears that funding research into the interaction of potentially toxic compounds in the environment, on which surer protection depends, is being inhibited by the recognition that even if results show that some regulations are inadequate or inappropriate, they are unlikely to be changed. There is, however, movement towards new approaches in toxicological testing some of which have already been mentioned (e.g. increased *in vitro* testing and simpler screening for existing compounds). An additional example is the proposal in The Netherlands not to require long-term carcinogenic studies for certain chemicals that can be shown not to be genotoxic.

There have been cases in which stringent controls have been imposed with little or no scientific evidence to support them and with no cogent argument. Not surprisingly, such regulations are resented and detract from the credibility of the regulators. To facilitate consultation and to carry conviction, documentation relating to decisions on the environment should be structured so that it is possible to trace decisions back through the arguments to the supporting evidence.

It is important, when regulations are made for the avoidance of harm from a particular cause, that consideration should be given to whether a more acceptable alternative exists. Proposals for the protection or improvement of health and the environment should be subject to the same detailed scrutiny of their consequences as any other proposal, to ensure that the best option is taken.

The belief that one should not be exposed to externally generated risks, and the consequent explosion of litigation, may well have a serious impact on progress in risk reduction. Toxicology and, indeed, patient treatment and care, could become frozen in 'best practice'. The risk increases as the contentious area broadens, for example through alleging adverse 'behavioural effects', which are difficult to specify precisely and difficult to test for in the laboratory.

Given the inevitable imprecision of some of the measurements on which toxicologists rely, the complexity of the systems under consideration and the possibility of differences in interpretation of data, informed expert judgement after consideration of all the evidence is likely to continue to provide a better basis for risk reduction and management than a mechanistic scoring or decision tree, desirable though these may be on legalistic grounds. This strengthens the need for public-interest participation in taking decisions on issues relating to risk.

3.8 CONCLUSIONS ON THE EFFECTIVENESS OF TOXICITY TESTING

The question is often asked 'How successful are toxicity tests in preventing harm to humans, to other animals and to the environment?' It is surprisingly difficult to document an answer, because of the paucity of published data on adverse effects and because the avoidance or limitation of exposure as a result of toxicity tests has, as intended, prevented harm to humans and consequently the possibility of comparison of effects in the test species with those in man. There are, in consequence few published analyses of predictive success and failure.

The conditions that are sought in laboratory experiments (controlled, precise, careful investigation and a uniform test system) contrasting with the poorly controlled situation outside the laboratory (misuse, abuse as well as use, variation of response due to diverse physiological states and disease, concurrent exposure to other compounds and inadequate in-

formation) hinder general correlations between laboratory results and clinical experience. However, there is reason to believe that testing compounds for toxicity has kept compounds with a high potential off the market. Many compounds have been marketed with recommendations, based on toxicity tests, for use under controlled conditions. Few, if any, of these have produced toxic effects other than in instances of clear misuse. The limitations placed on their use as a consequence of toxicology have provided protection.

Some pharmaceuticals constitute an exception. Despite thorough toxicity testing, and clinical trials, because the incidence of the effect is so low, and the onset slow, evidence of harm has not become apparent until these products have entered full clinical use. However, outside pharmaceutical products it is difficult to identify exceptions.

REFERENCES

BNF 1992 *Unsaturated fatty acids: nutritional and physiological significance.* Report of the British Nutrition Foundation's Task Force. Chapman and Hall.

CIA, 1987 *A guide to hazard and operability studies.* Chemical Industries Association.

CMAFP 1991 Dietary reference values for food energy and nutrients in the United Kingdom, Report of the Panel on Dietary Reference Values of the Committee on Medical Aspects of Food Policy. London: HMSO.

Gey, K.F., Pushka, P., Jordan, P. & Moser, U.K. 1991 Inverse correlation between plasma vitamin E and mortality from ischemic heart disease in cross-cultural epidemiology. *Am. J. clin. Nutr.* **53**, 326S–334S.

Key, A. 1980 *Seven countries: a multivariate analysis of death and coronary heart disease.* Harvard University Press.

Loasby, B.J. 1976 *Choice, complexity and ignorance.* Cambridge University Press.

Maltby L. & Calow P. 1989 The application of bioassays to the resolution of environmental problems; past, present and future. *Hydrobiologia* **188–189**, 65–76.

RCEP 1988 *Best practicable environmental option*, 12th report. London: HMSO.

RCEP 1989 *The release of genetically engineered organisms to the environment* 13th report. London: HMSO.

RCEP 1991 *GENHAZ, a system for the critical appraisal of proposals to release of genetically modified organisms into the environment*, 14th report. London: HMSO.

RCEP 1992 *Freshwater quality*, 16th report. London: HMSO.

Simon, H.A. 1969 *The sciences of the artificial.* MIT Press.

Spielmann, H. 1992 *Nature, Lond.* **357**, 432.

Steinberg, D., Parthasarathy S., Carew, T.E., Khoo, J.C. & Witzum, J.L. 1989 Beyond cholesterol: modifications of low-density lipoprotein that increase its atherogenicity. *New Engl. J. Med.* **320**, 915–924.

CHAPTER 4

ESTIMATION OF RISK FROM OBSERVATION ON HUMANS

Sir David Cox, F.R.S., and Sir Bernard Crossland, F.R.S. (Chairmen),
Dr S.C. Darby, Dr D. Forman, Dr A.J. Fox, Dr S.M. Gore, Dr E.C. Hambly,
Dr T.A. Kletz, N.V. Neill, Esq.

4.1 NEED FOR OBSERVATION ON MAN

Many hazards to which men and women may be exposed can be demonstrated and studied in animal experiments or, less convincingly, *in vitro*. To predict the risk before humans are exposed, as is often possible for a new machine or a newly introduced chemical, is obviously desirable. Should examination of an appropriate 'model' disclose a hazard that is unacceptable, either because the risk is estimated to be so large as to outweigh every possible benefit or because equal benefit can be obtained in another way at less risk, action can be taken immediately to prevent or minimize human exposure, if necessary by halting production.

Pre-testing in biological or physical models is not always practicable or adequate (chapter 3); observations may then have to be made on humans, despite the fact that disability and death may occur, before any risk can be quantified. Experiments on humans, in the true scientific sense of the term, may sometimes be done under carefully defined conditions (e.g. to investigate human physiology, to test methods of treatment or prophylaxis, or to examine whether a new drug brings the expected benefit without producing any greater harm). No experiment designed to produce serious disease is ever permissible, but with the consent of subjects, research involving, for example, intentional infection with the common cold may be allowed. Observations on humans, however, will often elucidate the reality of hazards to health. Such 'epidemiological' observations are required for five main reasons.

(a) Some hazards arise in contexts that are uniquely human (e.g. car driving). Here any realistic estimation of risk must involve observations on humans.

(b) A model may prove untrustworthy because it is based upon incomplete knowledge of the hazards. This has been demonstrated dramatically with several drugs whose effects on humans were not predicted from laboratory experiments. Examples are the effects of various drugs in pregnancy, the ocular and serous membrane reactions from practolol, the development of pulmonary hypertension from the use of the appetite depressant 'aminorex', and lung cancer and leukaemia resulting from use of arsenic and benzene respectively. The increasingly stringent requirements of regulatory agencies may have led to a reduction in risks of this kind in recent years, although, of course, in principle such gains have to be balanced against the costs and time delays in making new products available. Indeed, just as careful statistical review of related clinical trials is to some extent replacing subjective and qualitative medical editorials, so it is desirable that regulatory authorities seek quantitative assimilation of risks and benefits, in particular through more thorough analysis of clinical trials and post-marketing surveillance data to discern the characteristics of patients who experience side-effects.

(c) Biological models are of differing value in predicting the dose that produces a human risk or the risk associated with a specified level of exposure. In some circumstances, the mechanisms by which damage is produced are known in both humans and laboratory animals; models may then be highly reliable. In others, the mechanisms are not known, and the human risk can be estimated only directly. If extensive observational data are consistent with the absence of hazard, it may be possible to deduce that any detriment is small enough to be ignored. Whether epidemiological observations of this sort can ever be held to establish that no human hazard exists (e.g. that saccharin is not carcinogenic to humans, despite evidence that extremely high doses can produce tumours in rats) is a matter of judgement that depends on the state of development of theoretical knowledge and the strength of individual pieces of evidence. The IARC, however, does recognize a category of substance regarded as effectively non-carcinogenic. Observations on humans can demonstrate the size of the risk associated with a stated level of exposure (e.g. to ionizing radiations, or to the combustion products of coal); they then help to determine what exposure (if any) is socially acceptable in view of the accompanying benefits to society as a whole. This is especially valuable when the nature of the relation between dose and effects is uncertain, as it often is with laboratory carcinogens. Men and women may be exposed to small amounts of an agent, the effect of which could be demonstrated in animal experiments only if many thousands (even hundreds of thousands) of animals were used. Humans feed and house themselves, and their diseases are diagnosed for the epidemiologist by the normal medical services of the country. Paradoxically, therefore, it may be easier to observe directly the effect of small doses on man than to complete a sound and sufficiently large experiment on laboratory animals.

(d) Planned observations must continue after chemicals, machines and processes have been introduced so as to monitor the effect of control measures, and to check that any risk is contained within approved limits. Essential observations of this sort include current programmes to monitor morbidity from pneumoconiosis among coal miners, and lung cancer among asbestos workers and uranium miners after the implementation of new regulations.

(e) Perhaps most importantly, human observations provide a sense of perspective. They ensure that we do not devote disproportionate resources to problems that are likely to be minor while neglecting others likely to be far more important. Their value should not be judged solely by their ability to incriminate or exculpate particular sources of hazard. If it is, they may be downgraded undeservedly because they are more likely to fail to identify the many small effects of a multitude of agents than is laboratory science. Many epidemiological studies start, however, not from the many agents that occur in a region, but from the actual mortality or morbidity that has occurred in that region in a certain period; they seek to determine the major causes of these. Thus attention may be drawn to major determinants of current morbidity rates that have been overlooked by other approaches. Cigarette smoking was one example, and others may prove to be the effects of a sedentary life on mortality from vascular disease and of a low-fibre diet on morbidity from disease of the large intestine.

In addition, though not directly relevant to estimation of risk, observation on man is essential to the better understanding of the natural history of disease, and thus to the evaluation of any systematic screening procedures.

4.2 EPIDEMIOLOGICAL METHODS

By relating cases to the populations exposed and to the periods and levels of exposure, epidemiologists estimate probabilities for particular events. The population and hazard under study must be carefully defined, and a systematic count of the cases and exposures obtained. Initial assessments may be crude but, if results point to a problem worth following up, more sophisticated attempts to answer the basic question, 'does exposure to X cause disease Y?' will be made. These may include:

(a) Proportional mortality studies (deaths in a population are tabulated by cause of death and compared with the proportions of death from each cause in a standard population with the same age and sex distribution).

(b) Studies of deaths among workers employed at the time of death (the number of such deaths from various causes can be related to the average size of the work-force).

(c) Case-control studies (life histories of people who die of a particular disease are compared with those of people who do not die of the disease in question).

(d) Simple prospective studies (a cohort of persons exposed is followed until death, including periods after any member ceased to be exposed).

(e) Studies of spatial distribution.

Though (a) and (b) may sometimes be based on available administrative records, (c) and (d) require more detailed investigations. The methods are not restricted to the analysis of deaths but may be generalized to include cases of disease and disability.

Many important hazards may affect mortality years after exposure. Records of people exposed long ago are often incomplete, in the sense that they omit information about an individual's way of life and personal habits that could be relevant to his subsequent mortality or morbidity, and they seldom contain detailed exposure histories for each individual. Moreover, humans are seldom exposed as would be desirable in a planned experiment, with other factors held constant, so that the findings of epidemiologists' investigations are usually subject to many reservations although these can to some extent be dealt with by developments in statistical techniques. Unless the results of one study are particularly clear-cut, in trying to answer a question such as 'does X cause disease Y?' an epidemiologist will need to compare the results of several studies of people exposed in different situations and not to rely on a single study however detailed.

Once a situation is recognized as hazardous, epidemiological investigations become increasingly complex as they attempt to answer more detailed questions: What is the size of the risk for particular doses in different circumstances? Are there synergistic effects with other factors, such as alcohol consumption? What can be learned about the morbidity that precedes mortality, which might be used as the basis for screening programmes? Such studies would generally use the case-control or prospective approach, and would collect very full information about exposure and response.

The types of investigation described above tackle questions about specific exposures. Epidemiological methods are also used nationally for monitoring the environment for unsuspected effects on health. Agencies such as the Office of

69

Population Censuses and Surveys, the Department of Health, the Committee on Safety of Medicines, the Public Health Laboratory Service, and the Health and Safety Executive collect and publish regularly a wide range of health data. These data may receive systematic statistical analysis to detect changes in patterns, or may be used as the basis of time or geographic studies relating differences in health to differences in other factors. Other reporting systems, such as the yellow-cards for reporting adverse reactions to drugs, serve more to pinpoint issues for study than to provide quantitative estimates of risk.

4.3 RISK CRITERIA

The risks to health with which we are concerned, though commonly measured as risks of death, may also be measured as risks of developing a non-fatal disability or of failing to achieve a physiological norm of growth, mental development, or reproductive function. Mortality has great merit as an indicator because the fact of death is unequivocal even though the cause of death often is not. In the UK, moreover, as in many other countries where death certification is universal and accessible to study, to determine how many individuals in any group under observation have died (and hence to calculate the mortality rate) is relatively easy; this remains true even many years after the exposure to hazard and even though members of the group have been dispersed throughout the country (because deaths are registered and information about them is publicly available).

An increase in total mortality, however, is difficult to recognize as an attributable risk unless it either affects young people or is gross, because the normal risk of death due to causes common to the whole of society becomes appreciable in middle age (in England and Wales in 1989, rising from 1.3 per 1000 people at 35–39 years of age to 11.0 per 1000 at 55–59 years of age). To detect an increased mortality from one particular disease is much easier, although this requires that a specific diagnosis of the cause of death be made in each case. In a country like Britain, with a well-developed medical service, this is usually made accurately enough for the purpose, unless a hazard gives rise to some non-specific cardio-respiratory or mental degeneration that has not been clearly defined in pathological terms. In practice, many hazards have been first recognized by detection of increased mortality from a specific disease.

Hazards that involve risk of death may also involve greater risks of disability or interference with physiological function, but they are commonly described in terms of the associated mortality. If the risk of death is small, however, and other risks are large (e.g. bearing a physically deformed child as a result of medication with thalidomide in pregnancy, or sterility from exposure to the pesticide 1,2-dibromo-3-chloropropane (DBCP) during its manufacture), it is essential to measure risk in other terms. This may be relatively easy when the harm is great and the risk for those not exposed to the hazard is small. Often, however, it is difficult not only to decide whether an individual has developed the suspected disability (as with the mental effects that are believed to result from exposing infants to small amounts of lead in the environment) but also to determine the prevalence of the same disability in the population in the absence of the suspected agent.

Table 1 lists sources of evidence on physiological state or disease prevalence or incidence. Few provide reliable numerical information that can be used for comparison with that obtained for groups at hazard (Doll 1979). Consequently, risks that cannot be measured in terms of mortality commonly require *ad hoc* surveys for determining the spectrum of adverse events and estimating the probabilities of their occurrence.

4.4 SOME SPECIFIC RISKS

4.4.1 INTRODUCTION

There are many sources of risk on which empirical evidence is available and it is not the objective of the present report to embark on a comprehensive discussion. We shall therefore concentrate on a few specific issues, in particular radiation and AIDS, chosen partly because they are of considerable public interest and partly because they illustrate a variety of general issues.

4.4.2 RISKS FROM EXPOSURE TO RADIATION

All members of the population are exposed to ionizing radiation of natural origin, and some people may receive additional exposures as a result of medical procedures or occupationally. The estimated average annual dose to a person living in the UK is 2.5 mSv, and the contributions made by the various different sources are summarized in table 2. Natural sources dominate artificial ones, with the natural radioactive gas, radon, contri-

buting 48% of the total dose. Among artificial sources, medical procedures make by far the largest contribution. The contribution from the nuclear industry via occupational exposures or discharges is relatively small in comparison to other sources.

The estimates shown in table 2 have changed somewhat over recent years. To some extent this reflects real changes in the doses received. For example, doses from the testing of nuclear weapons in the atmosphere have declined since the mid-1960s. However, the most substantial change is due to increased knowledge of the extent to which the naturally occurring radioactive gas radon tends to accumulate in houses and other buildings after escaping from the soil, and to more precise estimation of the bronchial dose after the inhalation of radon under environmental conditions.

Table 1. Sources of data relating to physiological status and disease prevalence and incidence

national and area vital statistics (births, deaths, and census data)
hospital records (discharge diagnoses and operations)
general practitioner records
sickness benefit certificates
school medical examinations
health visitors' records
morbidity registers and notifications (congenital anomalies, cancer, blindness, infectious diseases, adverse reactions to drugs)
industrial medical records
General Household Survey
ad hoc surveys

Table 2. Annual exposure of the UK population from all sources of ionizing radiation

Source	Average dose /Sv
natural:	
cosmic	250
gamma rays	350
internal	300
radon	1200
thoron	100
artificial:	
medical	300
miscellaneous	10
fallout	10
occupation	5
discharges	<1
total (rounded)	2500

Source: Hughes *et al.* (1989).

71

There is ample evidence that most organs and tissues of the body experience an increase in the subsequent risk of cancer after substantial doses of ionizing radiation, and it seems likely that there is some increase in risk following any dose, however small. Several studies have been done on human populations who have received unusual and well-documented exposures, such as survivors from the atomic bombings of Hiroshima and Nagasaki, and uranium miners who have been occupationally exposed to high concentrations of radon. These studies have been used by various national and international committees to derive quantitative estimates of the risks involved, and a recent review by the National Radiological Protection Board has concluded that for a population with age and sex structure as in the UK, each Sv of exposure will induce a risk of about 4.5 fatal cancers per 100 persons and about another 2 non-fatal ones per 100 persons (Stather *et al.* 1988). This would imply that for the UK, with a population of 57 million and an annual average exposure of 2.5 mSv, about 6500 fatal cancers are caused by radiation each year and about a further 3000 or so non-fatal ones. The total number of deaths recorded in the UK each year is about 650 000, of which about 160 000 are due to cancer. Thus, on this basis, ionizing radiation is responsible for about 1% of all deaths and about 4% of deaths due to cancer.

Although these numbers are based on risk estimates extrapolated from the experience of populations exposed to substantially higher doses than those received by the majority of the population of the UK today, studies of groups exposed at lower doses have provided evidence to support the assumption that even at low doses risks are approximately proportional to dose (see for example, Kendall *et al.* 1992, Stevens *et al.* 1990, Muirhead & Kneale 1989).

The figure 4.5 fatal cancers per Sv per 100 persons is approximately three times greater than the estimate recommended by the International Commission on Radiological Protection in 1977 and given in the previous edition of this report. The increase is partly due to improved methodology for estimating the risks from the available epidemiological data, and partly, because as the period of observation in the various epidemiological studies has been extended, it has become clear that the increased risk of cancer following exposure to radiation can last a very long time. In the Japanese atomic bomb survivors, for example, even 40 years after exposure, mortality rates from cancer are still rising among those who received appreciable doses.

Although more is known about the quantitative effects of exposure to ionizing radiation than about any other carcinogen, considerable uncertainties remain including the duration of the increased risk following exposure, the effect of varying dose-rate on the subsequent risk, and the interaction of the radiation-induced risk with that of other carcinogens. The observation of an increased risk of childhood leukaemia in the vicinity of the Sellafield plant in Cumbria has also suggested that parental irradiation before conception might increase the risk of leukaemia in the offspring (Gardner *et al.* 1990) although the causal link is certainly not firmly established. Further revisions to the risk estimates can therefore be expected in future as additional knowledge on these issues becomes available.

Although the above estimates indicate that radiation may be the cause of quite a considerable number of deaths each year in the UK, prospects remain poor for any substantial reduction in the toll. Although there may be some scope for reducing doses received from medical procedures, for stricter control of radiation in the workplace, and for reducing radon exposures in houses and other buildings where the levels are likely to be raised, the vast majority of the collective dose is due to natural radiation, received at a relatively uniform rate throughout the population, and would be very difficult to reduce substantially.

The ultraviolet (UV) region of the electromagnetic radiation spectrum extends from 200 to 400 nm wavelength. It is adjoined at longer wavelengths by the visible region and at shorter wavelengths by ionizing radiation. The UV spectrum has been subdivided into three segments: UVA (320–400 nm), UVB (280–320 nm) and UVC (200–280 nm). In general, UV is increasingly active with decreasing wavelength, thus UVA is the least biologically damaging, whereas UVC is specifically used for its sterilizing (bactericidal) properties. The major source of human exposure to UV radiation is sunlight. Ozone in the stratosphere effectively absorbs all natural UVC and some UVB. The residual UVB which reaches the ground is responsible for several detrimental effects on the skin notably burning and cancer. Many factors affect the distribution of UVB, especially geographic latitude, altitude and cloud cover. Apart from sunlight, most artificial sources of UV predominantly emit UVA except for germicidal lamps, UVB lamps used in the treatment of psoriasis, and some of the early designs of sunlamps and sunbeds.

The UVB in sunlight is thought to be involved in the causation of more than 50% of malignant melanomas, more than 80% of other skin cancers (squamous cell carcinoma and basal cell carcinoma) and, in conjunction with pipe smoking, over 90% of all lip cancers. All skin cancers occur more frequently in white-skinned populations and at latitudes where UVB exposure is high. With the exception of malignant melanoma, the risk of skin cancer is directly related to length of sun exposure and the areas of the body most affected are those with the heaviest exposure. Malignant melanoma has, however, a more complex association with sunlight in that intermittent exposures carry a higher risk than long-term continuous exposures, and indoor workers who receive sudden, intense exposures on summer holidays are at greater risk than outdoor workers such as farmworkers etc. Also the distribution of melanomas on the body is not directly associated with the areas receiving most sunlight exposure.

Malignant melanoma is the only sunlight-caused cancer that is associated with a high mortality rate. Rates of malignant melanoma have risen in recent decades, approximately doubling every ten years, due mainly to changes in behaviour which lead to increased sun exposure (e.g. in clothing styles and in holiday patterns). In the UK there are now about 3000 new cases diagnosed each year. There is no doubt that the use of effective UV-blocking sun creams and avoidance of high UV-intensity sunlight will reduce both the risk of melanoma and the other forms of skin cancer. The depletion of stratospheric ozone has also led to concern about a subsequent increase in UVB exposure. A recent World Health Organisation estimate has predicted that a 0.6% increase in malignant melanoma and a 2–4% increase in other skin cancers will accompany each 1% decrease in the ozone layer. This is broadly equivalent to the annual rate of increase in UVB reaching the ground in Southern Hemisphere countries such as Australia. In the Northern Hemisphere, although there has been a build-up of ozone-depleting chemicals, there has been no significant decline in ozone outside the seasonal variation. Thus the current increases in skin-cancer rates cannot be attributed to depletion of the ozone layer. It seems likely, however, that there will be some depletion in future years before the phasing out of ozone-damaging chemicals exerts an effect.

By contrast with the biological and epidemiological information on the effects of ionizing radiation, knowledge of the effects of electromagnetic fields in the broad band of wavelengths from 1 mm to several kilometres is much less clear. Such fields are primarily man-made and arise, for example, from overhead power-lines, electric appliances, such as electric blankets, micro-wave ovens, TVs and computer displays, and span a wide band of frequencies. There is no strong experimental evidence for a potential carcinogenic effect and the results of reported epidemiological studies are difficult to interpret. Studies have focused especially on childhood leukaemia and brain cancer and the clearest evidence for an excess risk arises for brain cancer in certain occupations involving some kinds of electrical and electronic work. Even here whether any real excess risk is due to the electromagnetic fields or to other factors associated with the work is unclear. This is a situation where the costs of preventive action could be very high and yet the risks appear to be either zero or very small.

4.4.3 RISKS FROM AIDS
The risks associated with the AIDS epidemic are particularly difficult to specify for several reasons. There is extreme heterogeneity between countries, between risk groups within countries and between individuals. Infected individuals are not directly recognizable as such until they seek HIV testing or become symptomatic become during the long and variable incubation period. There is the further complication that although antibodies to HIV-1 are usually present within a few weeks of infection, their development, called sero-conversion, may be delayed up to six months. Infected individuals continue to be HIV-1 antibody negative on testing until sero-conversion. This has clear implications for the safety of donated blood and other tissues and also for the need for repeated testing of high-risk individuals.

Transmission of the infection can be via sexual intercourse (vaginal or anal) with an infected partner, by the injection of infected blood or blood products including the sharing of contaminated equipment by intravenous drug users and from mother to child at or around birth including via breast milk, and occasionally via an occupational hazard. The relative importance of these, in particular of heterosexual transmission, varies greatly between different regions of the world. Within the UK sexual intercourse between men is the commonest mode of transmission but, world-wide, vaginal intercourse accounts for perhaps 80% of infections. The total number of AIDS deaths in England and Wales in 1991 was about 1400 corresponding to a rate of about 27 per million. A general idea of the prevalence of infection with HIV is given in table 3.

In 1991 out of 2.95 million UK blood donations there were 26 who on test were HIV antibody positives. Of the 26, 12 had donated blood previously and 14 were new donors. HIV prevalence in new donors was thus 14 out of 443 000, i.e. 1 in 32 000. Note, however, that in the UK all intending blood donors receive a leaflet inviting those who regard themselves as having been at risk of HIV infection to withdraw.

Occupationally acquired HIV infection has been reported for a footballer, a prison officer and an American dentist, and is a concern for surgeons, especially those operating in locations with a relatively high proportion of infected patients.

Based on a survey of Lothian dentists, who experienced an average of 6.8 non-sterile inoculation injuries in the past five years, a probability calculation suggests that the chance of any of the 350 or so dentists in the Lothian area having been infected with HIV in the past five years is about 0.004 and of any of the 7000 or so dentists in London being infected is about 0.08. Such risks are evidently very small.

A probability assessment of the reverse risk – the chance of a patient being infected by an HIV-1 positive surgeon, made by Centers for Disease Control, Atlanta – is in outline as follows. Current evidence suggests that the chance of sharps exposure to one surgeon during one procedure is about 0.025 and the probability of the sharp object recontacting the patient's open wound is about one third. Further evidence suggests that whereas hepatitis B infection occurs in 30% of accidents involving hepatitis B virus and antigen positive individuals, considerably lower transmission risks are associated with HIV (0.3%). A surgeon may perform 500 procedures a year, and an infected surgeon might work for seven years before being symptomatic. The result of combining these pieces of information is that there is a chance per patient of about 25 per million that sero-conversion occurs after an invasive procedure when performed by an HIV-infected surgeon. This compares with a chance of between 7 and 25 per million for sero-conversion following transfusion with screened blood.

Such probability calculations, while tentative and based often on rather ill-determined numbers, are important in forming rational judgements.

4.4.4 LOSS OF LIFE EXPECTATION

Death and disability due to a specific hazard need not occur during the course of the hazardous activity, but may be delayed for many years. A coal miner's risk of death due to an accident at work might be less than an asbestos worker's risk of developing a fatal cancer due to asbestos; however, the one may occur the first time the miner goes down the mine, whereas the other is unlikely to occur for at least ten years after first employment, is more likely to occur 20–30 years later, and may be delayed for 40–50 years.

One way in which we can take account of the time of occurrence of the event is to calculate age-specific death rates, and thence to estimate the years of life lost by the affected individual relative to his normal expectation. This procedure requires precise observations on the whole of the exposed population, and some knowledge of the expectation of life of its members in the absence of the hazard. The life expectation may differ

Table 3. HIV: prevalence per thousand

source	prevalence	
1991	new blood donors, UK	0.032
1990	mothers of live-born infants in Scotland	0.29
	in Edinburgh	2.5
	in Dundee	1.4
	in Aberdeen	0.7
1991	male inmates of HM Prison, Saughton	45
	injecting drug user inmates	250
1990	antenatal clinics, inner London	1.9
1988–90	Dundee women having termination of pregnancy	8.5
1990	attenders at GUM (Genito Urinary Medicine) clinics, London and outside London	
	homosexual men	255 (60)
	heterosexual men	16 (2.6)
	heterosexual women	15 (1.2)
1987–91	European study group on heterosexual contacts of HIV-infected index cases (median duration of relationship three years, unsystematic use of condoms)	169

grossly from that of the general population of the country (for example, if the hazard results from attempts to correct a physical or mental disability by drugs or surgery). The necessary data are seldom available in sufficient detail, but a crude approximation to the true loss of expectation of life that an affected individual will suffer is commonly derived by subtracting the average age at which the induced death occurs from the average age at death from other causes in the whole population at risk. Precise estimates for the effect of six hazards obtained from life-tables for the whole population of England and Wales or detailed observations of men and women exposed to specific risks over many years, are shown in table 4.

The loss of life expectation by the affected member is very different from the average loss experienced by the group as a whole. The former is the relevant statistic for the person who is unlucky enough to suffer the specific effect, but it bears little relation to the latter, which is the detriment to be expected by any member of the group. To calculate this, we have to multiply the individual loss of expectation of life by the probability that the individual will be affected, perhaps nearly

Table 4. Loss of expectation of life from various hazards

population	adverse event: death from	average age at death if unexposed to specific hazard	loss of expectation of life if exposed from age 20 years	
			those dying from hazard/ yrs	average over all exposed to risk /yrs
all women[1]	complications of pregnancy	77.45	47.45	0.01
all men[1]	motor traffic accidents	71.97	27.07	0.30
blue asbestos-gas-mark assembling, female[2]	lung cancer mesothelioma, asbestosis	78.93	21.02	1.51
underground coalminers, male[3]	mining accidents, pneumoconiosis	68.90	18.22	2.40
nickel-refiners, male[4]	cancer or lung or nasal sinuses	69.28	14.18	3.97
doctors smoking 15 to 24 cigarettes a day, male[5]	all conditions associated with smoking	76.30	14.68	5.45[6]

1. Exposed to age-specific risks observed in England and Wales, 1978.

2. Exposed at various ages only during World War II, followed for 30 years (Wignall & Fox 1982).

3. Employed in Rhondda Vale at various ages before 1951 and followed for 20 years (Cochrane & Sweetham 1982). Risk of mining accidents assumed to be difference between observed risk and national risk of accidents.

4. Employed in Welsh refinery at various ages before 1925, alive in 1935, and followed to 1981 (Cuckle 1982).

5. Responded to questionnaire in 1951, continued to smoke, and followed to 1971 (Doll & Peto 1982).

6. A proportion of the risk (possibly 10 to 20%) attributable to other factors confounded with smoking.

100% in extreme cases (e.g. from distilling 2-naphthylamine), more often 1% or 0.1%, and sometimes as low as 1 or 2 per million (which is approximately the added risk of a liver tumour for young women who take oral contraceptives). The average losses of life that individuals may expect as a result of the same six specific activities are also shown in table 4; they are all smaller (some very much smaller) than the losses experienced by the affected individuals.

When evaluating and comparing different dangerous activities for purposes of regulation and control, the average loss of life experienced by all exposed individuals is probably the most appropriate index; when explaining a danger to an exposed individual, the best practice may be to describe separately the probability that the adverse event will happen (obtained by dividing the average loss by the loss to the affected individual) and the effect it will have on his expectation of life if he is unfortunate enough to suffer it. A further complication is that measures taken to benefit some members of a group may constitute a hazard to others. For example, a particular drug might reduce the risks of stress in pregnant women but increase the risk of harm to the fetuses; similarly, prohibition of alcohol or of addictive drugs may increase crime rates.

4.5 VARIATION OF RISK WITHIN GROUPS

In many industries, records show the number of fatal accidents to vary from year to year only in accordance with the limits of random variation of small numbers, or to have only a very small annual trend. To a reasonable approximation such a death rate defines the average annual risk of accidental death for individuals employed in the industry as a whole, and may be used predictively if working conditions do not change significantly. Often, however, the averaging will include sub-groups that differ substantially in risk, because of type of work, age, experience in work, or other factors. Any heterogeneity of risk within the population from which an average risk is estimated is therefore important, especially when comparisons are made between risks attributed to different industries in which the proportions of workers at high or low risks may differ.

Similar considerations affect comparisons of overall estimates of risks in different types of sport, travel, or medical procedure. These are likely to vary considerably within each activity examined. Comparisons will be strictly valid only when made between defined sub-groups within which the condition of exposure and individual response to the harmful agent can be regarded as uniform.

Further problems arise with harmful agents that have delayed effects. For example, the accidental death rate in coal mining reflects the safety of mining conditions today, whereas the death rate from pneumoconiosis reflects that of conditions over many years in the past. The yearly risk of accident may remain approximately constant throughout a working life, except for changes in safety standards or in individual care. The risk of pneumoconiosis, however, is initially negligible but increases as dust intake accumulates. Many symptoms or diseases that occur only after damage to a sufficiently large fraction of the cells of an organ are believed not to become manifest unless a 'threshold dose' of the harmful agent has been absorbed, or a given duration of constant exposure has been exceeded. The same situation may be produced if repair processes in the body can reverse the effects of a low rate of exposure to a harmful agent, but not of a more rapid exposure. On the other hand, if a hazard (such as induction of cancer or of genetic mutations) depends on cellular damage that escapes reversal by any repair process, even at the lowest doses the frequency of harmful effects may increase with the accumulated dose of the toxic agent. Total risk may then be proportional to duration of exposure, as with the risk of accidental deaths, even though the damage from each element of intake of toxic agent may be expressed only after a long interval. If the proportionality is linear, the risk can properly be stated only for each exposure level or distribution of exposure levels. The annual risk, indeed, may be proportional to a power of the duration of exposure; for cancer possibly proportional to the fourth power (Peto 1977).

In some circumstances, one harmful agent may have a potentiating or synergistic effect on the action of another, so that the detriment produced by both agents acting together exceeds the total that would result from the two acting separately. Such an excess may also occur in the absence of synergism if the relation between detriment and exposure is non-linear for either agent. The risk from exposure to either agent then cannot properly be stated without reference to the presence and amount of the other. More generally, one must note that risk, like all probabilities, is conditional on the segment of the whole population to which it refers, and therefore any measure of synergism may depend greatly on the characteristics of those at risk. Antagonism between two agents is conceptually possible, but is in practice rare for the types of situation considered here. An example is provided by the risks of malaria and inherited sickle cell disease.

4.6 TYPES OF ACTIVITY

Many published reports have revealed the large numerical differences in risks involved that may exist among activities ordinarily regarded as of broadly similar safety. This can be true even for apparently similar ways of life, for example in respect of diet and alcohol consumption.

4.6.1 TRAVEL RISKS
The risk of travel has commonly been assessed in terms of accidental deaths per 10^9 km travelled (table 5). For rail travel it will be noted that there is an increase in the most recent figures, which reflects two major accidents in that period: the King's Cross Underground fire (Fennell 1988) and the Clapham Junction railway accident (Hidden 1989). For road travel the risk will vary with many conditions (e.g. class of road, experience of driver, weather, lighting, wearing seat belt or crash helmet, as well as the type of vehicle). The reduction of risk for car travel noted in table 5 reflects the introduction of compulsory wearing of seat belts, greater enforcement of drink driving laws and the public attitudes to drink-driving, improvements in car design, a greater mileage on motorways which have lower accident and casualty rates, and slower traffic in towns due to increasing congestion. For air travel the risk per flight (or per sector of a flight) is arguably more significant than per 10^9 km travelled, as a substantial proportion of all fatal accidents occur during take-off or landing. The reduction in risk of air travel noted in table 5 reflect the improvement in reliability of aircraft and the extensive introduction of automatic landing of aircraft with a reduction of accidents due to pilot error.

Table 5. Deaths per 10^9 km travelled, UK.

	1967–71	1972–76	1986–90
railway passengers	0.65	0.45	1.1
passengers on scheduled air services on UK airlines	2.3	1.4	0.23
bus or coach drivers and passengers	1.2	1.2	0.45
car or taxi drivers and passengers	9.0	7.5	4.4
two-wheeled motor vehicle driver	163.0	165.0 ⎱	104.0
two-wheeled motor vehicle passengers	375.0	359.0 ⎰	
pedal cyclists	88.0	85.0	50.0
pedestrians*	110.0	105.0	70.0

* Based on a National Travel Survey (1985/86) figure of 8.7 km per person per week
Source: Department of Transport.

4.6.2 RISKS FROM MEDICAL PROCEDURES

Attempts have been made to review the range of risks, ordinarily of death, attributable to different medical procedures. In certain circumstances, however, the risk of a procedure will vary considerably between identifiable classes of patients, so that average risk estimates are of limited interest. For example, reports in the mid-1960s indicated an average risk of death following diagnostic needle biopsy of the liver as about 10^{-4}. The hazard results largely from bleeding from the liver following the biopsy, and therefore the risk is likely to be high in patients whose liver disease is associated with defects in blood coagulation or with raised portal vein pressure, and low in others. Nevertheless, estimates of average risk illustrate the orders of magnitude by which the risks of death appear to differ for different conventional procedures (table 6).

4.6.3 OCCUPATIONAL RISKS

In interpreting accidental deaths or other effects attributable to occupational conditions, it is often difficult to ensure that the same criteria are used for different occupations and for different countries. Moreover, as already discussed, there is no simple way of aggregating rates of death from accident and disease and rates of non-fatal effects or permanently disabling conditions into any single index that facilitates reasonable comparison between industries. The grosser differences, however, may be very obvious. The rates of accidental death per million employed vary through several orders of magnitude in different forms of manufacture, with annual rates ranging from a few deaths per million employed in some to several hundreds or even thousands per million in others (table 7). If deaths due to fatal cancers are included, rates of some tens of thousands per million per year have occurred in the past in

Table 6. Risk of death associated with medical procedure (per 10^6 cases).

procedure	risk
vaccination, England and Wales	1
surgical anaesthesia, England and Wales, 1970–73	40
surgical anaesthesia, England, 1986	5.4
childbearing, England and Wales, 1974–76	100
childbearing, England and Wales, 1987–89	69
needle biopsy of liver	200
former thiouracil treatment of thyroid over-activity	4 000
former treatment of ankylosing spondylitis by radiotherapy or by radium 244	10 000
former use of 'Thorotrast' as a radiological contrast medium	60 000

Sources: reviewed by Pochin (1981 *a*, *b*).

Table 7. Average annual accidental death rates at work in the UK per million at risk (1974–78 and 1987–90 except as stated)

	1974–78	1987–90
manufacture of clothing and footwear	5	0.9
manufacture of vehicles	15	12
manufacture of timber, furniture, etc.	40	22
manufacture of bricks, pottery, glass, cement, etc.	65	60
chemical and allied industries	85	24
shipbuilding and marine engineering	105	21
agriculture (employees)	110	74
construction industries	150	100
railway staff	180	96
coal miners	210	145
offshore oil and gas	1650*	1250
deep-sea fishing (accidents at sea)	2800**	840

* 1967–76 ** 1959–68
Source: Health and Safety Executive.

sections of industries dealing with carcinogenic chemicals (Pochin 1975). Comparison of recent data with those for 1974–78, given in table 7, shows some occupations in which there has been a significant reduction in death rate. This may reflect the increasing influence of the implementation of the Health and Safety at Work Act in enforcing safer practices. It should be noted that the recent death rate for the offshore oil and gas industry includes the 167 fatalities of the Piper Alpha disaster (Cullen 1990).

4.6.4 RISKS IN SPORT

Various estimates have been made of the risks to life involved in different sports, and several difficulties affect the interpretation of the values quoted. In the first place, participants differ in training, experience and skill. Second, in certain sports, the severity of the challenge encountered or sought, and of the conditions in which the sport may be carried on, will vary greatly. Third, participants may spend little or much of their time during the year in the activity: for this reason, estimates of risk per year are less informative than those of risk per hour engaged in the sport (table 8), or per event (e.g. per race, match, flight, dive or climb), even though a reliable estimate of the average number of hours, or of events, per year is difficult to obtain for participants in many sports.

Table 8. Accidental death rates attributed to sporting activities

Deaths per 10^6 participant-hours*	
school and college football	0.3
amateur boxing, UK, 1946–62	0.5
skiing, US, 1967–68	0.7
skiing, France, 1974–76	1.3
canoeing, UK, 1960–62	10
mountaineering, US, 1951–60	27
motorcycle racing, UK, 1958–62	35
rock climbing, UK, 1961	40
deaths per 10^6 participant-years**	
cave exploration, US, 1970–78	45
glider flying, US, 1970–78	400
scuba diving, UK, 1970–80	220
scuba diving, US, 1970–78	420
hang gliding, US, 1978	400–1300
hang gliding, UK, 1977–79	1500
power boat racing, US, 1970–78	800
sport parachuting, US, 1978	1900
association football, England and Wales 1986–90	1.2
climbing, England and Wales, 1986–90	130
motor sports, England and Wales, 1986–90	27

* Based on approximate estimates of participants' hours per year spent in the activity.

** Based on numbers of participants and deaths per calendar year, without allowance for hours actually spent in the activity.

Sources include: British Hang Glider Association (1981), British Sub-aqua Club (1981), K.S. Clarke (1966), Metropolitan Life Assurance Co. (1979) and F.D. Sowby (1965).

Table 9. Some risks of death expressed as annual experience per million of the population of the UK for 1989

average over entire population	11490
men aged 55–64	15280
women aged 55–64	9060
men aged 35–44	1730
women aged 35–44	1145
boys aged 5–14	225
girls aged 5–14	160
death by accident (all)	240
death by road accidents (averaged over population)	98
death by accident in the home	86
homicide, England and Wales (1990*)	12
homicide from terrorism, England and Wales (1982–90*)	0.2

Source: Health and Safety Executive, Consumer Safety Unit; * Home Office.

4.6.5 DISCUSSION OF RISK OF VARIOUS ACTIVITIES

Table 9 gives the risk of death by age and gender from all causes, from all accidents alone, for road accidents and accidents in the home. This may provide a perspective for the death rates given in tables 6, 7 and 8.

Death rates, even though they can be precisely quantified, do not provide a real feel for the risk incurred in particular activities, as the risk will depend on the duration of the individual's participation in the activity. The Fatal Accident Rate, (FAR), originally known as the Fatal Accident Frequency Rate, which is described by Kletz (1992), maybe provides a more individually related measure of risk. The FAR expresses the risk of any activity as the number of deaths per 10^8 man-hours of the people involved in a particular activity. An alternative interpretation is that it is the number of deaths per 1000 people involved in an activity during their working lifetime (which is approximately 10^5 hours).

Table 10 gives values of FAR taken from Hambly (1992) for various activities to which the individual can relate. Hambly suggests that the risk of being killed travelling in a car provides a useful reference for what many people will consider as acceptable in the light of the benefits imparted. He also notes that motorcyclists, whose risk, depending greatly on the length of time riding, is more than ten times greater than car drivers, might have more relaxed definitions of safe and unsafe.

Table 10. Risk from death of various activities in the UK in terms of Fatality Accident Rate (number of deaths per 10^8 hours of the people involved).

plague in London in 1665	15000
rock climbing, while on rock face	4000
fireman in London air-raids, 1940	1000
travel by helicopter	500
civilian in London air-raids, 1940	200
jack-up platform in winter at UK code limit	200
policeman in Northern Ireland, average	70
construction, high rise erectors	70
'tolerable' limit of 1 in 1000 per year at work	50
smoking, average	40
travel by air	40
travel by car	30
oil and gas extraction	15
average man in 30s from accident	8
average man in 30s from disease	8
radon gas natural radiation 'action level'	6
construction, average	5
travelling by train	5
factory work, average	4
accident at home, all ages	4
accident at home, able-bodied	1
all manufacturing industries	1
'tolerable' limit 1 in 10 000 per year near major hazard	1
'tolerable' limit 1 in 100 000 per year near nuclear plant	0.1
terrorist bomb in London area	0.01
target risk for major fire in public building	0.005
building falling down	0.002

Source: Hambly 1992.

4.6.6 BROAD TRENDS IN MOR-TALITY

Life expectancy in Britain has improved enormously over the past 100 years, and it is still improving rapidly (Peto 1992). At the UK death rates of 100 years ago about a quarter of the newborn children would die in infancy or early childhood and another quarter would die before middle age, so only half could expect to survive to middle age. At current UK death rates, however, less than 3% will die before middle age (and this proportion is still decreasing), and so more than 97% will survive to middle age. Even in middle age there has been (and continues to be) substantial improvement: 100 years ago half those aged 35 could expect to die before 70, whereas at current UK death rates only a quarter (male 30% and female 20%) will do so. It is only in old age that the UK death rates remain high, for death in old age is inevitable. In or before middle age (35–69) those who die often do so of just one particular disease, the prevention or cure of which would have given the affected individual an average of about 25 years extra life (Peto *et al.* 1992). At older ages, however, those killed by a particular disease might well have died soon of something else, and therefore lose on average 'only' about eight years of life (Peto *et al.* 1992).

Turning just to the past few decades, these downwards trends in premature death are still continuing in the U.K. For 1950–55 and 1970–75 the infant mortality rates were 28 per 1000 and 17 per 1000, and on current trends they will be about 8 per 1000 in 1990–95 (Peto 1992). Likewise, over the past 40 years U.K. life expectancy has risen steadily: 69 years in 1950–55, 72 years in 1970–75 and projected to be 76 years in 1990–95 (Peto 1992). In the first half of this century the increase in life expectancy was driven chiefly by the decrease in mortality before middle age, but this is now so low that even if all deaths before middle age were abolished it would have little effect on UK life expectancy. In the past few decades, however, the chief reason UK life expectancy has continued to improve is because of the decrease in mortality in middle age. At the death rates of the 1960s one-third of those aged 35 could expect to die at 35–69 years of age (42% male, 24% female), while the corresponding figure for 1990s is projected to be only one quarter (30% male, 20% female). The reason why the improvement is so much greater for males than for females is that for males the effects of tobacco are decreasing, whereas for females the effects of tobacco are increasing (see figure 1; Peto *et al.* 1992). The reasons for the male decrease in deaths from tobacco are threefold. First, fewer males now smoke; second, cigarettes now contain less cancer-causing tar (Doll & Peto 1981); third, progress is being made in other aspects of the prevention of death from vascular disease, and the main effect of tobacco on vascular mortality is to multiply up whatever other risks exist. The reasons for the female increase in deaths from tobacco are also simple; there is a long delay between cause and effect, and the large increase in female smoking during and after the second world war is now causing a large increase in death from the habit (Doll & Peto 1981) (which would have been even larger but for reductions in other risk factors for vascular disease and improvements in its treatment).

The effects of tobacco are so large that they must be subtracted out if the relevance of other risk factors to trends in UK mortality are to be considered. But, in subtracting them out a small correction is necessary, for what is wanted is the overall number of deaths that there would have been in the absence of tobacco, and a few of those killed by tobacco would have died prematurely of other causes (see figure 1: for example, for males in 1965 the risk of death at age 35–69 in the absence of tobacco would have been 25% not 22%). With this correction, in the absence of tobacco the risks of

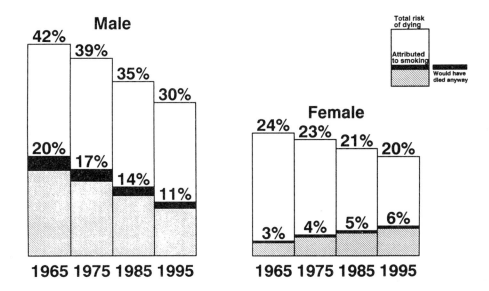

Figure 1. Risks of dying at age 35–69 in UK. (Source: data taken from Peto et al. 1992.)

death at age 35–69 in the 1960s and the 1990s would be approximately 25% and 20% for UK males, and 21% and 14% for UK females (or, taking the average for both sexes, 23% in the 1960s and 17% in the 1990s). This overall estimate of the reduction in mortality that would have been seen in the absence of tobacco includes a modest reduction in cancer mortality and a somewhat larger reduction in mortality from other diseases.

In discussing the avoidance of risk, it is useful to bear in mind this general context of risks, past and present; the present is much better than the past, and improvement continues; premature death in Britain is dominated by tobacco (which currently accounts for about one third of all UK deaths in middle age); we do not live in an era of increasing cancer mortality, nor in an era of increasing mortality from diseases other than cancer (indeed, decreases are still continuing in mortality from respiratory disease and from vascular disease). The prospect of a large eventual increase in death from AIDS (or from other new infective disease) is real, but if the effects of tobacco and new infections can be controlled then substantial further improvements can be anticipated.

4.7 CONCLUSIONS

If risk assessment is to be more than an academic exercise, it must provide quantitative information that aids decisions of many kinds, ranging from those made by the individual for his own health or for the welfare of his family, to those made by administrative bodies for the protection or benefit of sectors of the community, of the nation, or of mankind as a whole. Formal analysis of a class of risks can never be undertaken with perfect knowledge of relevant parameters or with exact prediction of the circumstances of its use. Results should therefore not be presented solely in terms of estimates of detriments, indices, or financial equivalents, useful though these concepts may be for the narrower purposes of cost–benefit analyses. All qualitative and quantitative assumptions must be explicitly stated and full information on constituent risks must be listed.

For the reasons sketched above, many epidemiological investigations focus on mortality. Attempts to measure health status (quality of life) have, however, a long history and in recent years have attracted much attention, both in connection with life-threatening diseases and more broadly. Measurement is preferably by patient self-assessment and there are now several reasonably well-tested questionnaires for this, some specific to particular diseases and others more general in nature. They frequently yield scores along several dimensions (e.g. referring to physical, social and psychological wellbeing).

There are essentially three types of application of such instruments:

(a) in connection with clinical trials to compare treatment regimes;

(b) for assessing changes in population characteristics;

(c) for resource allocation.

In clinical trials the object is detailed interpretation and ultimately the need to give individual patients (and their treating physicians) as clear a statement as possible of the likely consequences of different treatments, thus enabling individuals to make their own choice between, say, a treatment with relatively good survival prospects and relatively poor quality of life and one with poorer survival probability and good quality of life prognosis conditional on survival. Such comparisons are likely to be intrinsically probabilistic. Quality of life may well be assessed separately along several dimensions.

An example of (b) is the use of questions about limiting long-standing illness contained in the General Household Survey to assess expectation of life without dis-

ability. The general conclusion is that the quite substantial increase in life expectancy between 1975 and 1988 is not matched by a corresponding increase in expectation of life without disability. One of the assumptions underlying this conclusion is, of course, that the reporting of disability is reasonably constant over this period. Note that in this context the measurement of quality of life is a quite crude one.

A highly controversial aspect of the quality of life studies is their use in resource allocation. In essence, quality of life is reduced to a number between 0 and 1, corresponding respectively to death and complete health, although in principle negative values (fates worse than death) need not be excluded. Then for each patient treated by a particular route, the expected average quality is computed year by year, future years discounted and thus the consequence converted to a single number measured in QALYs (quality adjusted life years). Resources are then allocated to maximize the return in QALYs per million pounds spent, a form of cost–benefit analysis. Although such calculations, supplemented by careful sensitivity analysis, might well be valuable as a basis for discussion, there are overwhelming arguments against any kind of mechanical application of such a procedure. The conversion of the highly multidimensional concept of quality of life into a single number disguises major differences of preference between individuals, the basis for a discounting rate is very unclear and, most importantly, the comparison of major gains for a few individuals with small gains for many individuals raises very difficult issues which may be disguised rather than clarified by a calculation of QALYs. For example under a 5% discount rate the following highly idealized possibilities are roughly equivalent in terms of QALYs:

(a) To give 100 patients short-term therapy to relieve anxiety ($q = 0.75$) estimated to remove symptoms for an average of 7 months.

(b) To give the same patients surgery which if successful will remove symptoms for life but which has a 24% operative mortality.

Other more extreme comparisons in which the treatment of just one patient achieves the same number of QALYs can be constructed. The key issues are that any such calculation involves aggregation over time, over patient groups of different size and over uncertainty and it is implausible that any values can lead to widely acceptable conclusions.

Though statistics of cause of death are relatively easily recorded, they are inadequate as a measure of harm to individuals, their families and society. Major injuries and 'fates worse than death' are not so readily measured and the harm may be great, in some cases even more detrimental than death. Deaths in mining for example are serious, but the ill health among miners may well be more damaging. The cost resulting from accidents may be more unacceptable to society than the deaths that result, such as the high medical cost and use of scarce resources in treating the injured from road accidents.

Nevertheless death statistics given in tables 5–10 serve a useful purpose. They indicate glaring examples of what may be considered unacceptable death rates, such as those incurred by two-wheeled

motor vehicles or by the offshore oil and gas industry. These may provide guidance to the use of scarce resources to obtain the greatest benefit. Fatality accident rates may provide a better indication of risks incurred by an individual while pursuing a particular activity, be it rock climbing, travelling by air or living adjoining a nuclear power plant.

Table 5, which provides data over the period 1957–90, indicates the general improvement in safety of most forms of transport. With road accidents the improvement results from seat-belt legislation, drink-driving laws, better vehicle design, better roads, etc. Table 7 also shows the general improvement of safety at work, largely attributable to the implementation of health and safety at work legislation.

In summary, application of results will always involve elements of judgement, whether to take account of an individual's private scale of values or to allow for many factors that rightly concern the community, yet cannot be expressed numerically. At the level of decisions affecting populations, political considerations (in the good and in the bad sense) are inevitable. Yet, especially as regards mortality, we emphasize the central importance of careful estimation of risks from various sources. These provide the secure basis for action to deal effectively with serious risks and for the avoidance of costly over-reaction to risks of relatively minor importance.

REFERENCES

Bebbington, A.C. 1991 The expectation of life without disability in England and Wales: 1976-88. *Population trends* **66**, 26–29.

Bird, A.G., Gore, S.M., Jolliffe, D.W. & Burns, S.M. 1992 Anonymized HIV surveillance in HM Prison, Saughton in Edingburgh. *AIDS* **6**, 725–733.

British Hang Glider Association 1981 (personal communication).

British Sub-aqua Club 1981 (personal communication).

Card, W.I. 1973 Computer-assisted diagnosis and pattern recognition: the computing approach to clinical diagnosis. *Proc. R. Soc. Lond.* B **184**, 421–432.

Central Office of Information 1978 Quoted in *Nuclear Energy*, **17**, 12.

Clarke, K.S. 1966 Calculated risk of sports fatalities. *J. Am. med. Ass.* **197**, 894–896.

Clercq, A. de & Oeyen, L. 1991 HIV and surgeons. *Br. med. J.* **302**, 51.

Cochrane, A. & Sweetnam, P. 1982 (personal communication).

Cox, D.R., Fitzpatrick, R., Fletcher, A.E., Gore, S.M., Jones, D.R. & Spiegelhalter, D.J. 1992 Quality of life assessment: Can we keep it simple? (with discussion). *J. R. statist. Soc.* **155**. (In the press.)

Cuckle, H.S. 1982 (personal communication).

Cullen, The Hon. Lord 1990 *The public inquiry into the Piper Alpha disaster.* London: HMSO.

Department of the Environment 1978 *Transport statistics, Great Britain 1966–1976.* London: HMSO.

Doll, R. 1979 The pattern of disease in the post-infection era: national trends. *Proc. R. Soc. Lond.* B **205**, 47–61.

Doll, R. & Peto, R. 1981 The causes of cancer. *J. Natl Cancer Inst.* **66**, 1191–1308.

Doll, R. & Peto, R. 1982 (personal communication).

Fennell, D. 1988 *Investigation into the King's Cross Underground fire.* London: HMSO.

Gardner, M.J., Snee, M.P., Hall, A.J., Powell, C.A., Downes, S. & Terrell, J.D. 1990 *Results of case-control study of leukaemia and lymphoma among young people near Sellafield nuclear plant in West Cumbria.*

Gore, S.M., Felix, D.H., Bird, A.G. & Wray, D. 1992 Occupational risks and precautions among dental professionals in Lothian region of Scotland. *AIDS.* (In the press.)

Hambly, E.C. 1992 *Preventing Disasters. Proc. R. Instn. Gt Br.* (In the press.)

Health and Safety Executive 1978 *Mines and quarries*; 1979 *Mines*; 1979 *Quarries.* London: HMSO.

Health and Safety Executive. 1980a *Health and Safety Commission report 1978–79.* London: HMSO.

Health and Safety Executive. 1980b *Health and Safety Commission Report 1979–80.* London: HMSO.

Henderson, D.K., Fahey, B.J., Willy, M. *et al.* 1990 Risk for occupational transmission of human immunodeficiency virus type I (HIV-1) associated with clinical exposures: a prospective evaluation. *Ann. Internat. Med.* **113**, 740–746.

Hidden, A. 1989 *Investigation into the Clapham Junction railway accident.* London: HMSO.

Hughes, J.S., Shaw, K.B. & O'Riordan, M.C. 1989 *Radiation exposure of the UK population – 1988 review.* NRPB Report R227. London: HMSO.

International Commission for Radiological Protection 1977a ICRP publication no. 26, *Ann. ICRP* **1** (3), 1–53.

International Commission for Radiological Protection 1977*b* Problems involved in developing an index of harm. ICRP publication no. 27, *Ann. ICRP*, **1** (4), 1–24.

Kendall, G.M., Muirhead, C.R., MacGibbon, B.H., O'Hagan J.A., Conquest, A.J., Goodill, A.A., Butland, B.K., Fell, T.P., Jackson, D.A., Webb, M.A., Haylock, R.G.E., Thomas, J.M. & Silk, T.J. 1992 Mortality and occupational exposure to ionising

radiation: first analysis of the National Registry for Radiation Workers. *Br. med. J.* **304**, 220–225.

Kletz, T.A. 1992 HAZOP and HASAN. *Inst. chem. Engrs.*

Metropolitan Life Insurance Company 1979 *Statistical Bulletin* **60** (3), 2.

Muirhead, C.R. & Kneale G.W. 1989. Prenatal irradiation and childhood cancer. *J. Radio. Prot.* **9**, 209–212.

NRPB 1992 *Electromagnetic fields and the risk of cancer.* Documents of the NRPB 3 (1).

Peto, R. 1977 Epidemiology, multi-stage models and short-term mutagenicity tests. In: *Origins of human cancer. Cold Spring Harbor Conferences on Cell Proliferation,* vol. 4, pp. 1403–1428. New York: Cold Spring Harbor Laboratory.

Peto, R. 1992 Statistics of chronic disease control. *Nature, Lond.* **356**, 557–558.

Peto, R., Lopez A.D., Boreham, J., Thun, M. & Heath, C. 1992 Mortality from tobacco in developed countries: indirect estimation from national vital statistics. *Lancet* **339**, 1268–1278.

Pochin, E.E. 1975 The acceptance of risk. *Br. med. Bull.* **31**, 184–190.

Pochin, E.E. 1981*a* Risk–benefit in medicine. In: *Risk–benefit analysis in drug research* (J.F. Cavella, ed.). Lancaster: MTP Press.

Royal College of Pathologists 1992 *Report of a working group: HIV infection: hazards of transmission to patients and health care workers during invasive procedures.*

Schilling, R.S.F. 1979 Hazards of deep-sea fishing. *Br. Jl Ind. Med.* **28**, 27–35.

Sowby, F.D. 1965 Radiation and other health risks. *Health Physics,* **11**, 879–887.

Stevens, W., Thomas, D.C., Lyon J.L., Till, J.E., Kerber, R.A., Sion, S.L., Lloyd, R.D., Elghany, N.A. & Preston-Martin, S. 1990 Leukaemia in Utah and radioactive fallout from the Nevada test site. *J. Am. med. Ass.* **264**, 585–591.

Wignall, B. & Fox A.J. 1982 (personal communication).

CHAPTER 5
RISK PERCEPTION

Prepared by: Dr Nick Pidgeon, Professor Christopher Hood, Professor David Jones, Professor Barry Turner, and Ms Rose Gibson (Research Assistant).

5.1 INTRODUCTION AND BACKGROUND

5.1.1 PERCEIVED RISK

From the perspective of the social sciences, risk perception involves people's beliefs, attitudes, judgements and feelings, as well as the wider social or cultural values and dispositions that people adopt, towards hazards and their benefits. Hazards are defined here, following Kates & Kasperson (1983), as 'threats to people and the things they value'. This view of perceived risk is intentionally broad, and takes account of the fact that it is characteristics of hazards, rather than some single abstract concept such as risk, that people appear to evaluate. Furthermore, the perception of risk is multidimensional, with a particular hazard meaning different things to different people (depending, for example, upon their underlying value systems) and different things in different contexts. In some circumstances, important aspects of risk perception and acceptability involve judgements not just of the physical characteristics and consequences of an activity but also social and organizational factors such as the credibility and trustworthiness of risk management and regulatory institutions. What is clear is that risk perception cannot be reduced to a single subjective correlate of a particular mathematical model of risk, such as the product of probabilities and consequences, because this imposes unduly restrictive assumptions about what is an essentially human and social phenomenon.

There is no doubt that there has been an upsurge during the 1980s in social-science investigations of risk perception.

Significant new empirical work has been done, the scope of critical and conceptual thinking on the subject has broadened considerably, and application areas as well as policy implications of the basic research have been identified. During this period two new interdisciplinary international journals, *Risk Analysis* and *Risk Abstracts*, have been successfully launched; an uncounted number of conferences and scientific meetings on the topic have been held; and significant legislative changes, particularly with respect to the provision of risk information to the public, have occurred in the UK, the European Communities and the US. Reviewing the most significant published literature that has appeared over the past ten years has involved, inevitably, the inclusion in the current chapter of a relatively large number of references, although by no means all that have appeared are listed here. A recent bibliography of this area covering 1980–1989 compiled by Rohrmann, Wiedemann & Stegelmann (1990) lists almost 1000 publications.

As well as presenting a bibliography of significant literature for the benefit of the reader who wishes to explore the area further, the current chapter aims to summarize the emerging trends and debates in the social scientific study of risk perception. Four major trends can be charted in the recent literature, and these form the basis for the main chapter subsections. First, the view that a separation can be maintained between 'objective' risk and 'subjective' or perceived risk has come under increasing attack, to the extent that it is no longer a mainstream position (see section 5.2). Most people would agree that the physical consequences of hazards, such as deaths, injuries and environmental harm, are objective facts. However, assessments of risk, whether they are based upon individual attitudes, the wider beliefs within a culture, or on the models of mathematical risk assessment, necessarily depend upon human judgement. In this respect it can be argued that assessments of risk involve a degree of subjectivity, to a greater or lesser extent. Most contemporary social-science treatments of risk (and some recent engineering accounts too; see for example Blockley 1992) subscribe to this view either explicitly or implicitly. Second, the early psychological empirical studies of risk perceptions, and in particular those pioneered by the Decision Research group led by Paul Slovic, Baruch Fischhoff and Sarah Lichtenstein in Oregon, have been extensively replicated and extended (section 5.3). This approach to studying risk perceptions, deriving from the twin traditions of cognitive psychology (the study of human memory, sense perception, thought and reasoning) and the study of human decision-making behaviour, can be characterized today as a fully mature discipline, or to use Kuhn's (1962) well known phrase, a 'normal science'. A third trend, and perhaps the most significant one, is that many researchers have sought to look beyond purely individual, psychological explanations of human responses to hazards. Social, cultural and political processes are now acknowledged as all being involved in the formation of individual attitudes towards risks and their acceptance (section 5.4). This broadening of horizons has involved a higher profile for sociologists and anthropologists within the field of risk studies, together with attempts to adopt genuinely interdisciplinary approaches to this issue. Finally, part of the field has undergone a process of self-redefinition with the emergence of risk communication as a topic of concern. The study of risk com-

munication (section 5.5) relates theory and findings from basic risk perception studies to the formulation of policy (for example for risk managers and regulators), to the currently evolving legislative frameworks for dealing with hazards, and to the key question of public involvement in decision making about hazards.

5.1.2 THE 1983 CHAPTER

In approaching the subject ten years on, and so as adequately to chart the significant changes, it is useful to present first a brief appreciation of the state of knowledge as represented in the 1983 Royal Society report. A re-reading of this chapter with the benefits of hindsight reveals three significant themes. The first theme concerned the presumed disciplinary boundaries of the subject, which were represented as relatively narrow ones. The scientific investigation of risk perception was seen primarily as a question for the psychologist. This view accurately reflected the available literature, which with very few exceptions (see for example Conrad 1980) was the product of psychological investigations of individual perceptions of risk. Much of this early research, such as by Green and Brown in the UK (1980), Otway and colleagues at IIASA in Austria (Otway & Cohen 1975), and the Decision Research group in Oregon (Fischhoff, Slovic, Lichtenstein, Read & Combs 1978) had been conceived in response to and as critique of the classic paper by Starr (1969). Starr had utilized the method of revealed preferences (sometimes also referred to as implicit preferences) in his study of acceptable risk; that is, the investigation of the existing (implicit) preferences and trade-offs made within a society between the risk and benefits of a hazard, by the analysis of currently 'accepted' accident levels. In his paper Starr attempted to demonstrate that risk acceptance in the US differed significantly for hazards to which people are exposed involuntarily (e.g. energy generation) compared to those undertaken voluntarily (e.g. smoking). In contrast, the early psychological studies involved eliciting people's expressed preferences; that is the direct investigation, typically by questionnaire, of what people say risk means to them, what activities are risky, and which are acceptable or unacceptable. A major early finding from such work was that the concept of risk means much more to individuals than merely estimated fatalities in some unit of time (Slovic 1987). Individuals' conceptions of a wide range of hazards were found to involve several qualitative factors, such as an activity's voluntariness, its personal controllability and familiarity (see section 5.3.3), in ways not readily captured by the models traditionally used for mathematical risk assessment (Slovic, Fischhoff & Lichtenstein 1980). In addition, these studies revealed both differences and similarities between 'expert' and 'lay' judgements of risk although at that time the differences tended to receive more attention than the similarities (sections 5.2 and 5.3). The Oregon group had also begun to develop a theoretical framework, based upon the work of psychologists Tversky and Kahneman (see for example Kahneman, Slovic & Tversky 1982), to explain individual risk evaluations in terms of the intuitive mental rules-of-thumb, or short-cut judgement strategies (referred to in the technical psychological literature as cognitive heuristics) that people often use when judging the likelihood of every-day events.

The second theme in the 1983 chapter concerned the debate over the attempt to define a single expression of acceptable risk. This issue had motivated Starr's work, and the conceptual and empirical flaws in his revealed-preference approach to acceptability were soon extensively explored. One conclusion from the expressed-preference studies was that individual and social acceptability of risks might in part be related to the qualitative dimensions of hazard perception that were being identified in the psychology laboratory. Such findings pointed to the complexities inherent in any attempt to define a single measure expressing acceptable risk either in some 'objective' sense, or in more pragmatic terms for the purposes of public policy and decision making. However, the implications of such studies had not at that time been fully developed to their more general conclusion; that there are serious difficulties in defining a single measure of objective risk itself.

The third theme within the 1983 report concerned public perceptions of one hazard in particular; that of civilian nuclear power. Concern over nuclear power generation in Western societies had gathered momentum during the 1970s and early 1980s, although van der Pligt (1992) reports that, on general opinion-poll measures, US public acceptance of nuclear power appears to have been relatively stable prior at least to the Three Mile Island accident in 1979, but fell away sharply after this. One of the contested grounds between objectors to and proponents of civilian nuclear power development concerned the question of its risks. In this respect, studies of risk perception offered the possibility of an empirically grounded understanding of some of the psychological dimensions to this complex and highly visible social issue. Nuclear power also provided researchers with a key case to use in the comparative investigation of the structure of individual attitudes towards a more general range of societal hazards.

In the light of the subsequent developments in the field, to be reviewed here, it is clear that three of the conclusions drawn in the 1983 chapter displayed considerable foresight. These conclusions were, first, that the notion that all hazards could be scaled for magnitude of risk and an acceptable level established had largely foundered. Second, that the main achievement of risk-perception research was to demonstrate that the public's viewpoint must be considered not as error but as an essential datum. And third, that there was an administrative dilemma in studying individual risk judgements as the basis for policy-relevant recommendations, because these judgements are not necessarily a guide to aggregate decision making. Different sections of society might have different risk perceptions, and resolving such differences involved political as well as scientific choices. All three of these conclusions have, in different ways, been elaborated by subsequent research on risk perception.

5.1.3 ACCEPTABLE RISK AND TOLERABILITY

Arriving at consensus decisions over the question of acceptable risks in society is not a simple matter. At minimum, one might ask of any hazard, 'to whom might it be acceptable or unacceptable, when, and under what circumstances?' In practical terms, individuals, organizations and governments are faced constantly with the need to take decisions involving actual or projected hazards; and as a consequence with the problem of what is acceptable? Responsibility for environmental safety is a traditional part of government's 'police power' (in Continental European parlance) which has become increasingly salient in recent decades, with massive increases in bureaucracy and regulation which are discussed in chapter 6 below. Several methods have therefore evolved for the resolution of acceptable risk problems. Fischhoff, Lichtenstein, Slovic, Derby & Keeney (1981) have investigated this issue extensively. They suggest that there are three generic approaches that institutions typically use for resolving questions of acceptable risk. These are, first, professional judgement, as embodied in individual professional skills and knowledge or in institutionally agreed standards such as engineering codes of practice. Second, formal analysis such as cost-benefit analysis or decision analysis; and many of the techniques of mathematical risk assessment are founded upon this approach. Third, so-called 'bootstrapping' approaches, which include the method

of revealed preferences, and base acceptability upon extrapolation from statistics summarizing behaviour towards existing hazards. The assumption in this latter approach is that new hazards should not impose a greater risk than those already tolerated by society, and such an assumption often underlies the use of risk comparison tables (see for example Wilson 1979) for appraising acceptability. However, it should be noted that the bootstrapping approach gives no recognition to the ways in which a new hazard might increase the total risk-burden in society.

Fischhoff *et al.* evaluate each approach according to seven criteria: whether it is comprehensive; logically consistent; practical; open to evaluation; politically acceptable; compatible with existing institutions; conducive to society learning about risk; and improves decision making in the long run. They conclude that it is meaningless to speak of acceptable risk in isolation from the question of choice about alternatives. That is, acceptable risk is in their view best characterized as a decision problem, involving values, as well as both agreed-upon and contested facts. As a consequence 'there can be no single, all-purpose number that expresses the acceptable risk for a society. At best, one can hope to find the most acceptable alternative in a specific problem, one that will represent the values of a specific constituency' (1981, p. xii). They also conclude that none of the generic approaches to acceptable risk that they survey is fully comprehensive. Each makes different assumptions and omissions, and the use of any particular method inevitably involves a choice about what elements to include in an analysis. One practical suggestion that follows from this is that acceptability might be best approached by a dynamic or sequential process of evaluating an activity systematically against several criteria or methods, as recently suggested by Vlek (1990).

In the UK the use of acceptable risk as a guiding principle was criticized by Sir Frank Layfield, who chaired the 1983–5 public inquiry into the Sizewell B nuclear plant (see O'Riordan, Kemp & Purdue (1988), for an excellent analysis of this inquiry). Layfield argued that the term 'acceptable' failed to reflect the importance of the problem, and in particular the reluctance that individuals commonly show towards undertaking certain hazardous activities, particularly those involving the direct possibility of death or injury. He suggested that the phrase *tolerable risk* might better reflect the true seriousness of the question, and among his 'General conclusions on safety criteria' was the following:

The opinions of the public should underlie the evaluation of risk. There appears to be no method at present for ascertaining the opinions of the public in such a way that they can be reliably used as the basis for risk evaluation. More research on the subject is needed. As in other complex aspects of public policy where there are benefits and detriments to different groups, Parliament is best placed to represent the public's attitudes to risks. (Layfield 1987, summary paragraph 2.101h)

As a result of the Layfield inquiry the UK Health and Safety Executive (HSE) produced a report in which tolerable risk is defined as follows:

'Tolerability' does not mean 'acceptability'. It refers to the willingness to live with a risk to secure certain benefits and in the confidence that it is being properly controlled. To tolerate a risk means that we do not regard it as negligible or something we might ignore, but rather as something we need to keep under review and reduce still further if and as we can. (HSE 1988a, p.1)

In the HSE's approach this definition of tolerability is taken to imply that risks should be monitored, balanced against possible benefits, and wherever possible reduced to 'As Low As is Reasonably Practical' (the ALARP principle). The use of such a definition to guide regulatory decision making is clearly a significant development. It implicitly bridges technical and social science considerations of risk by acknowledging that it is individuals and groups in society who must live with hazards, and therefore may be granted a role in making decisions about risk; for example, in the trade-off between risks and benefits, and in investing trust in, and defining the responsibilities of, particular risk-management organizations and practices. In this respect the HSE is correct in stating that 'the judgement on what is tolerable is not a scientific but a political matter' (HSE 1991, p 13). The HSE approach has nevertheless been criticised on the grounds that it does not relate benefits clearly enough to tolerability (see HSE 1988b). More importantly, however, it does not address the critical issue of how public input to tolerability decisions might be achieved, beyond an implicit appeal to the restricted, and now much criticized (see for example O'Riordan 1977, Fischhoff, Lichtenstein, Slovic, Derby & Keeney 1981) revealed-preference criterion. The use of the tolerability concept might therefore be better informed by several of the findings from risk-perception research, which are summarized in the current chapter (see in particular sections 5.3.3). The findings from risk-perception research outline some of the characteristics of hazards (and the circumstances surrounding their management) that people may or may not be prepared to tolerate. The question of how future public input to tolerability decisions might be best achieved is also closely related to recent work on risk communication, which is considered in section 5.5.

5.2 THE OBJECTIVE–SUBJECTIVE RISK DEBATE

It is convenient to think that a clear and unambiguous separation can be maintained between 'objective' or statistical risk on the one hand and 'subjective' or perceived risk on the other. The belief that such a separation is indeed possible has been ironically – if perhaps tendentiously – termed by Watson (1981) the 'phlogiston theory of risk'. Watson's description of the phlogiston theory caricatures objective risk as a unique substance, given off by a physical process, and at a rate which can be determined precisely by risk assessment. Watson argues that this notion is unduly simplistic, and should be rejected, in the same way that the 18th-century notion of phlogiston ultimately was. If the objective/subjective distinction is conceptually simplistic it is far from trivial in its implications. It forms the foundation for a line of argument, most often heard when some social group appears to hold differing evaluations of hazards from those provided by technical models of risk assessment, which devalues the importance of public attitudes and beliefs in favour of an abstract statistical rationality (Otway & Thomas 1982). Given that the public may often also be the primary risk-bearers in society there are strong ethical and intellectual grounds for not accepting such arguments unconditionally and without very thorough critique. One important question that must be addressed concerns whether attempts at objective risk assessment can ever be totally free from elements of judgement, and hence from some degree of selectivity or subjective choice? An altogether more philosophical question, which will be considered later (section 5.4), concerns the possibility of 'plural rationalities' (that is, logical deductions stemming from different assumptions about human nature, distributive justice and the link between society and the physical environment), above and beyond the narrow economic

framework underlying much of statistical risk assessment, but each capable of providing individuals with logically defensible bases for decision making about risks (see for example Brown 1989).

The argument can be made that judgement is inherent in, and indeed essential to, all forms of risk assessment. Judgement can arise in the selection of a risk index, in the assessment of consequences and uncertainties, as well as in the initial structuring of a risk problem. Concerning the selection of a risk index, Vlek & Keren (1991; see also Vlek & Stallen 1980, Vlek 1990) identify ten different formal definitions of risk, which are listed in table 1. These definitions reflect the considerable diversity within the technical literature over a working measure of risk. It is clearly important therefore to establish whether conclusions drawn will be sensitive to the particular risk index adopted (Otway 1985). However, even if a core definition of risk can be agreed – for example either, as suggested by Vlek & Keren (1991) a function of the probability and seriousness of an undesired consequence (e.g. definition 4, table 1), or as adopted in the current report (Chapter 1) as the probability of a particular undesired consequence (definition 1, table 1) – the assessment of its parameters inevitably requires judgement.

As with any form of cost–benefit analysis, judgement enters into the assessment of the disutility of consequences over matters such as the appropriate balance between death, morbidity, and the long-term social and individual costs associated with debilitating injury and illness, as well as between effects upon humans and those upon the environment. Fischhoff, Watson & Hope (1984) illustrate how risk analysis might take into account factors over and above the estimated number of deaths from an ac-

Table 1. Some formal definitions of risk or riskiness

(1)	Probability of undesired consequences.
(2)	Seriousness of (maximum) possible undesired consequences.
(3)	Multi-attribute weighted sum of components of possible undesired consequences.
(4)	Probability x seriousness of undesired consequences ('expected loss').
(5)	Probability weighted sum of all possible undesired consequences (average 'expected loss').
(6)	Fitted function through graph of points relating probability to extent of undesired consequences.
(7)	Semivariance of possible undesired consequences about their average.
(8)	Variance of all possible consequences about mean expected consequences.
(9)	Weighted combination of various parameters of the probability distribution of all possible consequences.
(10)	Weight of possible undesired consequences ('loss') relative to comparable possible desired consequences ('gain')

Source: Vlek & Keren (1991).

tivity, pointing out, however, that the weight to be placed upon each factor (e.g. when, and by how much, will a particular long-term chronic condition be judged worse than death) is always a matter for a judgement about values. Furthermore, such analysis could be extended to take account of the well-established distinction between a rarely occurring event with potentially high kill size and frequently occurring accidents with small kill sizes. Ashby (1977) has explored this area, arguing for the use of 'large elements of intuition' on the part of administrators in construing from frequency statistics what risks are acceptable to the public. The need for an intuitive element arises, according to Ashby, because acceptability is in part dependent upon a balance of benefits over costs, and both are difficult to estimate (especially the benefits). Quantification of present returns is difficult enough, but it is easy by comparison with the measurement of long-term implications. He points out that we must first make a value judgement about which strata of posterity to cater for. Furthermore, some claim that the argument, that society should aim to spend money to save lives, assumes that economic efficiency in reducing fatalities is the universal value (Rayner 1989). Reinforcing these theoretical arguments, von Winterfeldt & Edwards (1984) assert that many conflicts about risk are at root conflicts about values.

Uncertainties are as equally difficult to measure as consequences. Traditionally, uncertainty has been discussed primarily in terms of probability. There are at least four conventional interpretations of probability to be found in the literature; classical, frequency, logical and Bayesian (or subjective). The probability calculus is relatively undisputed for these various types, although there has historically been a vigorous dispute over the relative merits of the frequency (statistical) and the Bayesian (subjective) views, and strong arguments can be found by proponents of both approaches (for a philosophical discussion of this debate see Hacking (1975)).

For most interesting risk problems, and certainly those for which formal risk assessment is typically utilized (that is, those involving low probability but high consequence events), there inevitably arises the problem of the combination of different types of probability. In particular the final numerical output of an analysis, involving the combination of both subjective and frequency inputs, might be interpreted as an empirically grounded statistical frequency. Funtowicz & Ravetz (1990) have developed a useful approach to this problem. They argue that the *process* of generating an item of quantitative scientific or technical information can be evaluated in terms of its overall dependability or quality; which they refer to as its pedigree. To take a hypothetical example, an overall failure 'probability' for a hazardous system may depend upon the combination of a well-corroborated frequency estimate (perhaps judged to be of high pedigree) of mechanical equipment reliability, with an acknowledged expert's judgement (medium to high pedigree) of the likely failure behaviour of a novel piece of control equipment, and a recent engineering graduate's guess (low pedigree) as to the levels of human or organizational reliability to be anticipated during maintenance operations. Clearly, the overall pedigree of any such combined assessment is open to debate, with one view being that it should only attain the pedigree of its weakest input. Perhaps a more fundamental issue however, and one requiring further investigation, concerns the question of whether probability is appropriate for modelling all of the potential uncertainties associated with complex hazardous systems. For example, Smithson (1989) presents an illuminating taxonomy of 'ignorance'. He points out that ignorance of the world may arise because our knowledge is distorted, incomplete (see also the related discussion of systemic uncertainties below) or even perhaps declared irrelevant. Within his taxonomy, probability is only one among several fundamental types of incompleteness, including also ambiguity and vagueness (or fuzziness).

Even the generation of seemingly uncontroversial 'statistical' estimates, such as the probability of harm associated with cycling, will depend upon a range of judgements; for example, decisions about the precise sampling space (what is to be counted as a cycling accident? Should the category include all accidents reported to the police, or only those for which an insurance claim is made?); the temporal units to adopt (accidents per hour of cycling, or per cyclist per year?); the methods for data recording and collation; and the assumption that the future will resemble the past in relevant respects. These all demonstrate how even the most straightforward of the risk tables (see also the comments on 'risk comparisons' in section 5.5.3), to which reference is often made in acceptable risk exercises, inevitably contain an appreciable element of judgement.

Perhaps the most fundamental point at which judgement is needed is during the qualitative structuring of a risk model. Before the assessment of consequences and uncertainties can commence, and the selection of a risk index be made, the basic components of the underlying risk model must be identified. Quantified risk assessment, and in particular event- and fault-tree analysis, is based upon the closed-world paradigm of decision analysis, which assumes that a complete and exhaustive set of pathways to failure can be unambiguously defined. However, although some consequences will be relatively easy to anticipate, others, particularly at the interface of human–technical systems (Collingridge 1980), may be more difficult to specify. In structural design Blockley (1980) distinguishes between parametric and systemic uncertainties. The former refers to stochastic uncertainties associated with random behaviours or measurement error, the latter to uncertainties due to the appropriateness or completeness of the structure of the risk model itself (that is, whether all relevant features have been included in a model). Vesely & Rasmuson (1984) make a similar distinction between physical and knowledge uncertainties in their discussion of nuclear probabilistic risk analysis. Green, Tunstall & Fordham (1991) have aptly characterized parametric uncertainties as 'what you know you don't know' and systemic (or knowledge) uncertainties as 'what you don't know you don't know' (p 228).

Systemic uncertainties may arise in several ways. For example, Pidgeon, Blockley & Turner (1986) describe a factory roof collapse under snow loading that was due in part to faulty tacit assumptions about snow distribution within the existing design code of practice. Incomplete understanding of the ways in which a system might fail can also arise as a result of the complexity, and dynamics of interaction, between the multiple elements within a large human–technical system. Such complexity can, under certain circumstances, mean that the precise pathways to failure may be particularly difficult to forecast or to control during the onset of an emergency (Perrow 1984). For many large-scale risk problems, systemic uncertainties are particularly associated with the influence of human and organizational factors (see Sjöberg 1980, Pidgeon 1988, Freudenberg 1988). The importance of the human element in large-scale failures is now widely recognized within engineering practice (Sibly & Walker 1977, Blockley 1980, Kletz 1985). However, human agency in popular treatments of the subject is often defined in terms of the rather restricted concept of 'human error'. There is now ample evidence that the behaviourial causes of accidents and disasters involve not just individual slips and lapses, but also, as demonstrated by Turner (1978), patterns of management and organizational failings such as failures of communication, information handling, coordination and error diagnosis. And although, as discussed by Reason (1990), traditional human reliability analysis may have had some success in defining and attaching probability estimates to certain classes of individual human error, modelling the organizational failings in this way would appear to set a more challenging task. The limited attention so far paid to the influence of organizational and management factors on reliability is a critical blind-spot in current risk assessment practice. This topic, and its implications for hazard management, are further discussed in Chapter 6.

The considerations above serve to illustrate the difficulties of measuring 'objective' risk, and force us to recognize the essentially conditional nature of all risk assessment. That is, it will necessarily depend upon a range of judgements and modelling assumptions introduced by the risk analyst. For example, Lathrop & Linnerooth (1983) describe how three separate risk assessments for the same proposed facility in the US differed widely in assumptions, presentation and implied conclusions. These arguments point to the 'open-world' nature of many risk problems (Blockley 1992), and they also serve to erode, to a certain degree, the presumed differences between 'expert' and public views of risk. In this respect Fischhoff (1989) suggests that the distinction between 'actual' and 'perceived' risk is misconceived, because, at a fundamental level, both inevitably involve human interpretation and judgement, and hence 'subjectivity', to a greater or lesser degree. He comments that 'In this light, what is commonly called the conflict between actual and perceived risk is better thought of as the conflict between two sets of risk perceptions: those of ranking scientists performing within their field of expertise and those of anybody else.' (1989, p. 270). This observation accords with the more general point, first made by the philosopher Polanyi (1958), that all scientific practice can be characterized by its reliance upon tacit or personal knowledge, as well as the more recent recognition from work on the sociology of scientific knowledge of the important role that social networks of scientists play in reviewing, evaluating and warranting scientific knowledge claims (see for example Latour 1987). In the context of risk perception studies some authors argue (section 5.4) for the radical position that all expressions of risk are derived from social and institutional assumptions and processes; that is, that risk is socially constructed (Douglas 1985, Johnson & Covello 1987).

5.3 THE PSYCHOLOGY OF RISK PERCEPTION

5.3.1 SENSE PERCEPTION AS A MODEL FOR RISK PERCEPTION RESEARCH

Within psychology the study of perception has traditionally been concerned with the ways in which the individual learns to know the environment through data from the sense organs. The early psychophysicists of the 19th century began a search for direct systematic relations between the physical energy of external stimuli (for example of light, heat and sound) and subjective responses, in different sensory modalities. The aims of such pure perception research are to establish law-like relations between characteristics of a stimulus input and an internal mental (that is cognitive) representation of that input. However, the most distinctive feature of an individual's cognitive system is its enormous capacity for storing the residue of past perceptions and for bringing these residues to bear on the processing of fresh input. Much contemporary work in psychology therefore operates with a model of mind that is not a passive 'convertor' of sensations but an active, seeking, 'constructor' of an internal representation of the environment. An important part of this constructive process involves the generation of understanding; that is, of endowing sensation with meaning. This process involves the assimilation of current input in the terms set up by past experiences (consider the difficulties of understanding a language that has not been previously learned), and in turn the extension and modification of stored experiences, or knowledge structures, upon receipt of novel stimuli.

The relations that the human sciences more generally seek to explain in the study of risk perception involve people's attention to and processing of a diverse range of information relating to hazards (and their benefits), and second-hand information from scientific communications, 'significant others' in the social world such as an individual's peers or other trusted figures, and, increasingly, from mass-media sources. Current psychological practice adopts the general assumption that external information is selected for attention and then interpreted upon the basis of organized knowledge structures by which all individuals make sense of the world, as well as with reference to the beliefs and systems of meaning that are shared more widely between members of a particular culture, society or social group.

The analogy between 'physical perception' and 'risk perception' is undoubtedly useful for guiding research, but has its limitations. Physical perception is typically associated with theories of the human perceiver as an isolated cognitive being (or processor of sensory information) which are grounded in purely psychological investigations. In contrast, as noted earlier, the field of risk-perception research today involves a far more diverse group of research specialities, together with theoretical and empirical foundations, not all of which take the individual as the basic unit of analysis. Furthermore, in traditional perceptual psychology the stimuli monitored by the five senses are relatively easy to measure, and therefore the properties of any external input can be objectively characterized. It is then possible to investigate in the laboratory the ways in which people's internal representations do and do not map onto pre-defined objective stimulus characteristics. And in this way the basic cognitive processes of perception can be identified. With risk perception research, however, stimulus definition is much more problematic, given the fact that defining the 'objective stimulus' characteristics of risk, as discussed in the preceding section, sets a contentious, if not impossible task. In this sense, therefore, the term risk perception is an unfortunate label, because one risks falling foul of Watson's (1981) phlogiston trap if the analogy with physical perception is taken too literally. It is for this reason that Otway (1990) has recently suggested that the field might more accurately be described as concerned with hazard or technology perception, rather than perception of risk.

5.3.2 Judged fatality estimates

One way to map a part of people's understanding of risk involves asking them to make fatality estimates for a range of hazards. In an influential study Lichtenstein, Slovic, Fischhoff, Layman & Combs (1978) asked educated lay subjects to judge the annual frequency of death in the US from 40 hazards, against the anchor reference point of annual motor vehicle accident deaths, for which the known rate was supplied. The results were then plotted against the best available (US) public health statistics estimating the deaths from such causes, as shown in figure 1. The results of this study were interpreted by the authors as showing two types of systematic difference between mean lay judgements and the statistical estimates. First, in comparison to the available statistical estimates, respondents tended to overestimate the number of deaths from infrequent causes such as botulism and tornadoes, but to underestimate the deaths from frequent causes such as cancer and diabetes. This can be seen in figure 1 in the 'flattening' of the best-fit curve relative to the identity line. Second, the precise amount of over- or underestimation for any specific activity

also displayed a systematic pattern. With the statistically infrequent causes figure 1 shows that approximately the same number of individuals die (less than ten per year in each case) in the US from botulism as do from smallpox vaccination. However, respondents in the study only slightly overestimated the number of vaccination deaths, but more heavily overestimated those from botulism. A corresponding pattern is evident for the frequent causes of death, where, for example, similar numbers of individuals die each year in the US from homicides as do from diabetes. Here, respondents heavily underestimated deaths from diabetes, but only moderately underestimated homicide deaths. Lichtenstein *et al.* (1978) note that the types of activity whose fatalities were judged to be relatively higher (at any given level of statistical frequency) were typically vivid, or imaginable causes of death (a result also found by Bastide, Moatti, Pages & Fagnanai (1989)), and go on to suggest that operation of the 'availability heuristic' might account for this secondary pattern in the data. The availability heuristic (Tversky & Kahneman 1973) suggests that an event will be judged probable or frequent to the extent that instances of it are easily recalled or imagined (i.e. are available in memory). Like all cognitive heuristics, this works well under most circumstances because events that are indeed frequently occurring in our environment will often become salient in memory. For example, the judgement that I am likely to obtain a taxi rapidly in the street outside my place of work is likely to be based upon considerable experience of observing the kinds of traffic in this particular street. However, it can be argued that if there is a selective presentation of information, so that some events are over-represented and others are under-represented, then reliance upon the availability heuristic may be misleading as a guide to frequency. For causes with which we have little direct familiarity mass-media reporting, particularly of vivid or sensational events, may

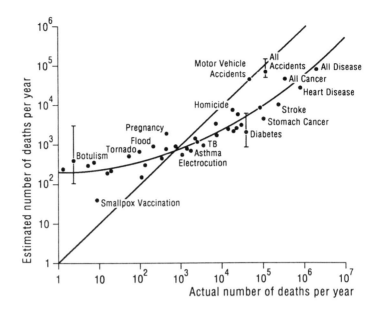

Figure 1. Relationship between judged frequency and statistical estimates of the number of deaths per year (US) for 40 causes of death. If judged and statistical frequencies were equal the data would fall on the identity line. The points, and the curved line fitted to them, represent the averaged responses of a sample of (US) lay people. To indicate the degree of agreement among the respondents, vertical bars depict the 25th and 75th percentile of individual judgements for botulism, diabetes and all accidents. (Source: Fischhoff, Lichenstein, Slovic, Derby & Keeney 1981.)

well be influential (Combs & Slovic 1979). The comparison of findings from studies of fatality estimation and characteristics of media reports are, however, clearly open to multiple interpretations.

Commenting retrospectively upon figure 1, Fischhoff (1990) observes that:

Typically, it has been described as proving the public's ignorance (or even 'irrationality') regarding risk issues with the attendant political ramifications. I have heard it described as proving the public's hopeless confusion about risks (e.g. nuclear power) that were not even in the study. Not only were these claims unwarranted by these results, but they went far beyond what could be shown in any single series of studies. (p. 648)

Fischhoff goes on to note that a subsequent study found that lay fatality estimates for the omitted activity of nuclear

power were broadly in line with the presumed number of deaths (to that date) from this energy source in the United States (Slovic, Fischhoff & Lichtenstein 1980). Other follow-up studies have confirmed that individuals' absolute estimates of fatalities do not correspond one-to-one with absolute statistical estimates, and are influenced systematically, as is commonly found in opinion polling research, by the way in which the researcher poses the question (that is, by the question response format). Neither of these are particularly surprising results given the difficulty of such an estimation task. However, these studies have also revealed that the rank ordering of lay fatality judgements (for example, comparative judgements of whether automobiles cause more, or less, fatalities than tornados) is relatively consistent across a range of response modes (Fischhoff & MacGregor 1983, Eiser & Hoepfner 1991), and that such orderings correspond quite well to the rank orderings implied by available statistical estimates (Daamen, Verplanken & Midden 1986). When response-mode effects are taken into account, therefore, it is clear that individuals are quite capable of providing well-founded judgements of the relative magnitude of expected fatalities in ways that are broadly in line with available statistical estimates.

5.3.3 QUALITATIVE CHARACTERISTICS OF HAZARDS: THE PSYCHOMETRIC TRADITION

Eliciting people's judgements of *risk* leads to much more complex findings than those for estimates of expected fatalities. In particular, it is clear that the concept of risk means far more to people than just expected fatalities. Empirical studies of individuals' risk perceptions reveal a pattern of quite complex qualitative understandings of the term risk. The suggestion that risk perception might involve qualitative characteristics is not a new one. As noted already, Starr (1969) made the important distinction between voluntary and involuntary exposure to risk, and Lowrance (1976) discusses several psychological dimensions of risk. The report of the Sunningdale Seminar (Department of the Environment & Health and Safety Executive 1979) held in the UK lists a set of characteristics held to underlie the acceptance of risks. Summarizing the work of the IIASA group on attitudes to nuclear risk during the 1970s, Otway and von Winterfeldt (1982) report that the acceptance of technological risks is in part based upon several qualitative dimensions. They note that there are several general characteristics of technologies and risk that are commonly valued negatively by all individuals. These are listed in table 2.

The early work of Green and Brown in the UK corroborates the claim that several of the qualitative characteristics shown in table 2 are important aspects of perceived risk. Green & Brown have extensively investigated the question of immediate versus delayed consequences (Green & Brown 1978*b*, 1980), catastrophic potential, which they term 'kill size' (Green & Brown 1978*a*, 1978*b*), as well as a range of low mortality but high disability consequences that might be said to impose 'fates worse than death'. In two studies Green & Brown (1978*b*) asked respondents to indicate their perceptions of the relative severity of several injuries. Of those included, permanent brain damage and permanent paralysis from the neck down were assessed as worse than death. There are doubtless other possibilities that could be placed in this category, such as protracted terminal cancer. The work of Green & Brown also makes the important distinction between individual and societal risk; for example, the risks from snakebite compared to those of the release of nuclear radiation. Green (1979)

Table 2. General (negative) attributes of hazards that influence risk perception and acceptance

(1)	Involuntary exposure to a risk.
(2)	Lack of personal control over outcomes.
(3)	Uncertainty about probabilities or consequences of exposure.
(4)	Lack of personal experience with the risk (fear of unknown).
(5)	Difficulty in imagining risk exposure.
(6)	Effects of exposure delayed in time.
(7)	Genetic effects of exposure (threatens future generations).
(8)	Infrequent but catastrophic accidents ('Kill Size').
(9)	Benefits not highly visible.
(10)	Benefits go to others (inequity).
(11)	Accidents caused by human failure rather than natural causes.

Source: Adapted from Otway & von Winterfeldt (1982).

has provided evidence that these two dimensions of perceived risk are independent, and in much of their subsequent work, Green & Brown use separate scales for 'personal safety' and 'threat to society'. It is interesting in this respect that in the UK the HSE (1988*a*) distinguishes between these two characteristics in its current approach to risk assessment. Referring to the qualitative dimensions listed in table 2, it is clear that several of these characteristics might differentiate between the perception and tolerance of societal and individual risk. For example, catastrophic potential (defined in terms of the possibility of several deaths) is likely to be a particular feature of societal rather than purely individual risks, as would be the distribution of risks and benefits, involuntariness of exposure, and personal controllability. Such examples point to the range of features that may underlie the cognitive representations that individuals construct of risks to which they themselves are personally exposed, and those imposed upon society as a whole. This observation has direct policy implications, as will become clear, both for risk communication and risk management.

The systematic investigation of the qualitative characteristics of the perception of hazards such as those shown in table 2 has been most actively pursued by researchers within the so-called 'psychometric' tradition. The most influential early work was done by the Decision Research group in Oregon (Fischhoff, Slovic, Lichtenstein, Read & Combs 1978). Good reviews of this work are provided by Slovic (1987, 1992), and Rohrmann (1991) gives a précis of the methods and findings from 30 recent key studies, many of which follow on directly from this work. As pointed out by Slovic (1992) this research began in part as an attempt to map the 'personality' of hazards; that is to identify the pattern of perceived qualities that characterize particular hazards, and through this to identify the relation between these characteristics and

the perception of risk. One significant question concerns whether, and how, the many potential qualities of hazards combine together to form a pattern in respondents' evaluations? A second is whether we can model the ways in which individuals construe hazards and give them meaning?

The label 'psychometric' derives from the methodology often employed to study individual risk perceptions. Typically, respondents are required to give their judgements (that is expressed preferences) of risk for a range of hazards. Groups of respondents rate sets of activities or risk sources (typically sets of pre-selected hazards) either in terms of their degree of similarity or dissimilarity to each other, or in terms of their perceived characteristics, such as the degree to which a source is personally controllable or not. The characteristics that have been investigated include overall risk and benefit, as well as qualitative dimensions such as are illustrated in table 2. In principle, therefore, the method maps aspects of the psychological meaning of the presented activities onto a set of rating scales (or metrics), as the first step in exploring the underlying structure of the psychological 'meaning space'. As Slovic (1992) notes, in these investigations risk is typically left deliberately undefined so as to elicit people's own understandings of the concept. The obtained similarity or rating data is then analysed statistically using exploratory multivariate techniques. Multivariate statistical techniques essentially analyse the patterns of correlations between the sets of ratings and this leads, in principle at least, to a model of the meaning placed by respondents on the rated hazard items. A variety of such statistical techniques have been utilized in this research, and the analysis can focus upon relations between the hazard items or the rating scales, as well as significant differences between respondents that arise as a result of individual or group differences (section 5.3.4).

In their most influential contribution Slovic, Fischhoff & Lichtenstein (1980) asked respondents to rate a total of 90 hazards, each with respect to 18 qualitative characteristics: for example, whether the risk from such sources as mountain climbing or exposure to asbestos was voluntary or involuntary; personally controllable or not; and known to those exposed or not. Slovic *et al.* employ 'principal components' factor analysis which is one of the most widely used multivariate techniques. With this method the initial rating scales are grouped in terms of their interrelations. Where strong relations between subsets of the rating scales are found these are expressed in terms of an 'underlying' small set of independent dimensions or 'factors'. The factors can then be used, graphically, to represent the psychological meaning, or factor, space (as illustrated in figure 2). The results of Slovic *et al.* indicate that ratings of the characteristics exhibit a systematic pattern, with three important factors emerging. The first factor was labelled by Slovic *et al.* 'dread' risk. This related judgements of scales such as uncontrollability, dread (or fear), involuntariness of exposure, and inequitable distribution of risks. Hazards which rate high on this factor include nuclear weapons, nerve gas and crime, in contrast to those that rate low such as home appliances and bicycles. A second factor, labelled 'unknown risk', relates judgements of the observability of risks, whether the effects are delayed in time or not, the familiarity of the risk, and whether the risks are viewed as known to science or not. Hazards that rate high on this dimension include solar electric power, DNA research and satellites, and those that rate low include motor vehicles, fire-fighting and mountain climbing. These two principal factors, the qualitative dimensions that they represent, and the location of the 90 rated hazards within the factor space, are illustrated in figure 2. The analysis also identified a third factor, primarily related to the 'number of people exposed'.

The authors conclude that perceptions of risk are closely related to the position of an activity in the factor space. Most important here is the dread risk factor, according to Slovic, because 'the higher a hazard's score on this factor (the further to the right it appears in the space in figure 2), the higher its perceived risk, the more people want to see its current risks reduced, and the more they want to see strict regulation employed to achieve the desired reduction in risk' (1987, p. 283). The findings of these studies indicated that the respondents were not satisfied with existing trade-offs between risks and benefits (as would be assumed in the revealed preference approach). In his review, Slovic notes (1987) that 'expert' perceptions were found to be more synonymous with their assessments of expected fatalities, and to be less influenced by the qualitative characteristics. Fischhoff (1990), however, points out that one important subsidiary finding of the research programme was that judgements from a group of risk experts produced a similar factor structure to that of the lay subject groups. This illustrates, as noted earlier, that the differences (and similarities) between expert and lay perceptions might be more subtle than a first reading suggests.

The early psychometric studies by the Oregon group have provided a model for a growing number of research efforts. As noted already, this effort has taken on the characteristics of a mature or 'normal' science as new researchers within the discipline have sought to replicate, extend and question the original findings. Interpreting the combined results of these follow-on studies is no simple task. Rohrmann (1991) identifies three classes of variables that have been manipulated in subsequent studies. First, the risk sources to be rated; second, the respondent groups participating (e.g. students, members of the public, professional groups etc.); and third, the risk dimensions used for rating the risk sources. A methodological complication

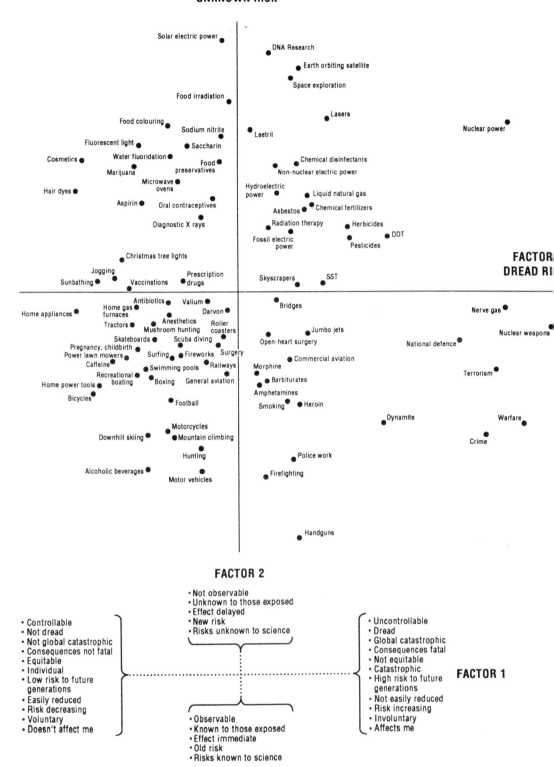

Figure 2. Locations of 90 hazards on factor 1 (dread risk) and factor 2 (unknown risk) of the three-dimensional factor space derived from the interrelationships among 18 risk characteristics. Factor 3 (not shown) reflects the number of people exposed to the hazard and the degree of one's personal exposure. (Source: Slovic, Fischhoff & Lichtenstein 1980).

derives from the wide range of statistical analyses adopted for these studies, and comparison of findings is further complicated by the different descriptions used for particular hazards (of which nuclear energy is a good example, as it is described in very different ways across many of the studies). Finally, the latitude available to the researcher in labelling the factors obtained from exploratory multivariate analysis must always be born in mind. Factor analysis, although in itself a well-defined mathematical technique, can lead to over-interpretation of the data and therefore to unwarranted generalizations. However, several replication studies are now available. In those which most closely follow the original Slovic *et al.* (1980) procedure, using similar analysis techniques and comparable sets of hazards and rating scales, a typical pattern is for a few factors to be found (two or three), often similar to the dread and known-unknown dimensions shown in figure 2. Where a third factor emerges it is typically related to the number of people exposed. In such studies judgements of riskiness tend, as also found by Slovic *et al.* (1980), to be positively correlated with the dread factor.

A criticism of both the Oregon work, and that of Green & Brown in the UK, concerns the relatively few respondents used. Larger-scale psychometric studies using respondents sampled from the general population include those in the US by Gardner & Gould (1989, n = 1021), in The Netherlands by Vlek & Stallen (1981, n = 679), in France by Bastide, Moatti, Pages & Fagnani (1989, n = 1000), and an opinion-type survey in the US by Pilisuk, Parks & Hawkes (1987, n = 429). However, in the last two studies participants were required to rate relatively restricted dimensions of risk, which limits the comparability of findings.

Gardner & Gould (1989) present perhaps the most comprehensive follow-on investigation, with a large representative sample of respondents from two US states. They ask respondents to rate six hazards (automobile travel, air travel, electricity, nuclear weapons, hand-guns and industrial chemicals) on several dimensions of risk, benefit and acceptability. Their method also permits the investigation of the influence of sociodemographic variables such as respondents' age, gender, education level and social class on these judgements, as well as the use of regression analysis (which allows the investigation of which of the qualitative characteristics best 'predict' a given target variable, such as overall riskiness). They find that the relations between 'overall risk' judgements and the other qualitative dimensions are different for specific hazards (e.g. 'catastrophic potential' is important for the nuclear and chemical technologies but less so for hand-guns, air and auto travel). They conclude that 'overall risk' is related mostly to judgements of 'number of deaths', and a risk's 'dread', as well as (more weakly) to the 'degree of scientific disagreement' about the risk and 'catastrophic potential'.

A similar activity-specific pattern emerged for the benefits: 'economic benefits' were positively related to judgements of 'overall benefits' for all hazards, but 'safety and security' as a benefit played a role only for nuclear weapons, hand-guns and industrial chemicals. With respect to acceptability judgements, without exception, a large majority (ranging from the lowest at 68% for air and automobile travel to 92% for industrial chemicals) of respondents wanted stricter regulation for every hazard in the study. Gardner & Gould, like Fischhoff *et al.* (1978), conclude that their comprehensive findings clearly cast further doubt upon the revealed preference approach to acceptability. However, Gardner and Gould also report that the qualitative risk and benefit dimensions only explain a relatively modest amount (one third) of the variance associated with respondents' judgements of the 'need for regulation'. Nor is the remainder of the variance explained by the influence of sociodemographic variables. They conclude that the sociodemographic variables appear to have only weak influence compared with the perceived qualitative properties of the technologies themselves.

Several methodological critiques of the psychometric paradigm revolve around the question of whether the findings might be dependent upon the hazards sets employed, the rating scales, or the forms of statistical analyses adopted. For example, the original study of Fischhoff *et al.* (1978) where respondents rate 30 hazards on nine risk characteristics, and the extended Slovic *et al.* (1980) study using 90 hazards and 18 characteristics lead to slightly different factor structures, which the authors acknowledge.

Regarding the hazards sets, subsequent work principally by Slovic & Kraus, finds broadly comparable factor structures from ratings of a set of railway transport hazards (Kraus & Slovic 1988) and medical hazards (Slovic, Kraus, Lappe, Letzel & Malmfors 1989). However, it may be that very different hazards sets (perhaps, for example, focusing upon non-technological activities) might lead to different factor structures. For example, Brun (1992) demonstrates a different factor structure for natural hazards as compared to man-made ones.

One drawback of rating scales, common to most psychometric methods in psychology, is that where questionnaire scales are defined in advance by the researcher, participants are not allowed to say what really matters to them about the question under investigation. In this regard the relatively modest amount of variance in risk acceptance explained by prototypical variables investigated by Gardner & Gould (1989), and discussed above, might be significant. This limited scope of explanation might be an indication that the psychometric approach is only

painting part (if nevertheless a highly significant part) of the story. Careful pre-testwork can often identify problems with particular rating scales. However, the issue remains critical if risk perception is to be properly investigated in terms of the personal experiences of respondents. Studies that have used more open-response methods, and which permit participants flexibility, are few and far between, but include the personal construct approach of Green & Brown (1980, see also Perusse 1980), the studies of Earle & Lindell (1984), MacGregor (1991), and Fischer, Morgan, Fischhoff, Nair & Lave (1991). The general lack of popularity of open-ended research methodologies in psychological inquiry stems partly from the extra levels of interpretation needed to analyse the more qualitative forms of data that are obtained. However, Henwood & Pidgeon (1992) argue that their potential for generating genuinely new insights into respondents' own systems of meanings are undeniable.

With respect to the statistical analyses used in psychometric risk studies, there are many multivariate techniques available, each highlighting slightly different features of a data set. Arabie & Maschmeyer (1988) discuss several of the alternative available models for analysis. They point out that a limitation of the factor analysis method used in the original Oregon studies is that it does not highlight differences between individuals that may be present (an important consideration, discussed further in section 5.3.4). Johnson & Tversky (1984) demonstrate how the use of several analytic approaches to risk perception data can yield different insights. For example, using cluster analysis (a multivariate technique for classification) they demonstrate that hazards can be classified into five categories; natural hazards, accidents, violent acts, technical disasters and diseases. As Vlek & Keren (1991) point out this classification implies that hazards may be differentiated by people in terms of the nature of the source or cause of damage.

This observation has implications for risk management given Brun's (1992) finding in a Norwegian sample that responsibility for managing natural hazards that are voluntarily undertaken (e.g. diseases caused by lifestyle) is seen primarily as a private responsibility, but for involuntarily undertaken man-made hazards (e.g. acid rain) as a public matter.

The psychometric tradition has undoubtedly generated an impressive body of empirical data on individual risk perceptions. The evidence shows that human judgements of hazards and their benefits involve multiple qualitative dimensions related in quite subtle and complex ways. However, it can be argued that this research tradition has not yet yielded substantive theoretical progress towards explaining risk perceptions and is a description of the perceived risk characteristics of hazards rather than of underlying psychological or social processes that could constitute an explanatory hypothesis (although two promising recent theoretical frameworks, 'social amplification of risk' and 'mental models', are discussed respectively in sections 5.4.3 and 5.5.3).

In the original 1983 Royal Society report the explanation of risk perceptions in terms of 'biases' of judgement, resulting from people's over-reliance upon cognitive heuristics, or mental rules-of-thumb, for frequency estimation (such as the 'availability' heuristic, see section 5.3.2) was discussed at some length. Heuristic theory (see Kahneman, Slovic & Tversky 1982) is clearly valuable for explaining several important aspects of how individuals arrive at judgements of subjective probability, although it does not, for example, provide a theoretical explanation for the motivational and emotional factors associated with risk perceptions and risk-taking behaviour discussed by Johnson & Tversky (1983) and Stallen & Tomas (1988).

One important practical finding from this research on heuristics is that experts themselves are not immune to biases of judgement; for example, they may be overconfident in their predictions. Hynes & Vanmarcke (1976) asked seven internationally known geotechnical engineers to estimate the height of an embankment that would cause failure in a clay foundation, and to set confidence limits wide enough to have a 50% chance of enclosing the true failure height. None of the engineers actually succeeded in establishing limits that enclosed the true height! Henrion & Fischhoff (1986) report similar examples of overconfidence in physicists, and Svenson (1989) outlines the forms of expert judgement bias that may enter into probabilistic risk assessments, suggesting ways in which these might be countered.

In discussing judgemental biases it is also important to note that the interpretation to be placed upon the findings from this research now occasions considerable disagreement among psychologists who study judgement and decision making. A good overview of some of the arguments is given by Jungermann (1986). One issue concerns the precise conditions under which judgemental 'biases' investigated under artificial psychology-laboratory conditions will generalize to real-world situations. To take two examples, the research on frequency estimation reviewed in section 5.3.2 indicates that individuals' probabilistic judgements appear, in this domain at least, reasonably well-founded. Similarly, some groups of experts have been found to be highly accurate in their predictions, as demonstrated in the studies of weather forecasters by Murphy & Winkler (1977). A key question, therefore, becomes the conditions under which accurate judgement can be fostered. Fischhoff & Svenson (1988) suggest that judgement as a learnt skill will improve with the provision to experts of 'prompt, unambiguous feedback that rewards them for candid judgement (and not, for example, for exuding confidence)' (p. 461).

5.3.4 INDIVIDUAL AND GROUP DIFFERENCES IN RISK PERCEPTION

There is now evidence that there may be significant individual and group differences in risk perceptions, for example in the differential importance placed upon particular hazards or their qualitative characteristics. In the human sciences, individual differences are generally held to be the result of relatively long-term psychological predispositions and are assumed to be stable for any particular individual, but to vary across members of a given population; for example, the notion of 'personality' is held to be an individual difference, and in gambling research a long-standing distinction is between risk-seeking and risk-avoiding individuals (see for example Lopes 1988). Group differences, on the other hand, are believed to reflect attitudes, beliefs and behaviours that result from an individual's identification with and membership of a particular social category, group or culture. Identification forms the basis for conformity with the norms, beliefs and behaviours of that group or culture, and an individual may identify with more than one group at any one time, as well as change affiliations over time. Cultural identification, however, is thought by some to be relatively resistant to change.

Orthodox social scientific evidence for individual and group differences in risk perceptions derives from a variety of sources, including psychometric, social psychological and cross-cultural studies, but some ambiguity remains. As noted earlier the psychometric approach of Slovic and his colleagues does not yield clear evidence of the influence of such factors, although it remains possible that this ambiguity is the result of the particular methods used. The apparent existence of such differences in risk perception is important because it suggests that the findings of psychometric

studies cannot be readily extrapolated to the population as a whole; and that risk perception is at least in part dependent upon person- and group-related variables. This observation has important policy implications for the questions of risk communication and risk management, and for attempts at arriving at a social consensus over tolerability.

Several cross-cultural studies of risk perception have been done, reflecting a growing interest in exploring risk issues from the perspective of cross-cultural psychology (see Cvetkovich & Earle 1991). In general terms, cross-cultural social science (see also the discussion in section 5.4.2 of 'cultural theory') aims to investigate and explain differences and similarities in beliefs and behaviours between different cultural (such as national, ethnic or institutional) groups. Risk perception studies have typically compared US samples (some using the original Oregon data sets) to equivalent data obtained in other countries, including Hungary (Englander, Farago, Slovic & Fischhoff 1986), Norway (Teigen, Brun & Slovic 1988), Hong Kong (Keown 1989), the former Soviet Union (Mechitov & Rebrik 1990), Japan (Kleinhesselink & Rosa 1991) and Poland (Goszczynska, Tyszka & Slovic 1991). The respondents in these studies are typically students (which increases comparability with the US findings but limits generalizability to the population at large), and some use relatively small respondent sample sizes. It is significant that the overall pattern of factors is similar to the US studies, although differences have also been found. For example, Kleinhesselink & Rosa (1991) in their comparison of US and Japanese samples closely replicate the factor dimensions of Slovic, *et al.* (1980) in both groups but also report differences between the two, particularly with respect to the ordering of hazards on the known–unknown dimension (e.g. nuclear power generation and AIDS risks are rated as 'unknown' in the US but 'known' in the Japanese sample), a result in line with the findings of Englander, *et al.* (1986). In his review, Rohrmann (1991) concludes that it is far from clear on the combined evidence whether the original US findings represent cross-cultural universals, despite the reported similarities across countries. Also the differences between countries that have been identified can only be interpreted with considerable caution. They might be due either to cultural differences or, as Johnson (1991) suggests, to other factors such as personal knowledge, experience or direct exposure to particular hazards, or different political and economic circumstances in the comparison countries.

In an early and influential paper Vlek & Stallen (1981), using a large representative sample drawn from the general population in the Netherlands, provided evidence of group differences within a national population. Respondents were required to complete a range of rating and similarity judgement tasks involving 26 separate hazards. Vlek & Stallen investigate several individual differences in the weightings of the obtained factor solutions. They find riskiness characterized by two dimensions which they label 'size of a potential accident' and 'degree of organized safety' (which might also be interpreted as lack of personal control over an activity). The former, primary, dimension accounts for the largest amount of variation in the riskiness ratings, and perhaps not surprisingly most of their respondents judge risk to increase for activities higher on this dimension. However, for the secondary 'degree of organized safety' dimension respondents are divided; for approximately half of the respondents, activities with a high degree of organized safety (e.g. a residential district near a petrochemical plant) are seen to be the most risky, whereas for the remainder of the sample activities with a low degree of organized safety are seen as most risky (e.g. smoking in bed). Vlek & Stallen also report two-factor structures both for judgements of

'beneficiality', and of 'acceptability'. As with the judgements of riskiness, in each case there is agreement about the implications of the primary dimension, and disagreement about the secondary. They also report that acceptability is less dependent upon perceived risk than upon the perceived benefits. Vlek & Stallen point out that the dimensions on which their respondents disagree tend to involve socially controversial issues, a point taken up since by Wynne (1989*a*) who argues that these dimensions are precisely the ones with contested institutional or political implications (see also section 5.5.4). Hence, the finding that for one group of respondents 'degree of organized safety' implies higher risk might indicate that such individuals view the existing institutional arrangements for risk management as inadequate. Conversely, the second group of respondents might view the existing arrangements as adequate. The design of Vlek & Stallen does not permit a full investigation of the source of these differences, but there is some evidence that occupation might predict part of risk acceptance; specifically, lower risk acceptance is reported for 'professional' groups such as the medical, social, scientific and arts-related occupations, higher for business, industrial workers and farmers. Vlek & Stallen conclude that 'the use of group average ratings makes far less sense than is often believed' (1981, p. 269).

Of the general sociodemographic variables that have been studied, there is a small amount of evidence that gender and age may influence evaluations of risk, although the precise interpretation to be placed upon such findings is uncertain. Several studies find that women perceive more threat to the environment than men (Schmidt & Gifford 1989, Pilisuk, Parks & Hawkes 1987, Fischer, Morgan, Fischhoff, Nair & Lave 1991). However, Eiser, Hannover, Mann, Morin, van der Pligt & Webly (1990) report that men show the greater involvement with Chernobyl. In their study of the perception of risks of prescription drugs, Slovic, Kraus, Lappe, Letzel and Malmfors (1989) fail to find gender differences but detect some age-related influence.

Using an open-response technique Fischer *et al.* (1991) find that students tended to emphasize risks to the environment, whereas older people emphasized health and safety issues (some of which could be explained by the immediate objective concerns of these particular groups of respondents). Regarding socio-political variables, as noted earlier Gardner & Gould (1989) in their large US survey report only weak effects of socio-demographic variables (including political affiliation) compared with that of the qualitative characteristics of technologies. In contrast, in a study in France, Bastide *et al.* (1989) find a complex pattern of sociodemographic differences associated with fatality judgements that appear to relate primarily to the social location of the respondents. They conclude that it is broad social factors, such as social position and general feelings of security, bound up with ideological and ethical legitimation of hazards, as well as the objective differential distribution of hazards within a society, that influence the risk evaluations of different groups.

The view that broader social factors, and in particular people's value orientations, might underpin perceptions of risk was discussed in Otway & von Winterfeldt's (1982) review of the IIASA work on perceptions of nuclear energy. They noted a group of economic, social and political attributes of technologies, such as their 'potential contribution to industrial and economic growth', or to the 'growth of centralized decision making' and 'lack of widespread public participation in the formal processes of risk management'. According to Otway & von Winterfeldt, this group of attributes can contribute either negatively or positively to overall attitudes towards a technological risk, depending upon an individual's particular value system or set of beliefs.

For example, Otway & Fishbein (1976, 1977) factor analysed the responses of an Austrian sample (n = 244) to nuclear power. Four distinguishable factors were revealed and were named respectively; 'psychological aspects', 'economic and technical benefits', 'socio-political implication' and 'environmental and physical risks'. The belief most closely identified with the psychological factor was 'using nuclear power will expose one to risks without one's consent', and this was closely followed in importance by 'once exposed to these risks one has little control over them'. The economic factor showed an association of the use of nuclear power with such benefits as 'creating new jobs' and 'raising the standard of living'. The third factor, socio-political, involved beliefs about the pollution of enduring noxious waste and the problems of its storage and transport, its security from terrorist attacks, etc. The factor obviously reflects a general concern that the acceptable harnessing of nuclear energy is crucially dependent on a stable socio-political system. Finally, the environmental and physical risks factor is concerned with the dangers of pollution, such as air and water pollution, and long-term modifications to the climate.

When the respondents were divided into pro- and anti-nuclear groups it was found that the evaluations or feelings of the two groups about these factors were not dissimilar; where they differed was on the extent to which they judged them to be applicable to nuclear power. The anti-nuclear group were markedly more inclined to regard harmful attributes as accurately applying to nuclear power and to ignore the benefits. The pro-group, on the other hand, saw attributes which loaded high on the benefits factor, and to a much lesser extent the physical environment factor, as important, while assessing the psychological attributes as relatively unimportant. Related conclusions are reported in the studies of belief salience in anti- and pro-nuclear groups by Eiser & van der Pligt (1979) in the UK, and van der Pligt, van der Linden & Ester (1982) in The Netherlands. Depending upon prior orientation on the issue of nuclear power, respondents saw different issues as salient or most important to them; pro-respondents saw the economic aspects of nuclear energy as most salient, and anti-respondents the risk of accidents and consequences for the environment. The findings of such social psychological studies on attitudes towards nuclear power are reviewed by van der Pligt (1992).

Another approach to the understanding of risk perception through examination of the broader social context has been made using empirical research based on 'worldviews', with the aim of investigating whether constellations of attitudes and beliefs surrounding issues of industrial, technological and population growth may be related in predictable ways to perception of risk and preferences for societal decision making. Results of research by Buss, Craik & Dake (1986) seem to indicate that those who favour a high-growth, high-technology society tend to see the benefits of technology as more important than its risks. The converse is found for a second group whose worldview emphasizes such matters as concern about social and environmental impacts of growth, and equity in risk distribution. With regard to decision-making methods, those in the first group were found more likely to approve of 'rational', quantified decision making, whereas those in the second group favoured more participatory methods.

The picture concerning value-orientation is, however, probably more complex than any simple categorization of individuals into pro- and anti-nuclear (or technology) groups might at first reveal. For example, Gardner & Gould (1989) note that they found that attitudes favouring stricter regulation often go hand-in-hand with the desire to see a technology more widely developed. This suggests that public calls for stricter regulation of a technology cannot be lightly brushed aside as solely representing an anti-technology bias.

5.4 SOCIAL AND CULTURAL APPROACHES

5.4.1 SOCIAL PROCESSES AND RISK PERCEPTION

Since the beginning of the 1980s, a consensus within the social sciences has been growing over the importance of social, cultural and institutional processes to the perception of risk, as evidenced, for example, in many of the contributions to the volume by Krimsky & Golding (1992). There are good *a priori* grounds for examining the role that social processes might play in risk assessment, risk behaviour and risk perception. The perceiver of risk is rarely an isolated individual, but a 'social being' who necessarily lives and works, plays and rests, within networks of informal and formal relationships with others.

Such relationships are manifest in a wide range of both small- and large-scale social and institutional arrangements within and across societies. These arrangements set constraints and obligations upon people's behaviour, provide broad frameworks for the shaping of their attitudes and beliefs, and are also closely tied to questions both of morality and of what is to be valued and what is not (Douglas 1985). There is no reason to suppose that beliefs and values relating to hazards are any different from other more general beliefs and values, and it follows from this that they will also be, in part at least, related to broader social factors and processes. Any comprehensive account of risk perception and behaviour, and in particular of social conflicts about risk, cannot exclude this claim (see for example Mazur 1981, Short 1984, Douglas 1985, Johnson & Covello 1987, Beck 1992). And the accumulated empirical evidence from psychometric and social psychological investigations supports the view that a purely psychological, individual-based analysis can account for only a part of risk perception and risk behaviour.

5.4.2 CULTURAL THEORY

One of the major challenges to orthodox psychological approaches to risk perception over the past ten years has come from the grid-group 'cultural theory' proposed by the anthropologist Mary Douglas and her colleagues. This approach did not feature in the 1983 Royal Society report, whose human science content was dominated by economics and psychology. But no balanced account of the field could ignore it today.

It is an assumption in much of sociology and anthropology that one of the things that people value most (and which shapes their perceptions and behaviour) will be the set of social arrangements or institutions that they personally strongly identify with or participate in. In the context of risk perception therefore, the hazards that are likely to be of particular concern are those that pose threats to locally valued social and institutional arrangements, or to other elements that are central to a particular way of life. The central claim of the cultural theory approach to risk perception is that human attitudes towards risk and danger are not homogeneous but vary systematically according to cultural biases. Cultural bias in this sense means attitudes and beliefs that are shared by a group (Douglas 1982). Cultural bias is what shapes the risks that groups choose to identify, in ways that cannot be explained by individual psychology or by natural science analysis of 'objective' risks.

The cultural theory school holds that there are a limited number of different and contradictory cultural biases which can be identified in diverse contexts and societies. It also holds, contrary to ideas that stress the effect of early conditioning, that cultural biases, and the life styles that go with them, are to some degree chosen rather than predetermined. An individual's cultural bias is linked with the extent to which he or she is incorporated into bounded groups ('group') and with the extent to which the interactions of social life are conducted according to rules rather than negotiated *ad hoc* ('grid').

By linking grid and group, four major cultural biases (or 'cosmologies') are identified, namely hierarchists (high grid/high group), sectarians or egalitarians (low grid/high group), fatalists (high grid/low group), and individualists (low grid/low group). In some variants a fifth category, autonomists, is added. The argument goes that individualists see risk and opportunity as going hand-in-hand; fatalists do not knowingly take risks but accept what is in store for them; hierarchists are willing to set acceptable risks at high levels so long as decisions are made by experts or in other socially approved ways; but egalitarians accentuate the risks of technological development and economic growth so as to defend their own way of life and attribute blame to those who hold to other cosmologies (Thompson, Ellis & Wildavsky 1990, pp. 62–66).

The implications of this approach for risk assessment and perception are revolutionary. It implies that people select certain risks for attention to defend their preferred lifestyles and as a forensic resource to place blame on other groups (see Douglas 1992). That is, what societies choose to call risky is largely determined by social and cultural factors, not nature (Johnson & Covello 1987). If the cultural theory approach is accepted, no 'single metric' for risk analysis can be developed on which the different cultural biases can find common ground. A hierarchist (high group/high grid) point of departure will always be challenged by those who identify with groups holding rival cultural biases, creating major challenges for the conduct of policy analysis and the design of institutions (cf. Schwarz & Thompson 1990).

Moreover, cultural theorists suggest that the very term and concept of risk is plastic and variable. Whereas risk once meant the probability of losses and gains, Douglas (1990) argues that it now just means danger, and serves the forensic needs of a new global culture, in politicizing and moralizing the links between dangers and disapproved behaviour, noting that:

The modern risk concept, parsed now as danger, is invoked to protect individuals against encroachments of others. It is part of the system of thought that upholds the type of individualist culture which sustains an expanding industrial system (p. 7)

The grid-group cultural theory, and its application to risk analysis, was developed in the early 1980s, and landmark publications included the work of Douglas (1966) and Thompson (1980). And there were other early approaches at that time which attempted to link risk perception with competing worldviews rather than to accept the orthodox psychological perspective. A notable case in point is the work of sociologist Cotgrove (1982) who adopts a position similar to the work, discussed in the previous section, of Buss, Craik & Dake (1986). Cotgrove argues, on the basis of considerable quantitative empirical evidence, that two cultural worldviews, of cornucopians and catastrophists can be identified in relation to perception of environmental risks.

However, it was not until the publication of Douglas & Wildavsky's *Risk & Culture* (1982), that the cultural theory began to

command more widespread attention; and at the same time produced some deeply polarized positions and argument. Since then, cultural theory has begun to become established as a major contributor to the risk debate, with important publications by Rayner & Cantor (1987), Thompson, Ellis & Wildavsky (1990), Schwarz & Thompson (1990), and Dake (1991). Recent exploratory research done in the UK by Adams & Thompson (1991) represents an interesting conjuncture between the grid-group cultural theory and Adams' (1985) risk compensation theory of risk regulation, to form the basis of a major challenge to orthodox ideas in the field of risk behaviour and safety.

The grid-group approach is not without its critics. The reception of *Risk & Culture* when it first appeared was not uniformly positive, and prompted Douglas to write a second volume on the subject (1985). Johnson (1987) claims that although the theory is potentially powerful, there remains a basic problem in unambiguously classifying existing social units in terms of the grid and group dimensions, that the basic four or five cultural types may oversimplify more complex shades of social difference, and in particular (a point also made by Funtowicz & Ravetz 1985) that environmentalism may not be just an egalitarian movement because 'different kinds of environmentalism can stem from all four posited social structures' (Johnson 1987, p. 160). Bellaby (1990) has claimed that the model needs more explicit recognition of the dynamic aspects of social life, and in particular an explanation as to why individuals might move from one 'risk culture' to another.

As yet, the grid-group cultural theory has involved the generation of much less systematic empirical evidence than that gathered by psychologists in their work on risk perception. Some qualitative work has been done in applying grid-group analysis to in-depth case studies of social groups in medical (Rayner 1986) and industrial (Bellaby 1990) settings. Attempts at direct quantitative tests are reported in Wildavsky & Dake (1990), Dake (1991), and Dake & Wildavsky (1991). However, in these studies fatalists are not considered, and it is not obvious from the evidence presented that individualists and hierarchists, as identified by these researchers, are very clearly distinguished from one another in their attitudes to risk. For example, Dake (1991) reports that hierarchy and individualism are both positively correlated with a pro-risk stance towards societal risk taking, and egalitarianism with an anti-risk stance. Furthermore, Dake's measures of hierarchy and individualism are themselves highly positively correlated. Dake's data suggests therefore that the main cleavage in risk attitudes may be between egalitarians and the rest, a finding that would support Cotgrove's earlier (1982) distinction of cornucopians and catastrophists as much as the four or five distinct types with which the grid-group school works.

It remains to be seen whether further research, perhaps integrating in-depth qualitative anthropological case studies of particular social groups with more quantitative ones, can differentiate more clearly among the risk attitudes of the non-egalitarian groups in the grid-group scheme. It also remains to be seen, as stressed by Kasperson, Kasperson & Renn (1992), whether the hitherto somewhat separate approaches of the psychological researchers and the cultural theorists can be more fully integrated. What is clear is that the cultural-theory approach has identified some very important aspects of the social fabric (Short 1984) for the understanding of risk perception and tolerance, and that the issues that it has raised are crucial for the future of the field, as well as for the issues of risk management that are discussed in the next chapter.

5.4.3 SOCIAL AMPLIFICATION OF RISK

To date there has been little direct interaction between the cultural and psychometric traditions of risk research within social science. A recent conceptual framework that makes a genuine attempt to unify psychological, social and cultural approaches to risk perception is the social-amplification framework developed by the Clark University group (Kasperson, Renn, Slovic, Brown, Emel, Goble, Kasperson & Ratick 1988, Kasperson, Kasperson & Renn 1992). These researchers adopt a metaphor loosely based upon communications theory, to explain why certain hazards (for example, public transport safety of trains or sea-going ferries) are a particular focus of concern in society, while others (such as motor vehicle accidents) receive comparatively little attention. They suggest that hazards and their objective characteristics (e.g. deaths, injuries, damage and social disruption) interact with a wide range of psychological, social or cultural processes in ways that intensify or attenuate perceptions of risk. At the heart of this suggestion is the observation that most of our knowledge, and this includes our knowledge of hazards and danger, is second-hand; that is, we come to know about the world through various communications that we receive in the form of signs, signals or images. In this sense, according to Slovic, Lichtenstein & Fischhoff (1984), hazardous events hold a 'signal value', which may differ for different people or social groups. An individual or group can in this way be conceptualized as a receiver of such signals about hazards. The key insight of Kasperson *et al.* (1988) is that such signals may be subject to predictable transformations as they are filtered through a variety of social 'amplification stations'. Examples of such amplification stations would include groups of scientists, the mass media, government agencies and politicians, as well as activist groups within a community. Each station will intensify or attenuate certain aspects of risk in ways predictable from their social structure and circumstances. Social amplification accounts in a very general sense for the differential interpretations that individuals and groups place upon hazardous events (as would be held to be the case by cultural theory, for example).

Kasperson *et al.* (1988) also argue that social amplification accounts for the observation that certain events, in their terms, lead to spreading ripples of secondary consequences, which may go far beyond the initial impact of the event, and may even impinge upon initially unrelated hazards. Such secondary impacts upon the original risk-managing organization include loss of sales (perhaps through a consumer boycott of a product), regulatory constraints, litigation, community opposition, and investor flight. A simplified model of the risk amplification framework, and the potential

secondary impacts upon a risk-managing organization, is shown in figure 3.

A drawback of the amplification idea, despite its *prima facie* plausibility, is that it may be too general to subject to direct empirical test. Furthermore, the source–receiver framework illustrated in figure 3 relies too heavily upon a simple conceptualization of communication as a one-way process; that is, from risk events, through transmitters, and then on to receivers. As discussed by Fitchen, Heath & Fessenden-Raden (1987), the development of social risk perceptions is always likely to be the product of more interactive processes between source and receiver of a message (see also the discussion of conceptual approaches to risk communication in section 5.5.2). In a subsequent paper, Renn (1991) acknowledges the important role that feedback (between receiver and source) inevitably plays in such communication

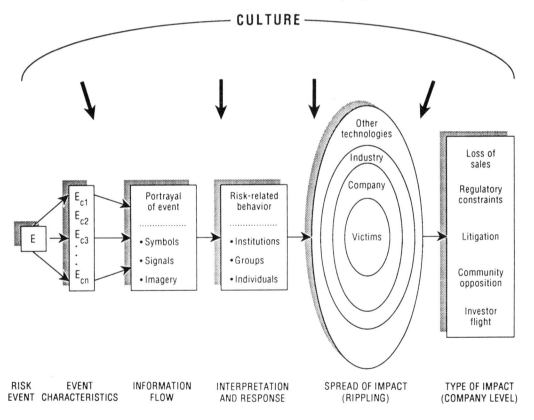

Figure 3. Simplified representation of the social amplification of risk and its potential impacts on a risk managing organization. (Source: Kasperson, Kasperson & Renn 1992).

processes. Renn's treatment also extends the social-amplification framework by suggesting that a risk event can be an actual occurrence (i.e. a physical disaster or near-miss) or a simulated event such as a scenario within a risk-assessment model.

Several criticisms of the amplification metaphor have been raised. First, it might be taken to imply that there is indeed a baseline or 'true' risk, which is then transformed, or distorted, by the social processes of transmission. However, it is clear that the proponents of the idea of risk amplification do not wish to imply that such a 'true' risk baseline exists, and their conceptualization of risk in terms of signs, symbols and images is compatible with the view, discussed earlier, that risk is a social construction (Johnson & Covello 1987). A semantic point, made by Rip (1988), is that the term amplification is typically associated, in its more common usage, primarily with the intensification of signals. However, the detailed framework, as formulated by the original authors, is intended to describe both the social processes that decrease (that is attenuate) signals about hazards, as well as those involved in intensification. Finally, although several plausible intensification and attenuation processes can be posited (see Renn 1991) it is not always clear what the behaviourial consequences of risk amplification might be. The link between perception and action may be more complex than implied in figure 3. For example, the original framework emphasizes possible ripples of secondary impacts that are, as Machlis & Rosa (1990) point out, typically of a negative nature. However, negative consequences are not an inevitable result of amplification. To take one obvious example, intensification of signals that point to a serious and perhaps new risk might lead to the prevention of a disaster by better technological design or risk management.

Despite these shortcomings, the social amplification of risk framework has to be recognized as a serious attempt to widen the conceptual debate on risk perception research. It emphasizes the important point that the subject must be viewed from a multi-disciplinary perspective rather than accepting the hegemony of any one particular approach. The framework will ultimately stand or fall on its ability to generate specific hypotheses that can be subject to empirical test, and its ability to provide new insights on risk perception and communication. A possible extension of the model, which would stress the role of attenuating phenomena, is to link it to the considerable empirical evidence of group and organizational processes that prevent warning signs from being effectively utilized before the onset of large-scale organizational failures and disasters (see for example Janis 1972, Turner 1978). Elucidating the conditions for such attenuation (and how it might be counteracted) would be a significant step in helping to prevent such events.

5.4.4 THE SOCIAL FRAMING OF RISK ASSESSMENTS

A third focus for the study of the role of social processes and risk arises from the fact, discussed in section 5.2, that expert risk and safety assessments always involve judgement. One less obvious aspect of this is that the assumptions that experts often make will set the underlying frameworks for the models used in the evaluation and assessment of risk. Assumptions are often implicit (and therefore difficult to detect), as well as being widely shared within a particular scientific or expert community; given that individual members are often exposed to a common core body of accepted knowledge and similar methods of training. Such assumptions can, therefore, be characterized as the product of social processes. The relevance of this to our understanding of aspects of societal conflicts about risk (see also Mazur 1981, Jasanoff 1987) is discussed by Wynne in his work on the social framing of risk.

As a result of his study of the UK inquiry into a proposed oxide fuels reprocessing facility at Windscale (now Sellafield) on the Cumbrian coast, Wynne (1982) observed that the expert and public frames of reference for the problem differed considerably. In particular, the expert definitions incorporated implicit assumptions about the social and institutional processes of risk management. By reducing issues of risk to technical matters, the expert view 'accepted existing decision making institutions as trustworthy, natural, impartial and open-minded about the future' (Wynne 1992). This frame of reference was at variance with that adopted by the groups objecting to the proposed expansion of the plant, who placed far less credibility and trust in the risk-management institutions. This observation throws further light upon some of the apparent discrepancies between public and expert views of risk. Wynne's point, however, is not that any particular framing is necessarily better or more 'accurate' than any other, but that alternative frames may express different aspects of the risk problem. In the Windscale case, the expert framing of the problem may or may not have been well-founded in the context of the then existing (or the current) Western nuclear risk-management practices. What is clear, however, is that it makes very strong assumptions about social behaviour both in the present and in the future. The disintegration of many of the institutions of the former Soviet Union, and the doubts that this now places over the management of nuclear and other hazardous facilities in the emergent states there and in Eastern Europe is a graphic illustration of how such social assumptions might rapidly be invalidated in any society by changed political and economic circumstances.

In a series of case studies following his Windscale work, Wynne (1989b) illustrates how expert framing of risk problems can incorporate a wide range of implicit assumptions about the risk-generating system. In one example he describes how the debate in the UK in the late 1960s and early 1970s over the safety of the herbicide 2,4,5-T (most widely known as a component of 'agent orange') was resolved only when it was realized that initial scientific evaluations of its safety were dependent upon the assumption that the product would always be used under stringently controlled conditions. According to Wynne, agricultural workers (whose arguments were initially dismissed by government advisers as 'unscientific' and anecdotal) were only too aware that their working environments rarely approximated the idealized 'laboratory' conditions assumed by the toxicologists. He notes that the expert framing of the safety problem assumed that:

'pesticides manufacturing process conditions never varied so as to produce dioxin and other toxic contaminants of the main product stream; drums of herbicide always arrived at the point of use with full instructions intact and intelligible; in spite of the inconvenience farmers and other users would comply with the stated conditions, such as correct solvents, proper spray nozzles, pressure valves and other equipment, correct weather conditions, and full protective gear. *As a model of the 'real' social world and thus of the typical risk system, this was utterly naïve and incredible* however good the laboratory science.' (Wynne 1992, emphasis added).

An alternative framing of the problem may sometimes reveal legitimate concerns about the social context that is an inevitable part of any hazard and its management. The human sub-system controlling a particular hazard is in this sense as much a part of the objective preconditions for the manifestation of that hazard as is the reliability of technical components. And under such circumstances both expert and 'non-expert' views can offer insight and inputs to the process of decision making and social learning about risk. Wynne (1992) also suggests that if this is not recognized technological controversies can slide into conflict and further polarization of positions. In this sense, therefore, controversies about technological risks can be conceptualized as a type of 'informal technology assessment' (Rip 1986).

5.5 RISK COMMUNICATION

5.5.1 THE NEW DISCIPLINE OF RISK COMMUNICATION

The study and practice of risk communication is a relatively new development, with most relevant literature appearing after the publication of the original Royal Society report in 1983. The increased interest in this particular topic, indicated by the many papers published and conferences held in a very short time-span, represents a significant proportion of the more general expansion of social science activity in the risk field since 1983. It is clear from a cursory survey of this literature that many of the researchers who were prominently involved in the early risk perception studies have subsequently turned their efforts to matters of risk communication. However, interest in risk communication does not reflect just a semantic re-definition of the activities of this particular research community. It is clear that several substantive issues, relating basic risk-perception research to public policy and decision making, as well as to the processes of risk management, are raised when risk communication is considered.

Contrasting overviews of many of the key contributions to risk communication research are provided by Krimsky & Plough (1988), the US National Research Council (NRC 1989), Handmer & Penning-Rowsell (1990), and Kasperson & Stallen (1991). Within the confines of the current discussion a comprehensive review of this literature is neither practical nor desirable. In part this is precluded by the large volume of available literature (which is of varying quality), as well as the fact that not all of the issues addressed by risk-communication re-

searchers are of central relevance to questions of risk perception. A further consideration is that, although much of the available literature purports to give practical advice for risk managers, to date few definitive empirical studies of risk communication, and in particular of its consequences and effectiveness are available. In this respect it seems unwise to reproduce here the practice of providing seemingly authoritative advice while the field is still relatively poorly grounded empirically, particularly in view of the important and practical questions that need to be addressed.

The more modest goal here is to raise several issues and concerns at the interface of risk perception and risk-communication research. Several issues will be explored, including: the different conceptual approaches that are taken to risk communication; the policy implications for risk communication of findings from risk-perception research; and the key issue of trust and risk communication. One objective in discussing these issues will be to highlight some of the emerging complexities in this field of study (see also NRC 1989).

Several interrelated factors have led to the emergence of interest in risk communication research. In practical terms there is an increasing requirement, both in legal as well as moral terms, placed upon government and private industry to inform populations about the environmental, technological, and health hazards to which they might be exposed. Such communications may have the goal of encouraging a particular behaviour to guard against an immediate individual risk (e.g. the use of condoms as a precaution against HIV infection), or in the context of large-scale societal risks, such as those of a flood or toxic release, communication may be a statutory part of the emergency planning process (see Handmer & Penning-Rowsell 1990). Emergency planning necessitates consideration first of what communications should be made in advance of a potential incident to inform and prepare those that might be affected, and secondly, plans for providing effective warnings in the event of an emergency. Legislation as a result of major accidents, such as the 1982 European Communities Seveso Directive, and the Emergency Response and Community Right to Know Act (third title of the Superfund Amendments and Reauthorization Act, sometimes known as SARA Title III) in the US have set specific requirements upon public bodies for information provision and preparedness in this respect. Although many parallels between these sets of legislation exist, there are also important differences; for example the SARA Title III specifies that information be provided, in practice at least (but see Hadden 1989*a*) on a 'right to know' basis, whereas the Seveso Directive operates on the 'need to know' principle (Baram 1991). Even within the EC the implementation of the Seveso Directive at national level has varied greatly from country to country. This in itself highlights the fact that the context within which risk communication operates may be highly specific to one culture or nation and that findings therefore should only be generalized to other contexts with considerable caution.

A second reason for the emergence of risk-communication research, noted by Krimsky & Plough (1988), derives from the highly visible public policy dilemmas that have arisen as a result of particular social conflicts over risks; for example, over the siting or expansion of hazardous facilities. Risk-perception research clearly illustrates the varied perceptions and frames of reference that different parties might be expected to bring to such disputes. And hence the possibility is held out that fostering appropriate forms of communication between the parties to such disputes might contribute in some way to better mutual understanding and hence to a resolution of conflict. In this case the question of who communicates what to whom (and in whose interests) raises potentially controversial ethical issues (see the discussion of ethics in risk communication by Morgan & Lave 1990).

5.5.2 CONCEPTUAL APPROACHES TO RISK COMMUNICATION

At first sight the task of communication might appear trivial given that most of us have little difficulty in conducting day-to-day interaction with colleagues, friends and associates. However, doing this effectively with diverse audiences, who possibly all hold different values and frames of reference with respect to the problem, where multiple feedback channels and competing messages (some out of our control) are available, and where interpretation is dependent upon subtle cultural factors, sets a more challenging task. It also raises several significant dilemmas and paradoxes (Otway & Wynne 1989). A particularly significant dilemma arises from conflicting goals in risk communications; for example, a message or messages about the same activity may need both to reassure (the risk from such an activity is indeed tolerable) while at the same time to warn (but if, in the unlikely event, that there is an emergency the following action will be necessary). Otway & Wynne refer to this as the reassurance–arousal paradox.

Therefore it is no easy matter to define risk communication, although this will have a crucial bearing upon the objectives set for any communication effort, as well as the related research questions that might be asked. At least four partially overlapping conceptual approaches to risk communication can be identified in the literature (see also Fisher 1991). The simplest approach defines risk communication within an 'engineering communications' framework; that is in terms of a 'top-down' or one-way transmission of some message about a hazard or risk from a particular 'expert' communicator to a target 'non-expert' audience. Typically, such an approach focuses upon characteristics of the source, channel, message and receiver that might enhance (or hinder) communication of any particular content. Initial discussions of risk communication were framed within the one-way model, and relevant research findings, many derived from work in social psychology on propaganda and persuasive communication techniques, are comprehensively reviewed by Lee (1986). The one-way model of risk communication has been the target of much criticism, in particular on the grounds that by assuming an altruistic communicator it implicitly devalues the perspectives and knowledge of the risk bearers (see for example Otway & Wynne 1989), as well as glossing over the political aspects to many of the risk conflicts in society (Stern 1991).

A second approach to risk communication therefore stresses the process of communication, typically within a two-way exchange or dialogue. The US National Research Council (NRC 1989) takes this view, noting the limited focus of the one-way approach, and accordingly characterizing risk communication as 'an interactive process of exchange of information and opinion among individuals, groups and institutions. It involves multiple messages about the nature of risk and other messages, not strictly about risk, that express concerns, opinions, or reactions to risk messages or to legal and institutional arrangements for risk management' (p. 21). Minimally, such a definition highlights the critical role that feedback and interaction play in any complex communication. Maximally, it implies that risk communication necessarily involves a fluid and dynamic interchange of information between the parties to a risk issue or conflict in the

search for mutual understanding. This also suggests that opportunities for learning exist on all sides to a risk debate or conflict. The NRC report also lists four principal reasons for conducting risk communication: first, desire by government to inform; second desire by government or industry to overcome opposition to decisions; third, desire to share power between government and public; and fourth, desire to develop effective alternatives to direct regulatory control.

A third approach to risk communication stresses not only exchange of information between actors, but also the wider institutional and cultural contexts within which risk messages are formulated, transmuted and embedded (Fessenden-Raden, Fitchen & Heath 1987, Krimsky & Plough 1988). By this account risk communication consists, to use Krimsky & Plough's phrase, of a complex 'tangled web' of messages, signs and symbols. This observation highlights the fact that intentional messages often compete with many other unintended signs and symbols relevant to a hazard. For example, Fessenden-Raden, *et al.* (1987) point out that action (and inaction) by a risk management institution can, depending upon the context, speak louder than words, sending important messages, and ones that may conflict with official communications. This implies that predicting the outcome of any intended communication may often be far more uncertain than is suggested by the simple one-way source-message–receiver model. In addition, within the cultural approach it is clearly recognized that all hazards have a history, and that this will influence the interpretations that are placed upon particular messages at any particular point in time. The onus is therefore placed upon the risk communicator to fully appreciate the context within which communication will occur.

A final approach to risk communication views it explicitly as part of the wider political processes that operate (or ought to operate) within a democratic society. Here communication is seen as an essential prerequisite to the enabling and empowerment of the risk-bearing groups in society in ways that allow them to participate more effectively in decision making about risks (see Hadden 1989b, Fiorino 1990, O'Riordan 1990). Defining risk communication in these terms highlights the important question of whether (and in what ways) public groups should be granted a right to know about the risks that they face (a position certainly not yet achieved in the UK), and the precise role of the public in risk-management decision making. As noted earlier the concept of tolerable risk implies that some such role is desirable if not essential. In this respect O'Riordan, Jungermann, Kasperson & Wiedemann (1989) comment that people may tolerate some risks 'insofar as they believe that the risks are reduced, and shown to be reduced, to levels as low as practical, that the benefits are clearly in the public interest, and that appropriate measures are in hand to cope with post-disaster effects' (p. 515).

5.5.3 APPLICATIONS
The findings from risk perception research hold several potential implications for risk communication, and several publications offer advice in this regard (see for example Hance, Chess & Sandman 1987, Covello & Allen 1988, Covello, Sandman & Slovic 1988). As observed by these and many other authors the content of any message must be sensitive to the receiver's frame of reference for the problem. Added to this must be the finding from social and cultural approaches to risk perception that there are many publics within any society each with possibly different worldviews and frameworks for approaching risk problems. Given this, the complexities of risk communication become clear.

A particular focus for the application of risk perception findings has been a critique of the use of risk comparisons. These have traditionally been utilized as a device for 'placing in perspective' a wide range of hazardous activities (see for example Wilson 1979, Wilson & Crouch 1987). Covello (1991) reviews the benefits and difficulties associated with this method of communicating about risks. One important psychological consideration, given that individuals distinguish between hazards along a range of qualitative dimensions (as discussed in section 5.3.3), is that some risk comparisons may fail to recognize these dimensions as significant. For example, when comparing two sources that have statistically similar probabilities, as well as comparable outcomes, but are not comparable in terms of whether they are voluntarily undertaken or not. Such a comparison may be rejected as inappropriate. Covello, Sandman & Slovic (1988) recommend that risk comparisons should, wherever, possible take account of the qualitative dimensions to risk. However, a major empirical question remains over whether this does indeed make risk comparisons both more understandable and acceptable to individuals, and empirical tests of this recommendation are now required (see for example Johnson & Fisher 1989, Roth, Morgan, Fischhoff, Lave & Bostrom 1990).

A novel, and highly promising approach to risk communication, which recognizes several of the complexities inherent in a receiver's frame of reference, is that of the mental-models approach, developed simultaneously in Europe (Jungermann, Schütz & Thüring 1988) and at Carnegie Mellon University in the United States (Bostrom 1990, Bostrom, Fischhoff & Morgan 1992). Mental models are conceptualized as small-scale psychological representations that individuals hold in their mind of some knowledge domain in the world. This concept has proven useful in applied psychology in understanding a range of specialized mental skills which individuals learn to use, for example when operating a particular piece of equipment or in problem solving (Gentner & Stevens 1983, Rouse & Morris

1986). Starting from the premiss that risk communications to lay people should provide individuals with what *they* actually need to know, the Carnegie Mellon work elicits individual mental models of a hazardous process (such as radon gas in homes) from both expert and lay subjects by means of open-ended interview techniques. These are represented using influence diagrams, a pictorial technique for illustrating the important concepts (and relations between concepts) that an individual associates with a problem domain. By using the expert model as a baseline for comparison (and assuming that this is accurate) the researchers can identify aspects of the lay subjects' models that are appropriate, those that are inappropriate, and important concepts that are absent entirely. The researchers argue that this then provides them with a better basis for developing a communication about risk (for example, a public information booklet on radon in the home) that addresses the framework of lay perceptions. In particular, the exploration of lay mental models allows correct beliefs to be reinforced, incorrect beliefs countered and absent information introduced. To date, however, as noted by Johnson (1992), this method has only been used in the context of individual risks, and it remains to be seen whether the technique has potential for understanding the bases for perceptions of (and in particular value conflicts about) larger-scale societal risks.

A final important practical issue related to the use of risk communications concerns the specification of effective means of programme evaluation. Several researchers have recently pointed to the importance of this issue (Kasperson & Palmlund 1987, O'Riordan *et al.* 1989, Rohrmann 1990, Handmer & Penning-Rowsell 1990, Morgan, Fischhoff, Bostrom, Lave & Atman 1992). As noted earlier, much of the currently available advice on how to communicate risk information lacks direct empirical validation either in terms of its effectiveness to meet set goals (e.g. to change beliefs and behaviour, or the timely distribution of warning messages during an emergency), or in its capacity to avoid unintended consequences. This latter consideration appears particularly important given that health and economic damage might flow from poor risk communications, and sets a significant future research agenda for risk communication researchers. As Morgan *et al.* (1992) succinctly comment: 'One should no more release an untested communication than an untested product.'

5.5.4 RISK COMMUNICATION AND TRUST

A current point of contact between risk perception and risk communication research, concerns the issue of trust in risk management institutions. This issue has relevance to a range of societal risks (see for example Renn & Levine 1991), but gained a particularly high profile during the late 1980s as a result of severe public opposition, in the US in particular, to the siting of hazardous waste storage facilities (Slovic, Flynn & Layman 1991, Kasperson, Golding & Tuler 1992).

Trust enters into the risk communication debate in two interrelated ways. First, as pointed out by Lee (1986), results from persuasive communication studies show that the credibility of a communicator is critically dependent upon the trust placed in him or her. If we do not trust the source (perhaps because of current evidence that contradicts past messages) then we will not trust the message! It is also the case that trust is hard to gain, but easy to lose. A particular dilemma is raised here by the uncertainties that often surround any particular risk assessment; under such circumstances too precise a prediction which unintentionally neglects areas of uncertainty or incompleteness in a risk model might, in the light of subsequent events, be interpreted to have been flawed, thus undermining the credibility of the risk analyst. Similarly, trust may be lost, following a serious incident or actual disaster, if the responsible authorities and institutions are not felt to be learning from, and responding to, the event in as open and public a way as is possible. It is for these reasons, among others, that many commentators, and the NRC (1989) in particular, advocate that early, on-going, open and honest interaction is a prerequisite to effective, as well as ethical risk communications.

The second, more complex argument stems from the observation, discussed earlier, that risk assessment incorporates social framing assumptions. The question of trust and risk perception was first raised by Wynne (1980, 1982) who argued that with technological risks some of the differences between expert and lay perceptions might be traced to differing evaluations of the relation between risk outcomes and the trustworthiness of risk-management institutions. This in turn involves a judgement as to the trustworthiness of the responsible authorities and institutions to act both in the public interest and with regard to the best possible technical and safety practices (a related issue, raised by Rayner & Cantor (1987), is the fairness of the processes of decision making about risk). By this argument, one interpretation to be placed upon several of the qualitative dimensions of perceived risk identified in the psychometric studies discussed in sections 5.3.3 and 5.3.4 is that they relate to important aspects of the social processes associated with hazard management (e.g. the 'degree of organized safety' dimension identified by Vlek & Stallen (1981), or the 'unknown to science' dimension of Slovic, *et al.* (1980)). Put this way, some aspects of public perceptions of

risk revealed by risk-perception research can be seen not as a nuisance variable to be countered by 'appropriate' risk communications, but as a datum to be considered in the processes of critical reflection upon and learning about technology (Wynne 1992). And this in turn suggests the need to consider more carefully the 'social rationality' of the risk perceiver (see also Krimsky & Plough 1988).

A recent study on public acceptability of food irradiation by Bord & O'Connor (1990) provides support for Wynne's view. They find that trust in institutions (industry in general, the food irradiation industry, government regulatory agencies, and science itself) has a clear impact upon judgements of the acceptability of food irradiation. The researchers report that their respondents frequently made the point that 'even if the scientific-technical plan were flawless, the people executing the plan and managing the technology would inevitably create serious problems. Bhopal, Chernobyl, Three Mile Island and even Nixon's Watergate were examples used to make this point' (p. 505). More generally, and as Laird (1989) has pointed out in the US context, lack of trust in risk-management institutions may be symptomatic of a more general loss of faith by the public in institutional arrangements, and an unwillingness to delegate responsibility for important decisions to institutions. What is clear is that the question of public trust in relation to risk management processes, and the role that the public should be accorded in risk decision making, sets a major future research agenda for social science research into risk.

5.6 CONCLUSIONS

Work on risk perception continues to play an important and expanding role in

our understanding of risk issues. The most important recent development has been the closer relevance of this work to questions of public policy and decision making, as reflected in recent work on risk communication, as well as on the relation between public perceptions and societal decision making about risk tolerability and risk management.

The field of risk-perception research now contains several well-defined schools of thought. The positions taken by these schools display both areas of agreement and disagreement. One constant theme, as noted earlier, is that most approaches now take the view that risk perceptions must be investigated, and perhaps more importantly be seen as valid, in and of their own right. A second clear consensus is that individual risk perceptions are shaped by a wide range of both social and cultural, as well as psychological factors. A third is that the 'public' should not be viewed as an undifferentiated entity; rather there are many groups within any society, and some may hold differing risk perceptions. One conclusion is that such plurality represents a desirable rather than a problematic situation. Diversity of view provides the basis by which decisions about risks can be informed (and subject to effective critique) from a wide range of perspectives. However, there remains the administrative dilemma of how, in the face of such plurality, societal decisions about risks may be made that are both equitable, and in some way in the interests of all.

Important differences between the various schools in risk-perception research are also evident. For example, the psychometric approach is well grounded empirically, but offers a relatively undeveloped theoretical framework, and in this respect has probably not progressed much from the position found in 1983. On the other hand the more recent social and cultural approaches to risk perception, such as cultural theory and the social amplification of risk framework, have been subject to far less direct em-

pirical testing than the psychological approach, but do, however, potentially offer more valuable, and wide-ranging, theoretical insights into the factors underlying risk perception. Bridging the gap between these two traditions (insofar as this is possible or desirable, and this remains a contentious issue among many of the researchers concerned), would seem a key research priority for the 1990s.

The initial one-way conceptualization of risk communication is now seen as too restricted. Risk communication can serve divergent goals over and above the mere provision of information about a specific hazard. These include the implementation of a general 'right to know' with respect to risks, conflict resolution, and the enhancement of societal and personal decision making about risk. Questions remain, however, with regard to identifying the contexts within which particular approaches to risk communication will be most appropriate, as well as the evaluation of the effectiveness of specific risk-communication programmes.

One emerging point of contact between psychology and the sociological and anthropological schools concerns the re-interpretations that can now be put on the established psychometric findings that individuals are sensitive to a range of qualitative characteristics of hazards. It is claimed that this aspect of individual risk perceptions may be in part related to the social contexts within which hazards arise. The question of the trust that people place in risk-management institutions appears important here, and is likely to prove to be a key determinant of public tolerance of large-scale societal risks. One policy question concerns the extent to which two-way risk communication, as well as the existence of an effective public right to know, might foster such long-term trust. A second concerns the nature of any wider future role that public groups might play in the processes of setting the parameters for risk tolerability and societal risk management. Meeting these two agendas, difficult though they are, might also contribute to a closer understanding between the technical and the social science approaches to risk assessment, perception and management.

ACKNOWLEDGEMENTS

The following have assisted the sub-group in its work by supplying papers, comments and suggestions for the revised chapter 5:

Dr John Adams (University College), Professor David Blockley (University of Bristol), Ms Wibecke Brun (University of Bergen), Professor George Cvetkovich (Western Washington University), Dr Karl Dake (University of California, Berkeley), Professor Mary Douglas (University College), Professor Richard Eiser (University of Exeter), Professor Baruch Fischhoff (Carnegie Mellon University), Dr Colin Green (Middlesex University), Professor Susan Hadden (University of Texas), Dr John Handmer (Australian National University), Dr Branden Johnson (New Jersey Department of Environmental Protection), Professor Roger Kasperson (Clark University), Dr Ray Kemp (University of East Anglia), Professor Terrence Lee (St Andrews University), Dr Harry Otway (Los Alamos National Laboratory), Professor Timothy O'Riordan (University of East Anglia), Professor Joop van der Pligt (University of Amsterdam), Ms Ana Puy (University Complutense, Madrid), Dr Stephen Reicher (University of Exeter), Professor Bernd Rohrmann (University of Mannheim), Professor Paul Slovic (Decision Research), Professor Ola Svenson (University of Stockholm), Dr Brian Toft (Sedgwick James, London, Ltd), Professor Charles Vlek (Groningen University), Professor Stephen Watson (University of Cambridge) and Dr Brian Wynne (Lancaster University).

Responsibility for the contents of the final chapter lies with the sub-group authors.

REFERENCES

Adams, J.G.U. 1985 *Risk and freedom: the record of road safety regulation*. Cardiff: Transport Publishing Projects.

Adams, J.G.U. & Thompson, M. 1991 *Risk review: perception, varieties of uncertainty, sources of information* (unpublished end of Award Report W100311002). Swindon: Economic and Social Research Council.

Arabie, P. & Maschmeyer, C. 1988 Some current models for the perception and judgment of risk. *Orgl Behavior and Human Decision Processes* **41**, 300–329.

Ashby, Lord 1977 The risk equations: the subjective side of assessing risks. *New Scient.* 19 May, 398–400.

Baram, M. 1991 Rights and duties concerning the availability of environmental risk information to the public. In: *Communicating risks to the public* (R.E. Kasperson & P.J.M. Stallen, eds). Dordrecht: Kluwer.

Bastide, S. Moatti, J.-P., Pages, J.-P. & Fagnani, F. 1989 Risk perception and the social acceptability of technologies: the French case. *Risk Analysis* **9**, 215–223.

Beck, U. 1992 *Risk society: towards a new modernity*. London: Sage.

Bellaby, P. 1990 To risk or not to risk? Uses and limitations of Mary Douglas on risk acceptability for understanding health and safety at work and road accidents. *The Sociological Review* **38**, 465–483.

Blockley, D.I. 1980 *The nature of structural design and safety.* Chichester: Ellis Horwood.

Blockley, D.I. (ed) 1992 *Engineering safety.* Maidenhead: McGraw-Hill.

Bord, R.J. & O'Connor, R.E. 1990 Risk communication, knowledge, and attitudes: explaining reactions to a technology perceived as risky. *Risk Analysis* **10**, 499–506.

Bostrom, A. 1990 'A mental models approach to exploring perceptions of hazardous processes'. (unpublished Ph.D. dissertation). Carnegie Mellon University, Pittsburgh.

Bostrom, A., Fischhoff, B. & Morgan, M.G. 1992 Characterizing mental models of hazardous processes: a methodology and an application to radon. *Journal of Social Issues.* (In the press.)

Brown, J. (ed) 1989 *Environmental threats: perception, analysis and management.* London: Belhaven.

Brun, W. 1992 Cognitive components in risk perception: natural versus man-made risks. *Journal of Behavioral Decision Making* **5**, 117–132.

Buss, D.M., Craik, K.H. & Dake, K. 1986 Contemporary worldviews and perception of the technological system. In: *Risk evaluation and management* (V.T. Covello, J. Menkes & J. Mumpower, eds). New York: Plenum.

Collingridge, D. 1980 *The social control of technology.* Milton Keynes: Open University Press.

Combs, B. & Slovic, P. 1979 Causes of death: biased newspaper coverage and biased judgements. *Journalism Quarterly* **56**, 837–843.

Conrad, J. (ed) 1980 *Society, technology and risk assessment.* London: Academic Press.

Cotgrove, S. 1982 *Catastrophe or cornucopia: the environment, politics and the future.* Chichester: Wiley.

Covello, V.T. 1991 Risk comparisons and risk communication: issues and problems in comparing health and environmental risks. In: *Communicating risks to the public* (R.E. Kasperson & P.J.M. Stallen, eds). Dordrecht: Kluwer.

Covello, V.T. & Allen, F. 1988 *Seven cardinal rules of risk communication.* Washington, DC: US Environmental Protection Agency.

Covello, V.T., Sandman, P. & Slovic, P. 1988 *Risk communication, risk statistics and risk comparisons: a manual for plant managers.* Washington, DC: Chemical Manufacturers Association.

Cvetkovich, G.T. & Earle, T.C. (eds) 1991 Special issue on 'Risk and culture'. *Journal of Cross-Cultural Psychology* **22**(1), 11–149.

Daamen, D., Verplanken, B. & Midden, C. 1986 Accuracy and consistency of lay estimates of annual fatality rates. In: *New directions in research on decision making* (B. Brehmer, H. Jungermann, P. Lourens & G. Sevon, eds). Amsterdam: Elsevier.

Dake, K. 1991 Orienting dispositions in the perception of risk: an analysis of contemporary worldviews and cultural biases. *Journal of Cross-Cultural Psychology,* **22**, 61–82.

Dake, K. & Wildavsky, A. 1991 Individual differences in risk perception and risk-taking preferences. In: *The analysis, communication and perception of risk* (B.J. Garrick & W.C. Gekler, eds). New York: Plenum.

Department of the Environment & Health and Safety Executive 1979 'Risk assessment and the acceptability of risk' (summary joint seminar held by DOE and HSE, Sunningdale, January). (Unpublished.)

Douglas, M. 1966 *Purity and danger: an analysis of concepts of pollution and taboo.* London: Routledge & Kegan Paul.

Douglas, M. 1982 Cultural bias. In: *The active voice*, chapter 9. London: Routledge & Kegan Paul.

Douglas, M. 1985 *Risk acceptability according to the social sciences.* New York: Russell Sage Foundation.

Douglas, M. 1990 Risk as a forensic resource. *Dædalus* **119**(4), 1–16.

Douglas, M. 1992 *Risk and blame.* London: Routledge.

Douglas, M. & Wildavsky, A. 1982 *Risk and culture: an essay on the selection of technical and environmental dangers.* Berkeley: University of California Press.

Earle, T.C. & Lindell, M.K. 1984 Public perceptions of industrial risks: a free-response approach. In: *Low-probability / high-consequence risk analysis* (R.A. Waller & V.T. Covello, eds). New York: Plenum.

Eiser, J.R., Hannover, B., Mann, L., Morin, M., van der Pligt, J. & Webly, P. 1990 Nuclear attitudes after Chernobyl: a cross-national study. *Journal of Environmental Psychology* **10**, 101–110.

Eiser, J.R. & Hoepfner, F. 1991 Accidents, disease, and the greenhouse effect: effects of response categories on estimates of risk. *Basic and Applied Social Psychology* **12**, 195–210.

Eiser, J.R. & van der Pligt, J. 1979 Beliefs and values in the nuclear debate. *Journal of Applied Social Psychology* **9**, 524–536.

Englander, T., Farago, K., Slovic, P. & Fischhoff, B. 1986 A comparative analysis of risk perception in Hungary and the United States. *Journal of Social Behavior*, **1**, 55–66.

Fessenden-Raden, J., Fitchen, J.M. & Heath, J.S. 1987 Providing risk information in communities: factors influencing what is heard and accepted. *Science, Technology and Human Values* **12**, 94–101.

Fiorino, D.J. 1990 Citizen participation and environmental risk: a survey of institutional mechanisms. *Science, Technology and Human Values*, **15**, 226–243.

Fischer, G.W., Morgan, M.G., Fischhoff, B., Nair, I. & Lave, L.B. 1991 What risks are people concerned about? *Risk Analysis*, **11**, 303–314.

Fischhoff, B. 1989 Risk: a guide to controversy. Appendix C in: *Improving risk communication*. Washington, DC: National Academy Press.

Fischhoff, B. 1990 Psychology and public policy: tool or toolmaker? *American Psychologist* **45**, 647–653.

Fischhoff, B., Lichtenstein, S., Slovic, P., Derby, S.L. & Keeney, R.L. 1981 *Acceptable risk.* Cambridge: Cambridge University Press.

Fischhoff, B. & MacGregor, D. 1983 Judged lethality: how much people seem to know depends upon how they are asked. *Risk Analysis*, **3**, 229–236.

Fischhoff, B., Slovic, P., Lichtenstein, S., Read, S. & Combs, B. 1978 How safe is safe enough? A psychometric study of attitudes towards technological risks and benefits. *Policy Sciences*, **9**, 127–152.

Fischhoff, B. & Svenson, O. 1988 Perceived risks of radionuclides: understanding public understanding. In: *Radionuclides in the food chain* (M. Carter, ed). New York: Springer–Verlag.

Fischhoff, B., Watson, S.R. & Hope, C. 1984 Defining risk. *Policy Sciences*, **17**, 123–139.

Fisher, A. 1991 Risk communication challenges. *Risk Analysis*, **11**, 173–179.

Fitchen, J.M., Heath, J.S. & Fessenden-Raden, J. 1987 Risk perception in community context: a case study. In: *The social and cultural construction of risk* (B.B. Johnson & V.T. Covello, eds). Dordrecht: Reidel.

Freudenburg, W.R. 1988 Perceived risk, real risk: social science and the art of probabilistic risk assessment. *Science, Wash.* **242**, 44–49.

Funtowicz, S.O. & Ravetz, J.R. 1985 Three types of risk assessment: a methodological analysis. In: *Risk analysis in the private sector* (C. Whipple & V.T. Covello, eds). New York: Plenum.

Funtowicz, S.O. & Ravetz, J.R. 1990 *Uncertainty and quality in science for policy*. Dordrecht: Kluwer.

Gardner, G.T. & Gould, L.C. 1989 Public perceptions of the risks and benefits of technology. *Risk Analysis* **9**, 225–242.

Gentner, D. & Stevens, A.L. (eds) 1983 *Mental models.* Hillsdale, New Jersy: Lawrence Earlbaum.

Goszczynska, M., Tyszka, T. & Slovic, P. 1991 Risk perception in Poland: a comparison with three other countries. *Journal of Behavioral Decision Making* **4**, 179–193.

Green, C.H. 1979 'Someone out there is trying to kill me: acceptable risk as a problem definition'. (paper presented at the International Conference on Environmental Psychology, University of Surrey, Guildford). (Unpublished.)

Green, C.H. & Brown, R.A. 1978*a Life safety: what is it and how much is it worth?* (CP52/78.) Borehamwood, Herts: Building Research Establishment.

Green, C.H. & Brown, R.A. 1978*b* Counting lives. *Journal of Occupational Accidents* **2**, 55–70.

Green, C.H. & Brown, R.A. 1980 'Through a glass darkly: perceiving perceived risks to health and safety'. (Paper presented at the workshop on Perceived Risk at Eugene, Oregon.) (Unpublished.)

Green, C.H., Tunstall, S.M. & Fordham, M. 1991 The risks from flooding: which risk and whose perception? *Disasters* **15**, 227–236.

Hacking, I. 1975 *The emergence of probability.* Cambridge University Press.

Hadden, S.G. 1989*a* Institutional barriers to risk communication. *Risk Analysis* **9**, 301–308.

Hadden, S.G. 1989*b A citizen's right to know: risk communication and public policy.* Boulder, Colorado: Westview.

Hance, B., Chess, C. & Sandman, P. 1987 *Improving dialogue with communities: a risk communication manual for government.* Trenton, New Jersey: Department of Environmental Protection and Energy.

Handmer, J. & Penning-Rowsell, E.C. 1990 *Hazards and the communication of risk.* Aldershot: Gower.

Health and Safety Executive 1988*a* *The tolerability of risk from nuclear power stations.* London: HMSO.

Health and Safety Executive 1988*b* *Comments received on 'The tolerability of risk from nuclear power stations'.* London: HMSO.

Health and Safety Executive 1991 *Major hazard aspects of the transport of dangerous substances.* London: HMSO.

Henrion, M. & Fischhoff, B. 1986 Assessing uncertainty in physical constants. *Am. J. Phys.* **54**, 791–798.

Henwood, K.L. & Pidgeon, N.F. 1992 Qualitative research and psychological theorizing. *Br. J. Psychol.* **83**, 97–111.

Hynes, M. & Vanmarcke, E. 1976 Reliability of embankment performance prediction. In: *Proceedings of the ASCE Engineering Mechanics Division Speciality Conference.* Waterloo, Ontario: University of Waterloo Press.

Janis, I.L. 1972 *Victims of groupthink.* Boston: Houghton-Mifflin.

Jasanoff, S. 1987 Contested boundaries in policy-relevant science. *Social Studies of Science* **17**, 195–230.

Johnson, B.B. 1987 The environmentalist movement and grid/group analysis: a modest critique. In: *The social and cultural construction of risk* (B.B. Johnson & V.T. Covello, eds). Dordrecht: Reidel.

Johnson, B.B. 1991 Risk and culture research: some cautions. *Journal of Cross-Cultural Psychology* **22**, 141–149.

Johnson, B.B. 1992 "The mental model" meets "the planning process": wrestling with risk communication research and practice'. New Jersey Department of Environmental Protection and Energy. (Unpublished.)

Johnson, B.B. & Covello, V.T. (eds) 1987 *The social and cultural construction of risk.* Dordrecht: Reidel.

Johnson, E.J. & Tversky, A. 1983 Affect, generalisation and the perception of risk. *Journal of Personality and Social Psychology* **45**, 21–31.

Johnson, E.J. & Tversky, A. 1984 Representations and perceptions of risk. *J. Exp. Psychol. (General)* **113**, 55–70.

Johnson, F.R. & Fisher, A. 1989 Conventional wisdom on risk communication and evidence from a field experiment. *Risk Analysis*, **9**, 209–213.

Jungermann, H. 1986 The two camps on rationality. In: *Judgment and decision making* (H.R. Arkes & K.R. Hammond, eds). Cambridge University Press.

Jungermann, H., Schütz, H. & Thüring, M. 1988 Mental models in risk assessment: informing people about drugs. *Risk Analysis*, **8**, 147–155.

Kahneman, D., Slovic, P. & Tversky, A. (eds) 1982 *Judgment under uncertainty: heuristics and biases.* Cambridge University Press.

Kasperson, R.E., Golding, D. & Tuler, S. 1992 Siting hazardous facilities and communicating risks under conditions of high social distrust. *Journal of Social Issues.* (In the press.)

Kasperson, R.E., Kasperson, J.X. & Renn, O. 1992 The social amplification of risk: progress in developing an integrative framework. In: *Theories of risk* (S. Krimsky & D. Golding, eds). New York: Praeger. (In the press.)

Kasperson, R.E. & Palmlund, I. 1987 Evaluating risk communication. In: *Effective risk communication: the role and responsibility of government and non-government organizations* (V.T. Covello, D.B. McCallum & M.T. Pavlova, eds). New York: Plenum.

Kasperson, R.E., Renn, O., Slovic, P., Brown, H.S., Emel, J., Goble, R., Kasperson, J.X. & Ratick, S. 1988 The social amplification of risk: a conceptual framework. *Risk Analysis*, **8**, 177–187.

Kasperson, R.E. & Stallen, P.J.M. (eds) 1991 *Communicating risks to the public.* Dordrecht: Kluwer.

Kates, R.W. & Kasperson, J.X. 1983 Comparative risk analysis of technological hazards. *Proc. Natn. Acad. Sci. U.S.A.* **80**, 7027–7038.

Keown, C.F. 1989 Risk perceptions of Hong Kongese vs. Americans. *Risk Analysis* **9**, 401–405.

Kleinhesselink, R.R. & Rosa, E.A. 1991 Cognitive representations of risk perceptions: a comparison of Japan and the United States. *Journal of Cross-Cultural Psychology* **22**, 11–28.

Kletz, T.A. 1985 *An engineer's view of human error.* Rugby: Insitute of Chemical Engineers.

Kraus, N.N. & Slovic, P. 1988 Taxonomic analysis of perceived risk: modelling individual and group perceptions within homogeneous hazard domains. *Risk Analysis* **8**, 435–455.

Krimsky, S. & Golding, D. (eds) 1992 *Theories of risk.* New York: Praeger. (In the press.)

Krimsky, S. & Plough, A. 1988 *Environmental hazards: communicating risks as a social process.* Dover, Massachusettes: Auburn.

Kuhn, T.S. 1962 *The structure of scientific revolutions.* University of Chicago Press.

Laird, F.N. 1989 The decline of deference: the political context of risk communication. *Risk Analysis* **9**, 543–550.

Lathrop, J. & Linnerooth, J. 1983 The role of risk assessment in a political decision process. In: *Analysing and aiding decision processes* (P. Humphreys, O. Svenson & A. Vari, eds). Amsterdam: North-Holland.

Latour, B. 1987 *Science in action.* Milton Keynes: Open University Press.

Layfield, Sir Frank 1987 *Sizewell B public inquiry: summary of conclusions and recommendations.* London: HMSO.

Lee, T.R. 1986 Effective communication of information about chemical hazards. *The Science of the Total Environment* **51**, 149–183.

Lichtenstein, S., Slovic, P., Fischhoff, B., Layman, M. & Combs, B. 1978 Judged frequency of lethal events. *J. Exp. Psychol. (Human Learning and Memory)* **4**, 551–578.

Lopes, L.L. 1988 Between hope and fear: the psychology of risk. *Advances in Experimental Social Psychology* **20**, 255–295.

Lowrance, W.W. 1976 *Of acceptable risk: science and the determination of safety.* Los Altos, California: W. Kaufman.

MacGregor, D. 1991 Worry over technological activities and life concerns. *Risk Analysis* **11**, 315–325.

Machlis, G.E. & Rosa, E.A. 1990 Desired risk: broadening the social amplification of risk framework. *Risk Analysis* **10**, 161–168.

Mazur, A. 1981 *The dynamics of technical controversy.* Washington, D.C.: Communications Press.

Mechitov, A.I. & Rebrik, S.B. 1990 Studies of risk and safety perception in the USSR. In: *Contemporary issues in decision making* (K. Borcherding, O.J. Larichev & D.M. Messick, eds). Amsterdam: North-Holland.

Morgan, M.G., Fischhoff, B., Bostrom, A., Lave, L. & Atman, C. 1992 Risk communication. *Environmental Science and Technology.* (In the press.)

Morgan, M.G. & Lave, L. 1990 Ethical considerations in risk communication practice and research. *Risk Analysis* **10**, 355–358.

Murphy, A.H. & Winkler, R.L. 1977 Can weather forecasters formulate reliable probability forecasts of precipitation and temperature? *National Weather Digest* **2**, 2–9.

National Research Council 1989 *Improving risk communication.* Washington, D.C.: National Academy Press.

O'Riordan, T. 1977 Environmental ideologies. *Environment and Planning* **9**, 3–14.

O'Riordan, T. 1990 Hazard and risk in the modern world: political models for programme design. In: *Hazards and the communication of risk* (J. Handmer & E.C. Penning-Rowsell, eds). Aldershot: Gower.

O'Riordan, T., Jungermann, H., Kasperson, R.E. & Wiedemann, P.M. 1989 Themes and tasks of risk communication: report of an international conference held at KFA Jülich. *Risk Analysis* **9**, 513–518.

O'Riordan, T., Kemp, R. & Purdue, M. 1988 *Sizewell B: an anatomy of the inquiry.* London: MacMillan.

Otway, H.J. 1985 Multi-dimensional criteria for technology acceptability: a response to Bernard L. Cohen. *Risk Analysis* **5, 271–273.**

Otway, H.J. 1990 How the public perceives technologies. (Paper presented at OECD/NEA workshop 'Communicating for tomorrow', Paris, March 1990.)

Otway, H.J. & Cohen, J.J. 1975 *Revealed preferences: comments on the Starr benefit–risk relationships.* (RM 75.5). Laxenburg, Austria: International Institute for Applied Systems Analysis.

Otway, H.J. & Fishbein, M. 1976 *The determinants of attitude formation in application to nuclear power* (RM 76.80). Laxenburg, Austria: International Institute for Applied Systems Analysis.

Otway, H.J. & Fishbein, M. 1977 *Public attitudes and decision making* (RM 77.54). Laxenburg, Austria: International Institute for Applied Systems Analysis.

Otway, H.J. & Thomas, K. 1982 Reflections on risk perception and policy. *Risk Analysis* **2**, 69–82.

Otway, H.J. & von Winterfeldt, D. 1982 Beyond acceptable risk: on the social acceptability of technologies. *Policy Sciences* **14**, 247–256.

Otway, H.J. & Wynne, B. 1989 Risk communication: paradigm and paradox. *Risk Analysis* **9**, 141–145.

Perrow, C. 1984 *Normal accidents*. New York: Basic Books.

Perusse, M. 1980 'Dimensions of perception and recognition of danger'. Ph.D. dissertation, University of Aston, Birmingham.

Pidgeon, N.F. 1988 Risk assessment and accident analysis. *Acta Psychologica* **68**, 355–368.

Pidgeon, N.F., Blockley, D.I. & Turner, B.A. 1986 Design practice and snow loading: lessons from a roof collapse. *The Structural engineer* **64**A (3) March, 67–71.

Pilisuk, M., Parks, S. & Hawkes, G. 1987 Public perception of technological risk. *The Social Science Journal* **24**, 403–413.

van der Pligt, J. 1992 *Nuclear energy and the public*. Oxford: Blackwell. (In the press).

van der Pligt, J. van der Linden, J. & Ester, P. 1982 Attitudes to nuclear energy: beliefs, values and false consensus. *Journal of Environmental Psychology* **2**, 221–31.

Polanyi, M. 1958 *Personal knowledge: towards a post-critical philosophy*. University of Chicago Press.

Rayner, S. 1986 Management of radiation hazards in hospitals: plural rationalities in a single institution. *Social Studies of Science* **16**, 573–591.

Rayner, S. 1989 Risk, uncertainty and social organization. *Contemporary Sociology* **18**, 6–9.

Rayner, S. & Cantor, R. 1987 How fair is safe enough? The cultural approach to social technology choice. *Risk Analysis* **7**, 3–9.

Reason, J.T. 1990 *Human error*. Cambridge University Press.

Renn, O. 1991 Risk communication and the social amplification of risk. In: *Communicating risks to the public* (R.E. Kasperson & P.J.M. Stallen, eds). Dordrecht: Kluwer.

Renn, O. & Levine, D. 1991 Credibility and trust in risk communication. In: *Communicating risks to the public* (R.E. Kasperson & P.J.M. Stallen, eds). Dordrecht: Kluwer.

Rip, A. 1986 Controversies as informal technology assessment. *Knowledge: Creation, Diffusion, Utilization* **8**, 349–371.

Rip, A. 1988 Should social amplification of risk be counteracted? *Risk Analysis* **8**, 193–197.

Rohrmann, B. 1990 *Analyzing and evaluating the effectiveness of risk communication programs* (Studies on risk communication, vol. 17). Jülich, Germany: Programme Group Men, Environment, Technology, KFA Research Centre Jülich.

Rohrmann, B. 1991 *A survey on social-scientific research on risk perception* (Studies on risk communication, vol. 26). Jülich, Germany: Programme Group Men, Environment, Technology, KFA Research Centre Jülich.

Rohrmann, B., Wiedemann, P.M. & Stegelmann, H.U. 1990 *Risk communication: an interdisciplinary bibliography*, 4th edn (Studies on risk communication, vol. 2). Jülich, Germany: Programme Group Men, Environment, Technology, KFA Research Centre Jülich.

Roth, E., Morgan, M.G., Fischhoff, B., Lave, L. & Bostrom, A. 1990 What do we know about making risk comparisons? *Risk Analysis* **10**, 375–387.

Rouse, W.B. & Morris, N.M. 1986 On looking into the black box: prospects and limits in the search for mental models. *Psychol. Bull.* **100**, 349–363.

Schmidt, F.N. & Gifford, R. 1989 A dispositional approach to hazard perception: preliminary development of the environmental appraisal inventory. *Journal of Environmental Psychology* **9**, 57–67.

Schwarz, M. & Thompson, M. 1990 *Divided we stand: redefining politics, technology and social choice*. Hemel Hempstead: Harvester Wheatsheaf.

Short, J.F. 1984 The social fabric at risk: toward the social transformation of risk analysis. *American Sociological Review* **49**, 711–725.

Sibly, P.G. & Walker, A.C. 1977 Structural accidents and their causes. *Proc. Inst. Civ. Engrs* **62** (1), 191–208.

Sjöberg, L. 1980 The risks of risk analysis. *Acta Psychologica* **45**, 301–321.

Slovic, P. 1987 Perception of risk. *Science, Wash.* **236**, 280–285.

Slovic, P. 1992 Perceptions of risk: reflections on the psychometric paradigm. In: *Theories of risk* (S. Krimsky & D. Golding, eds). New York: Praeger. (In the press.)

Slovic, P., Fischhoff, B. & Lichtenstein, S. 1980 Facts and fears: understanding perceived risk. In: *Societal risk assessment: how safe is safe enough* (R.C. Schwing & W.A. Albers, eds). New York: Plenum Press.

Slovic, P., Flynn, J.H. & Layman, M. 1991 Perceived risk, trust, and the politics of nuclear waste. *Science, Wash.* **254**, 1603–1607.

Slovic, P., Kraus, N.N., Lappe, H., Letzel, H. & Malmfors, T. 1989 Risk perception of prescription drugs: report on a survey in Sweden. *Pharmaceutical Medicine* **4**, 43–65.

Slovic, P., Lichtenstein, S. & Fischhoff, B. 1984 Modelling the societal impact of fatal accidents. *Management Science* **30**, 464–474.

Smithson, M. 1989 *Ignorance and uncertainty: emerging paradigms*. Berlin: Springer–Verlag.

Stallen, P.J.M. & Tomas, A. 1988 Public concern about industrial hazards. *Risk Analysis* **8**, 235–245.

Starr, C. 1969 Social benefit versus technological risk. *Science, Wash.* **165**, 1232–1238.

Stern, P.C. 1991 Learning through conflict: a realistic strategy for risk communication. *Policy Sciences*, **24**, 99–119.

Svenson, O. 1989 On expert judgements in safety analyses in the process industries. *Reliability Engineering and System Safety* **25**, 219–256.

Thompson, M. 1980 *An outline of the cultural theory of risk* (WP 80.177). Laxenburg, Austria: International Institute for Applied Systems Analysis.

Thompson, M., Ellis, R. & Wildavsky, A. 1990 *Cultural Theory*. Boulder, Colorado: Westview Press.

Tiegen, K.H., Brun, W. & Slovic, P. 1988 Societal risks as seen by a Norwegian public. *Journal of Behavioral Decision Making* **1**, 111–130.

Turner, B.A. 1978 *Man-made disasters*. London: Wykeham Press.

Tversky, A. & Kahneman, D. 1973 Availability: a heuristic for judging frequency and probability. *Cognitive Psychology* **4**, 207–232.

Vesely, W.E. & Rasmuson, D.M. 1984 Uncertainties in nuclear probabilistic risk analysis. *Risk Analysis* **4**, 313–322.

Vlek, C.J.H. 1990 *Decision making about risk acceptance* (executive summary: Report A 90/10H). The Hague: Netherlands National Health Council.

Vlek, C.J.H. & Keren, G. 1991 'Behaviourial decision theory and environmental risk management: what have we learned and what has been neglected?' Paper presented at the 13th Research Conference on Subjective Probability, Utility and Decision Making, Fribourg, Switzerland, August.

Vlek, C.J.H. & Stallen, P.J.M. 1980 Rational and personal aspects of risk. *Acta Psychologica* **45**, 273–300.

Vlek, C.J.H. & Stallen, P.J.M. 1981 Judging risks and benefits in the small and in the large. *Organizational Behavior and Human Performance* **28**, 235–271.

Watson, S. R. 1981 On risks and acceptability. *Journal of the Society for Radiological Protection* **1**(4), 21–25.

Wildavsky, A. & Dake, K. 1990 Theories of risk perception: who fears what and why? *Dædalus* **119** (4), 41–60.

Wilson, R. 1979 Analyzing the daily risks of life. *Technology Review* **81**(4), 40–46.

Wilson, R. & Crouch, E.A.C. 1987 Risk assessment and comparisons: an introduction. *Science, Wash.* **236**, 267–270.

von Winterfeldt, D. & Edwards, W. 1984 Patterns of conflict about risky technologies. *Risk Analysis* **4**, 55–68.

Wynne, B. 1980 Technology, risk and participation: on the social treatment of uncertainty. In: *Society, technology and risk assessment* (J. Conrad ed). New York: Academic Press.

Wynne, B. 1982 *Rationality and ritual: the Windscale inquiry and nuclear decisions in Britain*. Chalfont St Giles: British Society for the History of Science.

Wynne, B. 1989a Understanding public risk perceptions. In: *Risk analysis in nuclear waste management* (A. Saltelli *et al.*, eds). Brussels: ECSC, EEC, EAEC.

Wynne, B. 1989b Frameworks of rationality in risk management: towards the testing of naïve sociology. In: *Environmental threats: perception, analysis and management* (J. Brown ed). London: Belhaven.

Wynne, B. 1992 Risk and social learning: reification to engagement. In: *Theories of risk* (S. Krimsky & D. Golding, eds). New York: Praeger. (In the press.)

Chapter 6

RISK MANAGEMENT

Prepared by: Professor C. C. Hood, Professor D. K. C. Jones, Dr N. F. Pidgeon, Professor B. A. Turner, Miss R. Gibson (Research Assistant); with contributions from Mrs C. Bevan-Davies, Dr S. O. Funtowicz, Mr T. Horlick-Jones, Professor J. A. McDermid, Professor E. C. Penning-Rowsell, Dr J. R. Ravetz, Dr J. D. Sime, Dr C. Wells

6.1 INTRODUCTION: WHO MANAGES WHAT, WHEN, HOW?

6.1.1 THE 'RISK ARCHIPELAGO'

The term 'management' comes from the Italian verb *maneggiare*, meaning to ride a horse with skill. But it is hard to apply this beguiling metaphor to the handling of risks. Risk is ubiquitous and no human activity can be considered risk free. As the last chapter showed, social perceptions of risk vary widely. Both the subjects and the objects of the 'managing' process tend to be multiple and diverse. Indeed, many of the underlying principles are contested.

Some approaches, notably those of quantitative risk analysis, economics and the study of government regulation, address risk management in a generic way. However, the study of risk management also includes detailed investigation of how particular risks arise. For this purpose, risk management is typically broken up into distinct specialisms and subdisciplines. It is, for example, conventional to distinguish different levels of *scale* and *frequency* in the risk management problem. Some of the literature in risk management concentrates on the special problems associated with managing high-magnitude, low-probability (low frequency) events usually termed 'disasters' or 'catastrophes' (see Quarantelli *et al.* 1986). Disaster research (which first emerged as a recognizable subfield of the social sciences in the late 1950s) has mainly focused on the response phase of disasters, but is coming to give more attention to recovery and mitigation processes (see Drabek 1986, Comfort 1988).

Other work is more concerned with incidents of lower magnitude and higher probability (such as road accidents or accidents in the home), which may nevertheless have a larger absolute kill rate. Some attempts have been made to construct absolute scales for disaster using objective measurement (for example, the Bradford Disaster Scale; see Keller *et al.* 1990), but such scales are not widely accepted.

Traditionally, academic research in the field has been divided according to the specific types of risk being managed, notably into *natural hazards, technological hazards* and *social hazards. Natural hazards* emanate from the operation of natural or physical environmental systems extraneous to humankind, such as earthquakes or hurricanes, and there is a specialist field of natural hazard research which has tended to employ human ecological perspectives to examine the 'goodness of fit' between human societies and non-human physical processes (see White 1974, Burton *et al.* 1978, Kates 1978, Kates & Burton 1986, Bryant 1991, Smith 1992). The term 'environmental hazards' is increasingly coming to replace 'natural hazards', in recognition of the fact that many hazards in the environment are either produced or exacerbated by human activity (e.g. desertification, floods, acidification). *Technological hazards,* such as explosions or collisions, emanate from human-designed technological systems and there is a diverse literature on the causes

135

and management of such hazards which spans the social and natural sciences. *Social hazards* emanate from human behaviour, such as arson or terrorism. Although the special nature of each of these areas generates its own specialist literature and terminology, the distinctions cannot be absolute, because what is seen as the product of extraneous 'natural' forces as opposed to human behaviour is culturally variable. The three conventional types of hazard do not cover the entire field (e.g. health hazards, financial risk, etc.), commonly overlap, with many hybrid examples, and in some cases (for example in disasters) the impact characteristics of a hazard may be more important to risk managers than its causes. Indeed, generally similar consequences can often arise from very different causes.

6.1.2 THE TERM 'RISK MANAGEMENT' AND THE NATURE OF RISK MANAGEMENT

Because of the different dimensions of the field, sketched out in section 6.1.1, it is easier to say what risk management does – at least in an abstract way – than what it ought to be for. At the most general level, the process of risk management can be understood in terms of the three basic elements of organizational control theory (cf. Dunsire 1978, 59–60): the setting of goals, whether explicitly or implicitly; the gathering and interpretation of information, and action to influence human behaviour, to physical structures or both.

Each of the three elements is problematic and disputed. Who is to bear what level of risk, who is to benefit from risk-taking and who is to pay? Where is the line to be drawn between risks that are to be managed by the state, and those that are to be managed by individuals, groups or corporations? Where is the line to be drawn between minimizing accidents by anticipation and promoting resilience to cope with whatever failures may arise, and between attempts to influence the

causes of hazards as against measures to change their effects? What information is needed for 'rational' risk management and how should it be analysed? What actions make what difference to risk outcomes? Who evaluates success or failure in risk management and how? Who decides on what should be the desired trade-off between different risks? There is no general consensus on such questions, for reasons that have been explored in chapter 5. Yet life-or-death risk management does, and must, take place in all societies through some sort of institutional process (Douglas 1987).

Clearly, 'risk management' is a term that has no single meaning. Some adopt a rather restricted technocentric view, building on the technological hazards literature referred to earlier, and putting the emphasis on the safe operation of hazardous processes. Others take a wider view to include the effects of other adverse events. In a business context, the term means financial provision for risks. In politics, it is sometimes used to refer to the handling of issues that may affect a government's electoral fortunes, (see New Zealand State Services Commission 1991, 53–60). The 1983 Royal Society Report (149) recognized the diverse character of the subject but chose to adopt a technocentric view of risk management, stating that: 'Of particular public interest are those risks which arise from the activities of an industrial operator or manufacturer'. In this chapter, it has been decided to adopt the broader view and to attempt to present a synthesis, using the term risk management to denote regulatory measures (both in public policy and corporate practice) intended to shape who can take what risks and how.

Some have argued (National Research Council 1983) that risk *assessment* and risk *management* are overlapping, but separate, tasks. The claim is that the former is predominantly scientific and concerned with the establishment of probabilities, whereas the latter is primarily legal, political and administrative. But, as was shown in Chapter 5, this tidy distinction between 'scientific' assessment and 'political' management is contested by those who argue that it is impossible to disentangle social values and worldviews from the process of identifying, estimating and evaluating risks (Douglas 1985, Rayner & Cantor 1987, Zimmerman 1990, 9–10, Freudenberg 1992), and that, at least from a social viewpoint, it is unhelpful to conceive risk as if it were a single uniform substance, like 'phlogiston' (Watson 1981).

In public policy, 'risk management' has been commonly used to refer to an analytic technique for quantifying the estimated risks of a course of action and evaluating those risks against likely benefits. The assumption behind this approach is that a risk-free society is impossible, that all risk reduction involves costs, and that explicit valuation of benefits and costs (including the value of human life) can help to produce decisions that are consistent over different areas of public policy and that balance overall risks against overall benefits. This approach to risk analysis is well-established and influential, and it is therefore explained and discussed at some length in the appendix on costs and benefits of risk reduction at the end of the chapter. However, there are also broader institutional issues involved in the handling of risks, which are discussed in the remainder of the chapter.

6.1.3 THE AIMS AND STRUCTURE OF THE CHAPTER

The primary aim of this chapter is to provide a structured analysis of the risk-management debate. As indicated in section 6.1.1, the literature relevant to the field is large and diffuse. It spans the boundaries of many academic disciplines, meaning that the reader trying to get an overall perspective inevitably encounters much specialist terminology. According-

ly, this chapter has to be selective. Its objective is to map out some of the institutional dimensions that come into the risk-management debate and some of the contested positions within it. Some of the positions that are discussed are certainly unconventional, but to identify the poles of a debate is not to imply that each pole is of equal weight, and to identify a position is not necessarily to endorse it. What the reader should be able to gain from this chapter is a guide to the areas of debate and to the range of competing doctrines and beliefs impinging on a field which cannot be confined to scientific certainties but in which institutions do and must take life-and-death decisions in some way.

The chapter is structured as follows. First, section 6.2 addresses some of the elements of institutional design for the public management of risk. Up to now, questions of institutional design for risk management have tended to be considered only in a fairly *ad hoc* and fragmented way. This section aims to identify those institutional dimensions explicitly. Accordingly, we look at the institutional design problem from three different angles; the make-up of organizations in a risk management structure, the mix of regulatory instruments employed and the broader set of rules underlying the decision process.

Second, section 6.3 looks at seven of the major areas of contention that run through many of the diverse areas of the risk management debate. To bring them out, it uses the expository device of presenting seven differences of emphasis as opposed positions in debate. This expository device is used for convenience, but, as explained earlier, it does not imply that all positions carry equal weight, that debates are always polarized or that combinations are impossible.

Third, section 6.4 picks out six contrasting kinds of hazard, ranging from the management of human crowds to decision advice systems for global warming. The aim is to show the different ways in which the institutional and conceptual elements of hazard management come together into practical what-to-do debates on specific topics. Finally, section 6.5 offers a brief summary and attempts to identify some issues for future research in the area. The appendix outlines some economic approaches to risk management.

6.2 DIMENSIONS AND DYNAMICS OF RISK AND HAZARD MANAGEMENT

6.2.1 INSTITUTIONAL PLAYERS IN RISK AND HAZARD MANAGEMENT

Human handling of risks can be affected by a variety of institutions, both public and private. Indeed, for Douglas (1987, 4) an 'institution-free' approach to major risk management is not an option: 'individuals in crises do not make life and death decisions on their own. Who shall be saved and who shall die is settled by institutions. Putting it even more strongly, individual ratiocination cannot solve such problems. An answer is only seen to be right if it sustains the institutional thinking that is already in the minds of individuals as they try to decide.' Examples given by Douglas to support this contention (which contradicts an alternative view in institutional economics that it is individuals alone who take the 'big decisions') include the cases of nuclear medicine, behaviour in famines and the early history of kidney dialysis.

Douglas here uses the term 'institutions' to mean the social bases of shared classifications and ways of thought that underlie even apparently 'individual' decisions. At a more superficial level of analysis, of course, many types of risk appear to be handled as individual choices or as a by-product of market decisions. But even at this level of analysis, many large-scale risks involve substantial 'externalities' (cases where those who benefit from risks do not bear the full cost of their own actions). In principle, the law of delict might limit the problem (as it does to some extent) by requiring those who create risks to compensate those who suffer from them, for example by application of the 'polluter pays' principle. But such a legal framework cannot eliminate all externality problems because of the operation of well-known factors such as limited solvency, limited corporate liability, the problem of aggregating small claims and multiple-agent causation where the 'creators' of risk are hard to identify through a legal process (Brennan 1991, 31–32). Nor can it deal with any risks that are regarded as inherently 'uncompensatable'.

The social pooling of financial risks through insurance involves a system of incentives and signals that may significantly shape risk-taking behaviour by individuals and corporations (cf. Reuter, 1988: 19). For example, if insurers decide to 'red line' low-lying Pacific islands because of the postulated effects of global warming, such actions may be just as significant as any decisions that public bodies might take in shaping incentives for investment in hazard-prone areas. Similarly, the extent to which insurers find it profitable to differentiate premiums according to levels of estimated risk (for example in relation to marine accidents or building subsidence) could prove to have important impacts on risk-related behaviour.

However, the unavailability of insurance does not always have its theoretical effect of discouraging high-risk activity (see O'Riordan 1971, Arnell 1984, Handmer 1990). And insurance as a method of handling risk interacts with the broader framework of law and regulation, because the market for insurance is shaped by that framework, for example in obligation-to-insure requirements or in financial liability régimes for environmental pollution (cf. Katzman 1988). Insurance as a method of risk management is also limited in several well-known ways. Private insurance companies will not necessarily find it profitable to match insurance premiums narrowly to individual risks. Competition may prevent such companies from pooling the information needed to judge risks accurately. Solvency may limit the market and distort the signals. There is a large body of literature on the unwillingness of private insurers to offer protection against ambiguous risks such as environmental pollution (cf. Kunreuther 1989). Well-known difficulties in pricing risk properly include moral hazard and adverse selection. Moral hazard arises when incentives to take care are reduced by the fact of insurance. Adverse selection arises when risk premiums tend to be equalized in the insurance market, but insurees have more information about their risk status than the insurer, meaning that the insurer ends up with only the higher risks, as low-risk insurees defect under the pressure of rising premiums, and the basis of the insurance scheme ultimately collapses (cf. Arrow 1963, Akerlof 1970). The same problems can arise when risks are handled by quasi-insurers, for example through construction contracts (Ward, Chapman & Curtis 1991).

Risk management therefore does not stop with the activities of private individuals, corporations, associations and insurers. It has a public-management dimension too. But the point at which risks should be regarded as a public rather than an individual matter is a major area of debate in the field. And the effects of public management, as opposed to market or private handling of risks, are poorly understood. Some claim that public management through regulation and legislation is inherently vulnerable to 'rent-seeking' behaviour. 'Rent-seeking' means the capture of state regulatory or legislative power by those groups that have the motive and opportunity to organize collectively at relatively low cost, so as to transfer resources to themselves through the medium of state power at the expense of groups that do not possess a comparative advantage in low-cost organization. Institutional economists have paid particular attention to the vulnerability of regulatory bodies to capture by rent-seeking groups, particularly where the costs of regulatory action are diffused among a large group but the benefits of that regulation are concentrated into a smaller, easier to organize group (see Stigler 1988, Wilson 1980).

Public management of risks involves more than simply the rent-seeking issue. For example, the high sensitivity of public bodies to electoral pressures may make for special and volatile patterns of risk preference. When electoral considerations are paramount in public policy, for instance, harms to current voters are likely to be weighted much more strongly than harms to non-voters such as unborn generations or non-citizens. The result may be a policy bias towards discounting future harms and exporting pollution or health and safety risks to other countries.

Distinct preference patterns may also apply to the balancing of risks of 'Type I errors' against those of 'Type II errors' in public risk management. 'Type I errors' traditionally mean rejection of a true hypothesis (a term originally introduced into statistics by Neyman & Pearson (1967)) and the term is often extended more loosely to mean 'producer's risk' or sins of omission, for example the restraint or prohibition of products or practices that may in fact be harmless or beneficial. 'Type II errors' traditionally mean acceptance of a false hypothesis and the term is often extended more loosely to mean 'consumer's risk' or sins of commission, for example the release, approval or promotion of products or practices that may cause harm.

Is public risk management indifferent as between the two types of errors, and should it be? Brennan (1991, 33) claims that the two traditional types of error are generally not of equal political salience. His argument goes that 'governments will tend to be led to act too conservatively in Type I contexts and too casually in Type II contexts, and to trade Type I errors for Type II errors, even when the Type II error involves the greater expected loss'. The claim is that less rigorous standards of proof are typically required to justify action to prevent the possibility of a Type II error (in the extended sense) than those standards of proof that are typically required to justify action to prevent a Type I error. Hence the common observation of risk management decisions taken 'on the run', in which Type I errors are committed (sometimes involving very substantial cost and other negative effects) to avoid the possibility of a Type II error. Examples often cited in this context relate to drug testing and approval or to decisions to evacuate or close facilities in the face of terrorist warnings which may turn out to be hoaxes. But this key claim about public risk management remains to be systematically tested.

To the two traditional types of errors, Raiffa (1968, 264) has added what he terms 'Type III' errors, namely those errors that arise from faulty specification of the problem, leading to real solutions to what turn out to be the wrong problems rather than wrong solutions to the real problems (cf. also Ackoff 1974). Limited specification of the problem often dogs risk-management decisions, for example in the unanticipated destruction of the Lapp reindeer-meat economy and the associated social catastrophe that followed

the adoption of stringent regulations for radiation in meat following the 1986 Chernobyl disaster.

An additional feature of public risk management is that it is not done by a single unitary actor but involves many types of institutions. Within the UK, for example, a common pattern is for EC directives and regulations to be translated into national-level regulations and codes of practice negotiated by bodies like the Health and Safety Executive (HSE) and HM Inspectorate of Pollution (HMIP), with enforcement or other regulatory functions (such as licensing) undertaken by local authorities. As soon as more than one organization enters the risk management scene, different priorities and preoccupations must be resolved through bargaining. Problems of deadlock, jurisdictional tensions, ordering of preferences and varying levels of preference intensity become more acute. The policy 'packaging' processes involved in trading preferences, particularly in multi-level bargaining situations such as those involved in EC decision-making, may result in outcomes that do not match the preferences of any of the negotiating parties.

Many aspects of major risk management involve international politics (for example in the allocation of risks between wealthy and less developed countries through the dumping of wastes or distribution of polluting industry), and multiple levels of organization ranging from the international or supranational level through the national-government level to the subnational level. Institutional design debates often turn on the appropriate territorial level at which particular functions should be located. One example is the case of responsibility for the level of protection against coastal flooding and erosion, as discussed in section 6.4.1. Another is the debate over the appropriateness of EC-wide regulations or of the EC's 'mutual recognition principle' in regulation for application in different local environments (for example in the case of release of genetically modified organisms: see RCEP 1989, 89, paras 11.46–47).

On top of the territorial differentiation of institutional 'players' in risk management, functional differentiation also enters into the question of institutional design. A major dilemma of institutional design concerns whether to assign risk management to special-purpose institutions and specialized management units or to integrate it into general management and professional activity. Many public bodies involved in risk management are not part of the core executive structure, but are independent public bodies, such as independent regulatory bodies, advisory bodies or law courts, considered here in the American sense as the 'judicial branch' of government. The extent to which such bodies can operate as an independent counterweight to the core executive varies over time and from one country to another. Policy debate often turns on the extent to which regulatory bodies should be in-

sulated from core executive structures (as in the maritime and food safety debates in the UK). The presumption is that each particular type of organization has a characteristic incentive structure which may significantly affect its behaviour in risk management. But we have little systematic understanding of the way that regulatory behaviour in public risk management is related to organizational type.

Even the simple distinctions we have drawn on territorial and functional types of organizations may serve to show how far the institutional reality is from the simple equitational metaphor underlying the word management. Even with only nine basic types of 'player' (table 1), there are over 500 different ways in which these basic types could in principle be combined into an overall risk management régime. Inspection of this table suggests that it is wholly unrealistic to begin the analysis from the assumption that there is or can be any single 'Archimedean point' for managing risk. In contemporary society there is no

Table 1. Nine types of institutional player in public risk management, with examples

Territorial Level	Institutional type		
	'core executive' bodies	'independent public bodies'	'private or independent bodies'
Supranational	(1) example: EC Commission	(2) example: EC Court of Justice	(3) example: Greenpeace
National	(4) example: national Parliaments and Ministerial departments	(5) example: national courts and independent regulatory bodies like NRA	(6) example: national associations of insurers
Subnational	(7) example: state or local governments	(8) example: independent regional/local statutory bodies	(9) example: local firms & activists

single omnicompetent manager to whom scientific expertise should be directed. In the developed world today there is an established and ever-more densely institutionalized structure of many competing risk-managing organizations, each of which is in the market for scientific expertise to back up its case. The impact of such a structure on policy-making is not well understood. It seems likely that competition and other forms of interaction among multiple institutions located in the same policy domain promotes greater dynamism in the policy process than would otherwise occur. But we know little about the circumstances in which that dynamism takes the form of injecting greater rigour into policy argument, and the circumstances in which it takes the form of promoting instability, sensationalism and 'junk science'.

6.2.2 REGULATORY INSTRUMENTS

Another way to look at public risk management is to examine the array of regulatory instruments used in the process instead of the array of organizational players.

This aspect of the design problem can be framed in several ways. One is the balance between *active or corrective* measures (which are focused on modification of sources of risk, for example by hurricane seeding or slope drainage to limit landsliding) and *passive or preventative* measures (focused on the effects of risk, for example financial compensation or evacuation). Several intermediate steps can be identified between the extremes of 'active' and 'passive' management, and they are indicated in table 2, which is drawn from the natural hazard literature (see Burton *et al.* 1968). However, related issues also arise in other areas of risk management. Examples include the issue of whether to modify a drug that causes benefit to many but harm to a few, or whether to try to identify the high-risk individuals more carefully; whether to aim to influence human

Table 2. Regulatory approaches

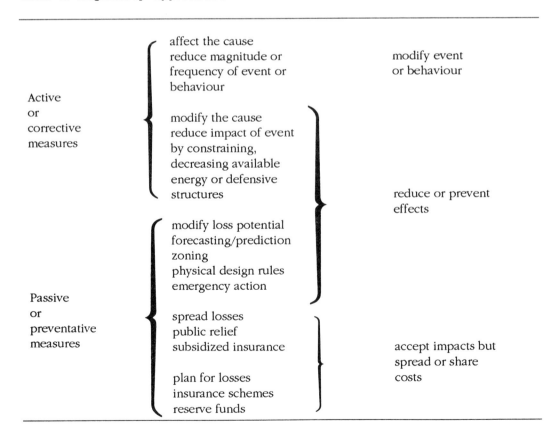

Active or corrective measures	affect the cause reduce magnitude or frequency of event or behaviour	modify event or behaviour
	modify the cause reduce impact of event by constraining, decreasing available energy or defensive structures	reduce or prevent effects
Passive or preventative measures	modify loss potential forecasting/prediction zoning physical design rules emergency action	
	spread losses public relief subsidized insurance	accept impacts but spread or share costs
	plan for losses insurance schemes reserve funds	

driving behaviour directly or whether to adopt measures designed to change the effects of that behaviour, for example by 'crumple zones' and compulsory insurance rules.

Another way in which the regulatory design problem can be framed is in terms of the basic resources available. Public authorities have four basic approaches available to them for risk management. They can operate through the medium of *information*, through deploying *resources* in some form, through laying down *laws or regulations* using the public power of the state, or they can take *direct action* through the state's own organizations such as police forces and armed forces.

In general, public management reform in OECD countries since the early 1980s has moved away from 'direct action' operations by the state, and towards arms-length regulation. The downfall of the Communist régimes in Eastern Europe and the former USSR appears set to produce a much more dramatic shift in the same direction. But direct action capacity is likely always to remain important for handling some crucial types of risk (for example those coming from crime and terrorism), and to figure large in emergency response operations. Indeed, hands-on public authority control has often been invoked for handling particular high-risk activities, from the days when the Venetian republic operated its own rope factory to limit the risks of shipwreck through use of poor-quality ropes, to the current exclusion of nuclear power plants from electricity utility privatization in the UK and debates about the use of private contractors (on a least-cost tender system) for safety-critical functions.

The provision and exchange of information is often of prime importance in risk management. Prediction and forecasting, for example, play a large part in the management of risk (see Smith 1992). But contestable issues arise in the interpretation of data for many kinds of hazard. Incorrect warnings or failure to issue warnings are costly, not only in money and disruption but also in the erosion of faith in future warnings through the 'cry wolf' effect. For example, the erroneous forecast of an eruption of the Soufrière volcano, Guadeloupe, in 1976, led to the evacuation of 72 000 people for several months; the erroneous 1980 forecast that Peru and Northern Chile would suffer their worst earthquake this century within in nine months, resulted in adjustments and loss of tourist revenue estimated at $50 million (Echeverria *et al.* 1986); and the failure of the Chinese to forecast the Tangshan earthquake of 1976 (*ca.* 242 000 dead) severely diminished the high status of earthquake prediction achieved in China following the successful evacuation of Haicheng and Yingkow in Liaoning province in 1975. 'Phased' warnings (as in the case of the UK Meteorological Office's Storm Tide Warning system) can in some cases avoid gross errors of this kind, but not all hazards lend themselves to a phased approach to warning.

Obviously, predictions and forecasts only have relevance if they can be communicated to those who are in a position to take action to avoid or mitigate the risk. Some of the social complexities that arise in the operation of warning systems are indicated in figure 1 (taken from Foster 1979, 172). Warning systems often evoke limited response from their target (see Penning-Rowsell *et al.* 1978), and perplexing issues arise of when to warn, who to warn and how to warn, which are independent of the sophistication of the hardware used to detect and analyse the technical data. The discussion of 'risk communication' in Chapter 5 suggests some of the difficulties of an 'information-centric' approach to risk management. Some of the specific problems in relation to crowd management and natural-hazard management are discussed in sections 6.4.1 and 6.4.4. Significant social barriers to effective pooling of information include the following.

> The existence of *fraud* or *malice*; for example in computer viruses;

> *Distrust*: for example, minimal information given by corporations to public regulators (Smith 1991); or fear of crowd 'panic' leading to delays in warning which in fact aggravate the flight and crushing that they are intended to prevent (see section 6.4.4);

> *Commercial confidentiality* and anti-trust considerations (as in the case of data held by competing insurance companies);

> *Rivalry* within the public sector (particularly with the trend towards corporatization of the public sector into a series of separate, competing and independently managed units operating use-pay principles for information);

> The potential effects of *legal liability*, for example in circumstances where false or inadequate forecasts or warnings are given. In spite of technological advance in areas such as weather forecasting or earthquake predictions, legal liability factors are most unlikely to diminish in importance and may well become more severe in the future under the pressures of juridification and growing litigiousness.

> Processes associated with *translation* and *interpretation*, particularly where 'expert' data and analysis is consumed by 'lay people', and barriers and amplifiers come into play. For example, the perceived threats posed by stratospheric ozone depletion due to a range of chemical pollutants (notably CFCs and halons), first raised in the early 1970s (Molina & Rowland 1974) led to unusually rapid international policy responses (notably the 1985 Vienna Convention for the Protection of the Ozone Layer, the 1987 Montreal Protocol and its 1990 amendment). Part of the rapidity of the response may

be explained by the dramatic way that the ozone threat was portrayed in public debate. The relabelling of the diffuse ozone layer as a 'shield' and the seasonal thinning as a 'hole' (Gribbin 1988), suggested a sudden emergency (Roan 1989), combining high levels of dread, uncertainty and surprise. The dramatic colour satellite imagery produced in 1987 by the Total Ozone Mapping Spectrometer (TOMS) carried on Nimbus 7 added enormous force to the message of impending global catastrophe conveyed by the media. Yet few scientists envisage more than a 20 % reduction in stratospheric ozone (see Benedick 1991, 13).

A third basic instrument for public risk management is the allocation of fungible resources. Many have claimed that safety levels are related to public spending and investment, notably in relation to transport, public utilities and investment in public infrastructure, and that resource pressures may contribute to vulnerability to major accidents (cf. Horlick-Jones 1990, Handmer 1992, 119). Such issues received much attention in the UK in the 1980s. For example, the Hidden Report which followed the 1988 Clapham train crash warned of the need to avoid compromising safety by delaying investment in safety-related projects. The problems of matching costs and benefits in project resource allocation are discussed in the appendix.

However, even apart from the cost–benefit problem, it is often difficult to show clear links between resources committed and risk outcomes, as a result of the operation of factors such as 'the law of anticipated reactions' and 'risk compensation' in human behaviour. Risk compensation is the idea that human beings (at least in some settings) adjust their behaviour in response to the inherent safety of their environment (see Adams 1985, 128–132). The implication is that the full risk-reduction potential of measures intended to promote safety will not be achieved if there are strong inter-

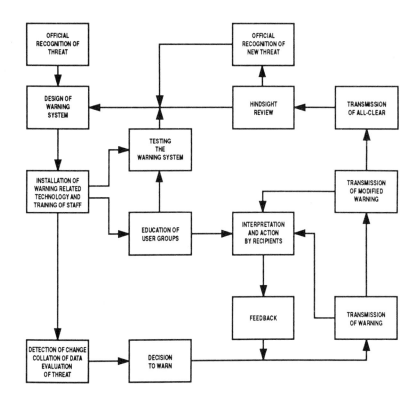

Figure 1. Components of an idealized warning system. (Source: Foster 1979, 172.)

active effects between human behaviour and outcomes, but that some or all of the expected safety gain will be traded for gains in performance or other values. For example, improved vehicle brakes might have the effect of making truck drivers drive faster down hills, consuming increased braking capacity as extra performance rather than extra safety; coastal hazard protection measures might have the effect of increasing investment and settlement in vulnerable areas. At the extreme is the hypothesis that each individual sets a target level of risk, so that safety measures that do not directly change human motivation will result in changes in behaviour which re-establish the original level of risk. The extent and nature of this kind of risk homeostasis has been much debated, particularly in the area of risk management in road safety, and is a crucial variable for risk management (Adams 1985, 1988, Adams & Thompson 1991, Asch *et al.* 1991, Evans & Graham 1991, Janssen & Ten-

kink 1988, Reinhardtrutland 1991, Wilde 1976, 1982, 1988).

It is difficult to make a clear assessment of all risk-related public spending, because of the way that government budget papers are laid out; and indeed all spending can be related to risk in some way. More narrowly, direct public spending on workplace safety and environmental regulation typically is small compared with defence, welfare and education, amounting to much less than 1 % of national government public spending. Some indicative data for the USA, drawn from Zimmerman (1990, 203–204) are presented in figure 2. They show that overall federal spending levels on pollution control and consumer and occupational health and safety rose sharply in real terms in the early 1970s and fell in the 1980s cutback era. For the UK, direct public spending on health and safety regulation amounts to about 0.1 % of total central government spending, and this proportion has remained fairly stable over 1978–9 to 1991–2 according to Supply Estimates.

Compared with the relatively small direct public spending on health, safety and environmental programmes, regulation is perhaps the most visible aspect of public risk management, and one that affects much larger resource commitments through the costs of regulatory compliance. Powers of command, permission, prohibition and penalty are exercised in the UK in the forms of EC directives and regulations, primary and subordinate legislation at national-government level and the regulatory decisions of local and other public

authorities. Some indicative figures on the incidence of UK and EC legislative activity in the area of environmental and health and safety regulation, are given in figures 3 and 4.

In the admittedly somewhat crude terms of the number of items of legislation, health and safety and environmental matters account for a much larger (and apparently growing) proportion of total legislation than the equivalent spend figures discussed above. But regulation also confronts the risk compensation problem. And against a background of globalized market competition, regulations (such as carbon taxes) that impose heavy costs of compliance may be unac-

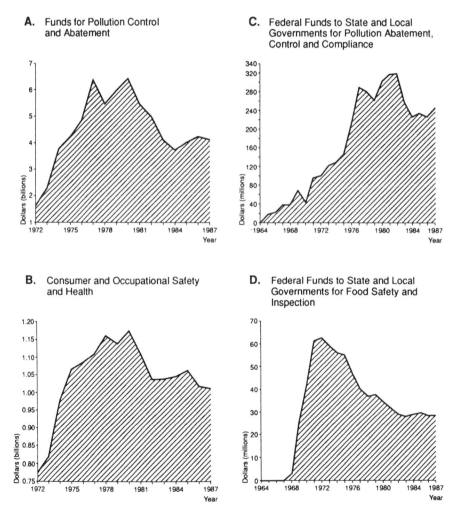

Figure 2. US Federal budget outlays (in constant 1982 dollars) for selected risk management functions. (Source: Zimmerman 1990, 203–204.)

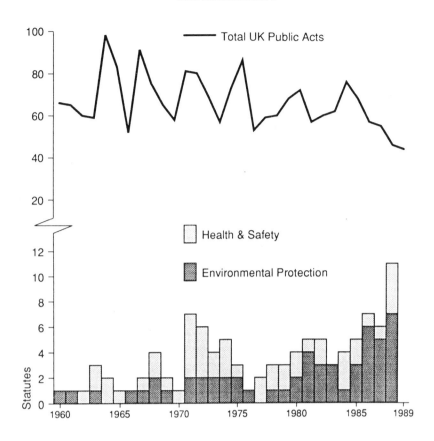

Figure 3. UK Public Acts and Statutes for England and Wales concerning health, safety and environmental protection 1960–88. (Source: UK Public General Acts; European Environmental Yearbook 1991; Fife and Machin 1990.)

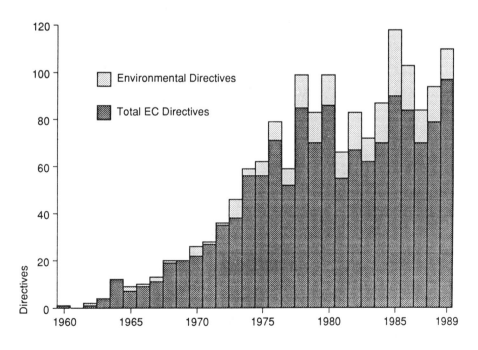

Figure 4. Total EC directives and environmental directives 1960–1989. (Source: European Communities Legislation Current Status 1990 and European Environmental Yearbook 1991.)

ceptable, provoking widespread evasion, patchy compliance, policy backlash or other forms of behavioural change that may limit the achievement of regulatory objectives. For example, it has been suggested that the imposition of strict regulatory controls on the release of genetically modified organisms (GMOs) may increase the tendency to select and develop naturally occurring micro-organisms for application in new environments, with the potential for a threat to the environment as great as those posed by some GMOs (RCEP 1989, para 5.49). Moreover, in some areas of risk management (particularly for highly politicized slow-onset hazards like global warming), there is no clearly demonstrated body of causal knowledge upon which a widely agreed regulatory régime can be based.

The appropriate use of regulatory instruments raises institutional design issues that are just as fundamental for public risk management as those about organizational structuring. Regulation – which imposes 'compliance costs' on the regulatees in one form or another – has commonly been substituted for public spending and direct action, as in the disengagement of UK government from direct operation of anthrax disinfection plants to process imported materials in the 1970s, and the more general process of utility privatization in the UK in the 1980s. In particular, the privatization of water utilities had the effect of moving out of the public sector some of the costs of management of the (non-marine) aquatic environment (Lomas 1990), costs which are certain to increase because of EC requirements. Of the £5.8 billion estimated environmental expenditure in the UK during 1990, 62 % (£3.6 billion) came in the form of costs to industry of compliance with legislation (*European Environmental Yearbook 1991*).

6.2.3 THE 'RULES OF THE GAME' IN PUBLIC RISK MANAGEMENT: SIX DIMENSIONS

Other features of risk management régimes can be seen if, instead of concentrating on the organizational components of risk-management systems as in section 6.2.1, we look at their structure in terms of the complex of underlying rules by which they operate. This analysis uses a six-dimensional model from a framework originally developed by Ostrom (1986, 468–470). Ostrom does not claim that the six dimensions are mutually exclusive, but she does claim that when they are considered together they encapsulate the essential 'rules of the game' involved in institutionalized decision processes, involving 'working rules' as well as formal rules. The six types of institutional rule are summarized briefly, if somewhat abstractly, in table 3, which also contains a tentative assessment of the overall direction of change in risk and hazard management on the six dimensions. Each dimension is then briefly discussed.

BOUNDARY RULES

Boundary rules are those rules that define who has access to the risk management process and who can count as a 'player', for example in legal rules of *locus standi*. Institutionalized risk management systems often involve restrictive boundary rules, effectively confining the debate to a small circle of officially approved experts charged with arriving at some optimum risk level for the public at large (as for instance with drug approval or food safety standards). The decision process in some regulatory institutions is in practice only accessible through high-cost lobbying activity or through approved expert groups. In general, the more one goes from local level through national to supranational institutions the more restricted public access to the process is likely to be.

The 'boundaries' of risk management systems are sometimes ambiguous and frequently disputed. As was noted in

Chapter 5, and will be discussed further in section 6.3.2, there are many who would like to open up public debate about risk management beyond the bounds of a narrow group of 'experts', whereas others see in such a proposal the seeds of an indiscriminate over-extension, and deem such a move likely to lead to ill-judged decisions based on populist prejudices. In many areas, new players have actually come on to the scene. For example in the UK environmental lobbying groups and groups such as Disaster Action have had an increasing presence, and influential pressure groups were formed in the wake of a number of public transport disasters to which we refer in section 6.4.2. The growth of such interest groups may be a significant development because, having an element of middle-class, educated and articulate people who have learned a lot about accidents, they are well-placed to challenge the boundaries of the established risk-management system, and to some extent have done so (for example in pressing for the development of legal systems of blame to focus on the responsibility of corporations rather than of individual operators for disasters). On the other hand, the shifting of the location of some key risk-management decision making from national governmental to EC level tends to increase remoteness and thereby place restrictions on general access to the decision-making process, thus representing a move in the opposite direction.

SCOPE RULES

Scope rules govern what comes within the province of risk management and the limits of what 'risk managing' institutions may decide. For instance, as is shown in

Table 3. Dimensions of risk management (after Ostrom 1986) and putative trends

#	Rule type	Explication	Range of keys types	Characteristic trends
(1)	boundary	who is counted as a player?	technocratic/ participative	more participation
(2)	scope	what is managed and what can be decided?	broad/narrow	extension of scope
(3)	position	what is the hierarchy of players?	single organization/ multi-organization	more multi-organizations
(4)	information	who is entitled to know what from whom?	open/closed	more open
(5)	authority and procedure	under what conditions must decisions be made?	formal/informal	more formal
(6)	preference merging	how are individual preferences aggregated into collective decisions?	consensus (integration)/ conflict (aggregation)	more conflict

section 6.4.2, the ability of post-disaster inquiries to attribute blame as opposed to establishing facts, and the ways in which blame can be attributed through the legal system, has occasioned much discussion in the English law over the past decade. Frequently, too, the scope rules surrounding regulatory institutions are in debate. Hazards and disasters that span more than one national jurisdiction (such as the 1984 Bhopal accident and the Lockerbie air crash of 1988) often throw up major scope-rule issues, because they involve international relations and interpretations of the powers of international bodies.

Over the past decade, there have been tendencies to widen the scope of what counts as risk management well beyond that considered in the 1983 Royal Society report, partly because, as was noted in Chapter 5, significant social pressures have developed to redefine risk as danger or threat rather than as mathematical probability (Douglas 1990, 7). Certainly there has been some tendency towards wider scope of regulatory responsibility in institutional terms, and towards merging of risk management with other dimensions of management. Examples include the UK's adoption in the late 1980s of the goal of 'integrated pollution control', the creation of HMIP within the Department of the Environment (DOE) in 1987 to pursue that goal, and its statutory underpinning by the 1990 Environmental Protection Act. This shift towards an attempt at greater integration parallels the equivalent move in health and safety regulation in the 1970s, when the HSE was created as an intendedly all-purpose body for the regulation of workplace hazards. But the shift towards integration is far from complete. For example, the National Rivers Authority (NRA), created in 1989 along with water utility privatization, is currently another regulatory player in pollution control, with an ill-defined interface with HMIP in sewage-treatment works, and even the HSE's

remit does not extend to 'workplaces' in ships at sea or aircraft in flight.

Of course, there is no truly all-purpose public authority for risk management in any developed country (and, given that risk is not a uniform substance but a set of distinct management problems that require detailed and systematic analysis, such an authority could exist only on paper). Public regulators are often tightly constrained by finances and legal limitations of their powers and, typically, the institutional landscape of risk management is a highly fragmented one. The legislative process tends to identify risks piecemeal and to deal with each one separately. For instance, emerging risks (such as those associated with safety-critical software or GMOs) often do not fit readily into existing institutional frameworks because of scope restrictions. And institutional systems often tend to draw a fairly rigid distinction between decision advice procedures for artificial and natural hazards, even though, as noted in section 6.1.1, it may plausibly be argued that the traditional distinction nowadays obscures as much as it illuminates in terms of the underlying management issues. Similarly, management of slow-onset international-impact hazards such as AIDS or global climatic change (Couch & Kroll-Smith 1988) will necessarily tend to be distinguished from management of rapid-onset local-impact hazards such as explosions, collisions or tornados (Turner 1978).

POSITION RULES
Position rules identify the decision points in the risk-management process (for example, who decides whether to bring forward public prosecutions and on what charges); how those decision points are arrayed in terms of hierarchy or precedence (for example, in the decisions of one court against another or between local authorities and central governments); and how individuals are appointed to or dismissed from those positions. For example, many regulatory

bodies in the UK are statutorily distanced from the core executive and their directors are directly accountable to parliament, with limitations on the ability of ministers to dismiss them.

The increasing involvement of the EC in risk management has been a notable recent influence on this dimension, affecting the position rules applying in its member states. For example, the 1989 Framework Directive (89/391/EEC) contains a general 'substitution principle', that the employer has an overall duty to replace the dangerous by the non-dangerous or less dangerous and that the improvement of workplace health and safety 'should not be subordinated to purely economic considerations' (see Neilsen & Szyszczak 1991, Haigh & Baldock 1989).

One important milestone in the changing role of the EC in risk management was the Seveso Directive (82/501/EEC, amended by 87/216/EEC and 88/610/EEC; see also Baram 1988). The Directive requires that premises storing or using more than certain specified quantities of particularly hazardous substances be designated as 'major hazard sites'. It further requires that the operators of such sites prepare emergency plans, and communicate the potential dangers and appropriate responses in an emergency to the nearby public likely to be affected by an accident. The EC's Major Accident Reporting System (MARS) collates reports on accidents occurring at such sites on an EC-wide basis (Drogaris 1991).

INFORMATION RULES

Information rules specify who is entitled to what information from whom and under what conditions, for example in rules of confidentiality and secrecy, in requirements to inform the public, employees, insurance companies or public authorities of potential hazards, incidents or accidents such as radioactive releases. Some of these rules are embodied in confidentiality provisions for commercial and public bodies, in labelling rules, or regulations regarding the provision of safety signs. Other requirements may cover applications for official permission to undertake risky activities, as in the case of the registration procedures under the UK Control of Industrial Air Pollution (Registration of Works) Regulations 1989. There may be formal requirements to express information in quantitative or monetary terms, as is the case with the 'compliance cost' assessment of proposed new legislation in the UK since the 1980s, currently undertaken by the DTI Deregulation Unit.

Another key element of information rules in risk management is the extent to which the public is entitled to have access to documents or meetings. The effects of secrecy in risk management are not well understood. For obvious reasons, increasing demands for 'freedom of information' have been particularly strong in the area of risk and hazard; influential practitioners have pointed to the possible positive consequences of freer access to information in raising the level of informed debate; and in some areas more openness has been introduced into the regulatory process. For example, recent EC legislation embodies moves towards freer access to environmental information, and under the UK's Environmental Protection Act (EPA) 1990, all operators of large plants must apply for licences and submit details of polluting activities to HMIP. But the EPA also contains a clause continuing the long-established practice of allowing some details to be kept secret if their disclosure would harm competitiveness, and some companies have attempted to use this clause as reason for not publishing their emissions. Terrorist threats are also often cited as a reason for limiting release of information, and may explain why bodies like the Channel Tunnel Safety Authority are statutorily prohibited from releasing information. Even in the USA, where the public availability of information has been considerably extended in the past decade, the legislation which enshrines 'right to know' (SARA Title III) contains significant exceptions.

AUTHORITY AND PROCEDURAL RULES

Authority and procedure rules define the ways in which decisions must be made, in specifying the order or timing of decisions, and what counts as 'evidence'. Thus in terms of risk management, authority and procedure rules may determine where the emphasis is laid in policy making between quantification and calculation on the one hand, and the weighing of qualitative arguments on the other. Such rules may also determine whether decision advice procedures are to be adversarial, with rival points of view to be advanced before passive hearers along the lines of a criminal trial, or inquisitorial, with a directing intelligence. Authority and procedure rules may also determine whether decision advice procedures are formal, (with elaborate constraints on what information may be admitted and in what form), or informal (with fewer constraints on admissible information). As risk-management procedures become more 'juridified', increasing formality in the process is to be expected.

Another area governed by authority and procedure rules concerns the phasing of inquiry or deliberation: the question of where risk-management systems should be focused to achieve the most effective solutions is a matter of considerable debate (cf. Tait & Levidov 1992). In many areas of risk management, such as environmental assessment, heavy institutional emphasis has been laid on *ex ante* controls, with an elaborate anticipatory process designed to predict and evaluate potential sources of risk. In others, the emphasis shifts towards *ex post* inquiry, on the assumption that effective risk management involves a learning process derived from forensic examinations of past accidents. This debate is further explored in section 6.3.

PREFERENCE-MERGING RULES

Preference-merging rules define the ways in which the individual preferences of each player or stakeholder concerned in the management of a particular risk are to come together into a collective decision. For example, unanimity rules are sometimes used to introduce a bias towards caution in high-risk decisions (for an example, see RCEP 1989, 60, para 8.14). Indeed, many aspects of risk management have traditionally involved preference merging by a process of consensus built on consultation within a small group of experts. As the process of risk management has become more politicized, juridified and institutionally complex over the past decade or so, and more 'players' have attempted to enter the fray, this traditional model of élite consensus has become harder to sustain.

For a different reason, unanimity rules have traditionally governed decision making in the EC Council of Ministers. But although many EC decisions still require a unanimous vote, qualified majority voting has been adopted for some issues, including health and safety directives and some environmental issues. Such a preference-merging rule can be wide ranging in its implications for risk management in member states, because its bargaining effect is to substitute minimum winning coalition strategies among member states for the generalized log-rolling that the unanimity rule engenders (that is, the adoption of insincere preferences by one member in exchange for the adoption of insincere preferences by another). The use of majority voting for decisions over the harmonization of standards where there are different requirements in member states (for example in emissions or waste disposal) may result in standards more stringent than those currently existing in – or deemed necessary by – many member states (Haigh 1989, Haigh & Baldock 1989), and less attuned to specific local environments.

More generally, preference-merging procedures can be distinguished according to whether they have the 'integrative' effect of pulling a community together and strengthening social cohesion by arriving at the broadest possible consensus, or whether they have the 'aggregative' effect of dividing a community by procedures that give the decision to one party at the expense of others (see March & Olsen 1989, 189 ff). Preference merging will necessarily be less problematic when only one 'worldview' is involved. But when many and conflicting ideas about blame, causation, responsibility and levels of harm and loss are involved, preference merging will raise more difficulties. The developments such as increased judicial interventions and a move towards majority voting and cross-policy log-rolling in the EC may signal a shift in preference-merging procedures towards the aggregative rather than integrative approach.

6.2.4 THE DYNAMICS OF RISK AND HAZARD MANAGEMENT

The institutional components of risk management outlined in the past three sections provide a way of arraying possible or actual types of risk-management structures. In principle, the problem of institutional design for risk management can be stated in rational terms as the choice of settings for: the combination of organizational types (section 6.2.1), the combination of regulatory instruments (section 6.2.2), and, the combination of institutional rules (section 6.2.3) to produce outcomes of the least-cost mix of Type 1, Type II and Type III errors when traded off against other social values.

It is not a problem that has received much rational attention. One possible reason for the lack of attention is that the notion of *institutional* design (as opposed to the design of safe products or structures) has only recently begun seriously to penetrate discussion of risk management. Another reason, which need not be laboured here, is that the risk

management debate has become heavily politicized around different cosmologies or worldviews of the types described and discussed in Chapter 5.

However, some broad trends can be hypothesized. In terms of organizational types (6.2.1), the trend seems to be in the direction of more complex, multi-level and multi-organizational structures occupying most or all of the categories in table 1, so collective action and preference-merging processes become harder to predict and less controllable by any one set of actors. In terms of regulatory instruments (6.2.2), the emphasis seems to be laid heavily on public authority and the structuring of information, rather than on major growth in public spending or 'direct action' public organization, so that issues of balancing risk and benefit in compliance costs become increasingly salient. In terms of institutional rules (6.2.3), table 3 gives an estimation of general trends in public risk management.

Since publication of the 1983 Royal Society report, the UK risk management world could be argued to have changed significantly in many, if not all of the dimensions characterized by the six types of rule. The boundary-rule structure faces pressures for more participatory styles of dealing with risk and hazard in preference to *ex cathedra* pronouncements from a small, remote group of experts. For the same reasons, the scope-rule structure faces pressures for a broadening definition of what is to be covered by 'risk management', its interrelation with other forms of management, and of where blame may be apportioned through the legal and official inquiry process. The position-rule structure has changed dramatically in the direction of increasing participation and authority by the EC rather than national government acting alone. The information-rule structure faces pressures for increased general access and for increasing 'obligation to notify' requirements on hazard-monitoring and hazard-creating organizations. The authority and procedure rule structure faces pressures for increasing procedural formality, as the risk management field has become further juridified as a result of the flow of EC directives, and the increasing involvement of the law courts in the risk management process. And the preference-merging-rule structure seems to be moving away from a traditional 'integrative', consensus-seeking emphasis (albeit within small communities of trusted experts) towards the adoption of processes in which one side 'wins' at the expense of another or others.

This tentative assessment of the direction of institutional change should be qualified in at least three ways. First, the picture varies from one specific field to another, as is illustrated in section 6.4. Second, to identify trends as having oc-

curred is not necessarily to say that they are universally desirable or will make for risk management that is 'better' in some general sense. Third, the claim that such shifts appear to have taken place in the recent past does not necessarily mean that they will continue in the future. Reversal is entirely possible, as in other areas of public policy. Against that, however, the pattern of change identified above does not seem to be a random set of movements. Juridification, demands extra access to information and decision making, and a shift away from consensual modes of decision making may well be linked processes related to larger cultural shifts. At the very least, therefore, the continuation of such trends is a strong possibility, and has to be taken into account in any informed discussion of the institutional context of risk management.

6.3 SELECTED DIMENSIONS OF THE RISK MANAGEMENT DEBATE

6.3.1 A CONTESTED AREA

This section examines risk management from a different perspective, discussing some of the competing positions taken up by practitioners, academics and other participants in debates about the principles that should govern the identification, measurement and regulation of risk.

From what was said about the social factors in risk perception in Chapter 5, it should be no surprise to find that current debates about risk management reflect competing worldviews. For those engaged with practical risk management or those involved in policy development in the area, it may be difficult to understand the significance of the disputes about different options in risk management, especially because these views are often expressed forcefully and emotively. It may be helpful to try to identify elements

that keep cropping up in these debates, and for this reason we set out here seven recurrent sets of opposing views about how risk management should be handled. For the sake of clarity, we present each of the seven issues here as a choice between two options.

But four important caveats need to be entered at the outset about this expository device. First, splitting the discussion into opposing pairs in this way helps to present the ideas involved, but it is not meant to suggest that all the pairs are evenly balanced, or that each of two opposing views should be given equal weight. There are orthodoxies and heresies, and typically one side of the debate carries more weight than the other. Second, the opposing views are not necessarily irreconcilable in every case. Risk management practitioners often 'mix and match' or adopt compromise positions. Third, some of the seven areas of debate are interlinked, and they do not, of course, exhaust the field of disputed issues. Fourth, labelling the rival doctrines has required taking some liberties with ordinary language. But a degree of neologism is unavoidable, as elegant ready-made terms are not available, and typically, the debates in each area of risk management are usually conducted in a vocabulary which is specific to that area. A summary of the debates is presented in table 4.

6.3.2 SEVEN AREAS OF DEBATE

ANTICIPATION IN RISK MANAGEMENT
Risk management in practice typically involves some mixture of anticipation and resilience, and one key element of the risk-management debate turns on where the emphasis is to be laid at the margin. In this context, 'anticipationists' argue for extra weight to be given to measures designed to detect in advance the clues that signal potential threat in physical or organizational structures. Such an approach means laying more emphasis on methods of *ex ante* detection and prevention, and on regular 'health checks' (audits) of potentially dangerous organizations or locations.

The case for adopting a more anticipationist or proactive approach is made in different ways. Some argue that high complexity and uncertainty require an extension of precautionary 'just in case' regulation, particularly in the field of pollution control. For example, Tait & Levidov (1992) note: 'The Versorgensprinzip, or precautionary principle, originally enunciated by the West German Government in 1976, has gradually become a focus for creative thinking on these subjects throughout the EEC and more widely. The precautionary principle is proactive in that it advocates the implementation of controls of pollution without waiting for scientific evidence of damage caused by the pollutant(s) con-

cerned, and without necessarily requiring consideration of the relative costs and benefits of regulation to industry or the public.'

Clearly, there are difficult issues as to exactly how far the 'precautionary principle' ought to be taken, and how far public policy should run ahead of clear scientific findings. For example, the maximum acceptable level of 50 mg l^{-1} nitrate in drinking water in the 1980 EC directive on the subject (80/778/EEC) and the subsequent draft directive to control nitrates entering water likely to suffer eutrophication (Draft Directive on Nitrates in Ground and Surface Water) is built on concerns about the causal link between nitrate, stomach cancers and infantile methaemoglobinaemia ('blue baby' syndrome). This precautionary measure involves substantial compliance costs and the target will take some time to achieve in the UK (see Royal Society 1983), yet a link between nitrate and cancer has not been confirmed by recent epidemiological research (Wheeler 1987) and no evidence has been produced to suggest that 'blue baby' syndrome is caused by bacteriologically sound water supplies containing less than 100 mg l^{-1} NO_3.

A very different argument for a more 'anticipationist' stance goes that in hindsight disasters can often be interpreted as 'waiting to happen' and may even be linked to particular types of organizational culture and structure. Those who adopt this view point to research on systems failure, done in several countries, showing that major incidents are typically produced by a concatenation of smaller slips, errors and malpractices, which themselves could have been reduced if not eliminated by improved everyday work practices, better training, better 'safety culture' and more frequent and more adequate safety audits (cf. Baldissera 1987, Pidgeon 1988, Turner 1978, 1989, 1991, Turner, *et al.* 1989, HSE 1990). Failure to learn effectively from previous errors is often claimed to be at the heart of many disasters (see Handmer 1992, 117). Horlick-Jones, Fortune & Peters (1991) interpret the 'system' concept more broadly, examining organizations within their environment, which includes such factors as resource allocation, task overload and regulation. It is the complex interaction of organizations and their environment that creates vulnerability. This second strain of anticipationism bases its claim on developments of knowledge about the chains of causation leading up to both rapid-onset and slow-onset disasters. Specifically, the argument is that particular patterns of organization, such as regulatory conflicts of interest, secrecy and lack of broad participation, tend to be regularly associated with major failures; and that research designed to identify such associations can be fed back into risk-management practice through an extended process of 'hazard audits' (Toft 1990). The same general arguments can be found in debates about the management of geophysical hazards (earthquakes, hurricanes, floods), where there is a strong body of opinion that various types of anticipatory planning are essential to risk reduction (Foster 1979, Wijkman & Timberlake 1984).

Against this position, institutional analysts like Wildavsky (1985, 1988) argue that disasters and system failures often look 'predictable' only in hindsight, and that many such cases involve high-dimensional dynamic systems whose behaviour is inherently impossible to forecast, because of the complexity and stochastic character of the systems. The implication is that, at the margin, risk-management régimes should be designed to promote resilience against unexpected catastrophes rather than to rely on being able to spot them coming in time to take action to prevent their occurrence or lessen their impact. From this viewpoint, it can even be claimed that attempting to place the emphasis on anticipating risks may itself contribute to the crises it seeks to

avoid, by a 'Titanic effect' (or the related 'levée syndrome' in natural hazard management) which reduces the capacity to respond to the unexpected and increases the surprise when the 'inevitable' disasters actually happen. For resilienists, the emphasis of a risk-management régime at the margin should be laid more on promoting the capacity to cope with the unexpected, for example by relief, emergency action, rescue and insurance (see Cuny 1983).

The anticipation–resilience debate in risk management, we stress, is typically about what should be done at the margin, not about absolutes. Few serious contributors to the debate would put all the emphasis on one approach rather than the other, and it is a normal principle of sound design to incorporate both the lessons of previous failures and forethought about likely future ones. Practitioners use devices of piloting and monitoring (for example in post-occupancy evaluation of building use, discussed in section 6.4.4) as means of bridging anticipationism and resilience. Moreover, the anticipation–resilience issue has many possible shades and variants. For example, growing design complexity leads to debates about the extent to which the behaviour of safety-critical software can be reliably predicted in advance (as we will illustrate in section 6.4.3), and also to discussion of whether in some cases it is advisable to limit design complexity. Essentially, the issue comes down to a discussion of the extent to which system failures (particularly those involving human organization) are low- or high-dimensional dynamic systems, or more precisely what kinds of failure involve the one and what involve the other. It remains to be seen whether the issue can be clarified by more systematic investigation, or whether it must remain a 'trans-scientific' issue: that is, a problem which in principle is investigable by the orthodox methods of science but in practice cannot be so investigated because of limits on time, resources or morally sanctioned behaviour (Weinberg 1972).

LIABILITY AND BLAME

A second key area of debate on risk management turns on the extent to which risk-management régimes at the margin should be more or less 'blame oriented'. Those who favour a high-blame approach argue that effective risk management depends on the design of incentive structures that place strict financial and legal liability for risk on to those who are in the best position to take action to minimize risk. This principle has a long history in law and economics, particularly in discussion of the famous 'Hand formula' in American law and its analogues (see Posner 1986, 147–151). The claim is that if liability is not precisely targeted on specific and appropriate decision makers, a socially inefficient system will allow avoidable failures to occur. There is then too little incentive to take care on the part of the key decision makers in organizations that are capable of creating hazards, and (the argument goes) 'risk externalization' will be encouraged. The policy implication is to support expanded corporate legal liability, more precisely targeted insurance premium practices, regulatory policies that have the effect of 'criminalizing' particular management practices and of laying sanctions on key decision makers within corporations (cf. Fisse & Braithwaite 1988).

The 'blame' argument manifests itself in several ways. Some large business corporations build into their corporate safety policies a strategy of dismissal of individual employees found to be responsible for safety violations. Some argue that avoidable accidents and failures may result from insufficiently individualized insurance (as in the case where government acts as its own insurer), so that financial penalties for negligence are either non-existent or not discriminatory enough (cf. Perrow 1984). Others think that social efficiency in limiting risk externalization requires the ability to target

legal blame on the designers and managers of a *system*, rather than on operators of its component parts, because blaming the operator will not necessarily create the appropriate incentives on designers and managers in relation to inherent system safety and system tolerance to minor human errors.

As we will see in section 6.4.3, this issue is becoming increasingly salient in the field of safety-critical software. And in recent years, a spate of transport accidents affecting UK citizens has led some jurists and other contributors to the debate to argue for changes in the legal system, making it easier to bring corporate manslaughter charges against those who are responsible for designing and directing organizational systems that are judged inherently unsafe, instead of focusing blame narrowly on an individual – for example a driver or a pilot – who is not responsible for the broader corporate policies that create the setting for major system failures (cf. Field & Jorg 1991, Wells 1988, 1991, 1992*a*). The sinking of the car ferry *Herald of Free Enterprise* at Zeebrugge in 1987 led to a corporate manslaughter suit against P&O Ferries being brought to court in 1990, partly as a result of pressure-group activity. Though that particular case collapsed, it may well be that further corporate-manslaughter suits may emerge in the future, and such developments may significantly affect the incentive structure of senior corporate executives in relation to risk management.

Against the strict liability approach, proponents of the opposing no-blame view are sceptical of the argument that a move towards more general 'criminalization' of management or system-design activity rather than penalizing specific errors by operatives will make for more effective risk management, and hold that it may be ineffective or even counter-productive. Such critics can point to other areas of policy where criminalization leads to the adoption of artificial legal devices to limit liability rather than to real changes in behaviour; promotes tendencies to 'go by the book' rather than to flexible approaches to adopt the most appropriate behaviour in the circumstances (see Bardach & Kagan 1982); results in the export of risky activities to jurisdictions without criminalization policies rather than overall reductions in risk; or may remove the motivation to undertake particular activities at all.

More positively, those of this persuasion believe that effective risk management means on balance a move away from mechanisms for pinning down blame after accidents. Some major corporations (such as Shell International, which aims for a 'no-blame culture' (Shell International 1988)) base their corporate safety policy on such a declaration of principles, and the same argument can be found at the level of public management. Studies in the USA of so-called 'high-reliability organizations' (LaPorte 1982, Roberts 1989 Roberts & Gargano 1989, Weick 1989) have suggested that some complex systems can only function efficiently if all incentives to hide information about errors are removed so that near-misses and minor malfunctions can be fully analysed and discussed so as to head off major malfunctions.

Thus, those who favour a no-blame approach claim that in situations where the institutional process relating to disasters or accidents is primarily focused on apportioning blame, facts will be concealed or seriously distorted by the adversarial process, with negative consequences for risk management. If emotional responses in the media and management paralysis take the place of calm stock-taking in such circumstances, crucial information which could be relevant to learning will not be pooled. The result, the argument goes, is that hindsight reviews, tougher corporate penalties and after-the-fact blaming processes will fail to deliver the results in risk management that blamists expect. Following the prosecution of a

pilot whose plane came close to colliding with a Heathrow hotel, there were reports of a 'drying-up' of information provided by pilots on civil air mishaps and near-misses, thus confounding the purpose of the reporting systems, which is primarily to increase safety by preventing similar accidents occurring. This reluctance to provide information in the face of possible prosecutions is exactly what those who favour a no-blame approach would expect when such reports are linked with blame and punishment.

As with the anticipation–resilience issue, few contributors to the risk management debate would put all the emphasis either on strict liability or on a no-blame approach. The real debate turns on precisely where the emphasis is to be laid on information and incentives in risk management. Those who incline to a strict liability approach think that legal and other blaming processes are inevitable and at the margin they are prepared to sacrifice the free-flow of *post-hoc* information in the wake of disasters or mistakes to achieve strong enough incentives on managers and other actors to limit avoidable risks through the legal and insurance régime. From the opposite camp, the proponents of a no-blame approach argue that as failures and near-misses are inevitable, the opposite trade-off should be made so as to achieve maximum learning from failures as they occur.

THE CONTRIBUTION OF QRA TO RISK MANAGEMENT

A third major aspect of the contemporary risk-management debate turns on the extent to which management régimes should rest on quantified evaluation of risk as against more qualitative assessment; on which areas or aspects of risk management are most suitable for the application of quantitative risk assessment (QRA); and on the most productive mix of QRA with other inputs to the decision-making process.

Table 4. Seven doctrinal contests in risk management policy summarized

Doctrine	Justificatory argument	Counter-doctrine	Justificatory argument
anticipationism	apply causal knowledge of system failure to ex ante actions for better risk management	resilienism	complex sytem failures not predictable in advance and anticipationism make things worse
absolutionism	a 'no-fault' approach to blame avoids distortion of information & helps learning	blamism	targeted blame give strong incentives for taking care on the part of key decision-makers
quantificationism	quantification promotes understanding and rationality, exposes special pleading	qualitativism	proper weight needs to be given to the inherently unquantifiable factors in risk management
designism	apply the accumulated knowledge available for institutional design	design agnosticism	there is no secure knowledge base or real market for institutional design
complementarism	safety and other goals go hand in hand under good management	trade-offism	safety must be explicitly traded off against other goals
narrow participationism	discussion is most effective when confined to expert participants	broad participationism	broader discussion better tests assumptions & avoids errors
outcome specificationism	the regulatory process should concentrate on specifying structures or products	process specificationism	the regulatory process should concentrate on specifying institutional processes

Much of the running in risk-management policy has been made by quantificationists. The argument for quantification is that any rational system of risk management must rest on systematic attempts to quantify risks and to assess them against a pre-set array of objectives by methods analogous to cost–benefit analysis (for example, the 10^{-9} failures per hour standard for flying-control systems in modern aircraft to which we refer in section 6.4.3). The development of QRA into a major instrument of public policy was a feature that the 1983 Royal Society report described in considerable detail, and need not be rehearsed here. Rigorous quantification of risk, it is held, helps to expose anomalies and special pleading and in that sense promotes policy rationality, for example, by pointing to the very different value-of-life settings that are implicit in different areas of UK transport policy, notably road and rail transport (cf. Jones-Lee 1990, Evans 1992). The technical sophistication to which the QRA approach lends itself fits well with legal and bureaucratic requirements for standard operating procedures and the approach has been systematically adopted by bureaucratic organizations (Mitchell 1990). The approach remains the backbone of 'rational' risk management in the UK, particularly in areas of complex socio-technical risk and for many types of natural hazard too (as we describe in section 6.4.1). Supporters of quantification argue that there is no real alternative to QRA as the primary tool of resource allocation in corporate and public management. We look at some of the issues involved in the appendix on risk–benefit analysis.

However, there are important shades of opinion among those who favour an emphasis on quantification in risk management. Few practitioners of risk analysis would put all the weight of policy resolution in risk management on ever-more refined approaches to QRA. Many who favour a quantificationist approach stress the importance of understanding the causes and characteristics of different types of risk and not simply of establishing probabilities (important though that is). Many would concede that QRA has many limitations in practice and needs to be combined with other, broader forms of information and analysis (for example in qualitative techniques of risk identification which feed into or complement QRA), while still maintaining that QRA offers an essential tool for promoting rational risk management and exposing key policy questions

(cf. HSE 1990, Reason 1990, Brogan 1991).

In the (rather less influential) opposite camp are those who are uneasy about placing heavy emphasis on QRA in risk management (cf. Wilpert 1991). Those who are of this persuasion point out that the assumptions involved in some QRA procedures are often both value-laden and implicit (cf. Chapter 5, section 5.2). They are sceptical of claims to be able to quantify risks with very high degrees of accuracy, particularly where changing human behaviour can make a crucial difference (for example, where responses to safety measures or human-induced environmental change defeat predictions based on extrapolations of past data (see Adams & Thompson 1991)). Lave and Malès (1989) have argued that no single decision framework can cater for all the relevant values that come into play in risk regulation, and that cost–benefit analysis and risk–benefit analysis, although high on the economic-efficiency value relative to other approaches to policy, typically score low on the values of equity, administrative simplicity, public acceptability and risk reduction. But such scepticism does not necessarily mean outright dismissal of all attempts at quantification. More commonly, it involves a different judgement as to what the balance should be as between QRA and other sources of information and judgement. It may involve interest in ideas of modifying and extending orthodox QRA techniques, giving the approach 'extra vitamins' by the inclusion of explicitly qualitative elements which might eliminate or at least compensate for some of its more obvious deficiencies (for example in the temptation to avoid inclusion of values of infinity in the analysis because of their mathematical intractability).

Some radical critics even consider that QRA is not simply limited but actually harmful as a tool for risk management. The claim is that QRA, although convenient for organizations facing public attack for their handling of risks, tends to exaggerate the ability to quantify risks reliably and may direct attention away from 'safety imagination' for rarely occurring, hard-to-quantify areas (Toft 1990). In effect, the argument is that QRA may make the risk-management system more vulnerable to Type III errors, as described in section 6.2.1. This view (which is closely paralleled in critiques of over-reliance on economics in other areas, such as that by Gorz (1989)) holds that QRA's calculative techniques are not simply neutral decision aids but actually define the way that problems are perceived and addressed.

The radical critics' position is a minority one, with little influence in risk-management practice. But risk-management practice often involves interaction between quantitative and qualitative techniques. An example of the latter is HAZOP (hazard and operability study), a procedure in which a team of engineers and managers carefully consider the possible consequences of a range of malfunctions of each component in a proposed system, as well as reviewing safety aspects of start-up, shutdown and maintenance requirements. HAZOP has been widely used in chemical-plant design to facilitate the identification of risks associated with the operation of a system outside its intended limits (Kletz 1986, Chemical Industries Association 1987), and a derivative GENHAZ has been proposed for the assessment of risks associated with genetic engineering (RCEP 1989, 1991). Much of the debate is therefore about how the two approaches can feed into one another rather than simple advocacy of one or the other.

THE FEASIBILITY OF INSTITUTIONAL DESIGN IN RISK MANAGEMENT

A fourth key element in contemporary risk-management debates (more often implicit than fully articulated) turns on the extent to which there is a reliable knowledge base on which to ground effective institutional design for risk management, and the extent to which the orthodox engineering approach to 'design' can feasibly be extended to complex organizational structures, especially in social and socio-technical systems. The majority of recommendations for change that come in the aftermath of major accidents tend to be social and administrative, but it is in this area (especially where complex systems are involved) that doubts about ability to fashion effective arrangements are most prominent.

At one end of this spectrum are those who argue that there is a sufficient accumulation of understanding about how institutional design affects vulnerability to system failure and risk-taking behaviour for principles of good practice to be articulated with some degree of confidence. Research in this area includes work on organizational vulnerability to major system failure to which we have already referred (Horlick-Jones 1990, 1991, Horlick-Jones & Peters 1990, Horlick-Jones, Fortune & Peters 1991); work on 'high-reliability organizations' (Halpern 1989, Roberts 1989, Roberts & Gargano 1989, Rochlin 1989, Weick 1989); and the work of Reason (1990) and his colleagues on human error. Those who see considerable scope for the development of established principles of institutional design point to what they see as the cumulative growth of a recognized practice of corporate safety-management over the past decade, particularly in multinational corporations which have become concerned about the growing visibility and rising costs of large-scale accidents.

Spearheaded by some of the major corporations in the chemical and process industries, such practices tend to stress a commitment to safety at the highest organizational level, the adoption of low or zero accident targets on a corporation-wide basis and the provision of training and resources to back up such attention. Corporate safety-management programmes include regular safety audits, the inclusion of more safety elements in 'total quality management' programmes, and the promotion of such arrangements as quality circles and 'toolbox safety meetings' to raise safety consciousness in all parts of the corporation. The standard of a corporation's 'safety culture' has also occasioned considerable discussion following the introduction of this term as part of the assessment of the after-effects of the 1986 Chernobyl nuclear power station meltdown (cf. CBI 1990).

At the other end of the spectrum are those who are much less sanguine about the scope for, or the knowledge base underlying, institutional design claims in risk management, especially in large socio-technical systems. The sceptics point to sharp limitations in the current state of knowledge about how risk is handled in human organizations, and consider that there is a much less robust knowledge base on which to ground design than applies to traditional engineering. However, assumptions about human and organizational design become increasingly crucial as the development of technology comes to involve constructing more complex systems and human–machine interfaces. For example, as we show in section 6.4.3, some software specialists are sceptical about the extent to which an analogy with other branches of engineering can provide a reliable basis for design integrity, where the issue in question involves the interaction between complex technology and the dynamics of human response to that technology. In addition, some are sceptical of claims that organizational 'safety cultures' can be deliberately engineered by management or that they are grounded in systematic investigation of cases. Such sceptics note that in practice there are considerable variations in corporate safety policies in transnational corporations, and sometimes even apparently contradictory approaches seem to yield similar outcomes (as in the cases referred to in the discussion of liability approaches above).

Whereas those who favour an emphasis on institutional design in risk management are entitled to question whether it is helpful merely to bring scepticism to the risk management debate, the sceptics have sharp questions to ask how much straw the designists have in their bricks. But the growing volume of research in areas such as human–computer interfaces and user-oriented architecture ought to enable those who wish to expand the scope of institutional design to make some ground; and in principle, a constructive dialogue between the two approaches ought to guide experimentation and to enable each to develop its position well beyond first principles.

THE COST OF RISK REDUCTION

A fifth area of debate in risk management concerns the cost of risk reduction and the extent to which reduction in risk has to be traded off against other basic goals. The doctrine of BATNEEC (Best Available Technology Not Entailing Excessive Costs) explicitly recognizes the trade-off problem.

The conventional 'no-free-lunch' trade-off model of economics offers a clear starting point for risk management, as it focuses attention very sharply on discounted costs and benefits. Those who adopt a trade-off position argue that increases in safety must normally come at the expense of other valued objectives such as wealth creation, international competitiveness in productivity or economic dynamism, and environmental degradation (see section 6.4.1). The debate over the costs of risk reduction has included discussion of the economic consequences of extended product liability in the USA, although there is no clear overall evaluation of the economic effects of those legal trends (see Reuter 1988). At the limit, the cost of risk reduction can be framed not simply as the trading off of risk reduction against other competing values, but also as the trading off of some kinds of risks against others (for example, botulism risks *versus* cancer risks in relation to nitrites in food).

As is shown in the appendix on risk–benefit analysis, public policy can be represented as an implicit trade-off between safety and economic surplus, and by analytic techniques designed to make the trade-off explicit, an effort can be made to assess the consistency with which the trade-off is made in different areas of public policy, and why it varies from one case to another; for example, why the trade-off appears to be different in public transport as against road transport (see section 6.4.2).

Against this orthodox view is an alternative position which holds that high safety standards may be achieved in conjunction with other goals, and also that good risk management is one of the signs of good management in general. The claim here is that badly managed organizations are likely to have poor safety records along with poor performance in other dimensions. From this viewpoint, increased attention to safety can pay for itself, because prevention through good design, good training and good practice will be cheaper than the costs incurred by disruption, damage claims and insurance premiums, poor public image and a loss of goodwill from employees (cf. Kloman 1990). Such arguments have figured prominently in the justification for the wide-ranging corporate safety programmes to which we have just referred, and have even been enshrined in the OECD chemical industry guidelines for the handling of hazardous materials.

In the environmental pollution area, Tait & Levidov (1992) argue that regulation that requires developments in technology does not necessarily come at the expense of profits, and that 'where such an approach has been adopted, as for example in the German car industry, there is no evidence that it has disadvantaged the companies concerned'. And the RCEP report on *Best practicable environ-mental options* (1988, para 1.12) points to 'sound business sense' arguments for increased efficiency and waste reduction through better environmental management. In relation to crowd safety (see section 6.4.4) some have argued that expensive safety-related investments in physical facilities can achieve compensatory returns, as an increasingly safety-conscious public comes to select venues according to their levels of safety provision, and perhaps is prepared to pay higher admission prices in return for improved facilities.

The debate over the extent to which risk reduction needs to be traded against other values, and how such a trade-off should be made, was a notable feature of discussion on UK transport safety in the 1980s and the issue is also very important in the safety debate for hazardous process industries. The debate turns on the precise shape of industrial production functions and of the risk-related characteristics of broader technical, ecological and macroeconomic functions. Up to now, the view that risk reduction can come without sacrifice of other major goals has been more in evidence in debates over risk management by corporations than in public management more generally. It remains to be seen whether further research can elucidate the shape of the social and corporate production functions that are in dispute in these debates.

THE DEGREE OF PARTICIPATION APPROPRIATE TO RISK-MANAGEMENT DECISIONS

A sixth area of debate concerns the optimum size and composition of the groups involved in risk-management decisions. In one camp are those who are critical of narrow participation in decisions such as nuclear-waste transportation (cf. Kirby 1988) and who advocate extension of the 'peer community' involved in risk management. The case for extension can be put in several ways. One is that opening up the relevant decisions and monitoring processes to wider scrutiny and attention from the multiple stakeholders involved will result in better-informed and less error-prone decisions. For example, the RCEP report on *The release of genetically engineered organisms* (1989, 47, para. 6.39) notes that, 'The discovery of the environmental effects of DDT, leading eventually to its banning, is attributed to amateur ornithologists who noticed the decline in populations of peregrine falcons and other birds of prey', and proposes a broad basis of environmental monitoring activities. Extension of participation may also be argued to bring different scientific perspectives to bear. For example, some social scientists argue that engineering-based crowd-safety designs which treat human movements as analogous to the motion of physical objects will fail to model the essential characteristics of human crowds as interactive communication systems, and hence that broader participation in crowd-safety decisions will avoid serious errors that would otherwise arise (see section 6.4.4).

Apart from its claimed effects in improving the information base of risk management, the case for broader participation is sometimes put in terms of increasing the accountability of the technical decision-makers (Beder 1991), or on moral or 'spillover' grounds. OECD guidelines on the management of chemical plants suggest that risk-management decisions should explicitly consider suppliers, clients, customers and local residents as well as corporate managers and employees.

The case for broader participationism is often linked to the development of challenges to the traditional positivistic view of scientific knowledge in the mould of 18th-century physics. Such challenges have developed in analyses of science (Wynne 1992), of decisions about technology (Latour 1987, Collingridge 1980), and of the operation of the regulatory process (Stigler 1988). Funtowicz &

Ravetz (1991, 1992) argue that in circumstances such as global warming (see section 6.4.6), where facts are inherently uncertain, values in dispute, stakes could be high and policy decisions presumed to be urgent, the institutional characteristics of 'normal science' need to be significantly modified. In cases where neither conclusive scientific proof nor effective technology can be expected within the critical time-horizon of the decision, they claim, quality assurance of the (uncertain) scientific inputs to the policy process requires an 'extended peer community'. Such extension is already the accepted practice where the ethical complexities of scientific work cannot be resolved within the boundaries of science, and where non-scientists representing special perspectives and interests set permissible limits on scientific work; embryo research is a most notable example. Similarly, in epidemiology there is increasing participation of citizens in the identification of new medical problems from local and anecdotal data (Brown 1987).

In 'trans-scientific' settings of this kind, the extension of participation in decision making is not, according to Funtowicz & Ravetz, prompted by benevolence. It is a functional necessity for improving the quality of both decision making and implementation, by broadening the base, first of knowledge and criticism, and then of consensus and responsibility. In this way, they claim, a new 'social contract of science' can be achieved, in which there is a common respect for a plurality of competences, perspectives and commitments among the different stakeholders in a risk-management issue.

Against this view are those such as Yalow (1985) who are sceptical of the benefits to be gained from broader participation in risk management decisions and argue instead for the continuation of those decision-making methods that involve a few scientifically well-informed participants, and which are still the most widely used in many areas of risk-management. Those of this persuasion hold that proper risk-management decisions require the application of the best available technical expertise to the reaching of consensus on the balance of the evidence. Yalow sets her argument in the context of what she sees as unfounded public fears about radioimmunoassay, and holds that extension of participation in decision and policy-making processes may lead to quality scientific expertise being over-ridden by ill-informed contributors, so that risk management would thereby become both impoverished and irrational as it is subjected to whipped-up scares and to over-politicization. In addition, it can be claimed that broad participation may be counter-productive in achieving its aims, if the only people who understand a risky project are those who are involved and that broad participation diffuses responsibility away from those who essentially make the decisions and makes it possible for them to lay the blame when things go wrong on poorly informed participants.

THE REGULATORY TARGET

Finally, there are differences of opinion as to where the emphasis in risk management should be placed at the margin as between the specification of physical products or structures on the one hand and the specification of institutional processes (by appropriate settings of the six types of rules discussed in section 6.3.3) on the other. The difference of emphasis is in part related to the debate about the appropriate degree of 'anticipationism' in risk management which was noted earlier.

Like the institutional design issue, this dimension of the risk-management problem is not characterized by sharp and explicit debate. But there is a spectrum of possible positions which vary according to the emphasis that they place on the specification of *outcomes* (in the sense of laying down physical standards) as against the specification of decision *pro-*

cesses. In the traditional regulatory paradigm of natural science, risk management is conceived of as essentially about the design of products or physical structures that are safe within a specified set of functions, or 'safe enough', within cost–benefit constraints. The emphasis is on incorporating the expertise of natural science, medicine or engineering into authoritative research-grounded standards and specifications (as with the specification of rules about maximum daily intakes of certain food additives or chemical residues in food or pharmaceutical products, or permitted levels of exposure to radiation for workers in radiology departments). Such an approach is deeply embedded in much of the institutional structure of risk regulation and its surrounding decision-advice procedures.

In practice, such standards often rely heavily on socially negotiated notions of 'feasibility', 'practicality' and 'reasonableness', for example in the idea that particular hazards or contaminants should be rendered 'As Low As is Reasonably Possible' (ALARP) or 'As Low As is Reasonably Attainable' (ALARA). A related goal which balances the aspirations of science with both the practical demands of technologists and the social concerns of other groups, is that set by the principle, already mentioned, of BATNEEC. Such goal definitions for product specification clearly hinge on it being possible to find legally or socially agreed interpretations of what exactly constitutes 'reasonableness', 'excessive cost', 'best available', 'practicable'. The discussion of cultural variability in attitudes to risk suggests that it is dangerous to assume a homogeneity of social attitudes to such matters.

At the other end of the spectrum are those who argue that a regulatory emphasis on the design or composition of products and structures is of limited usefulness, and may at some point become self-defeating, given irreducibly high levels of uncertainty, limited opportunities for laboratory testing in some crucial areas of risk management, difficulties of extrapolation from a small number of data points or animal experiments, and declining popular faith in the authority of natural science (Wynne 1992). The claim is that in circumstances where uncertainty cannot be entirely eliminated, the traditional physical-standards approach needs to be supplemented or even replaced by an emphasis on specifying organizational processes that will ensure careful balancing of arguments. Such an approach to organizational design is exemplified by the philosophy supporting BS5750, which offers a standard for quality assurance within corporations. Those who favour the process-based approach argue that the emphasis must inevitably be placed on structuring the way that decisions are taken rather than on specifying physical output in circumstances of ineradicable uncertainty; as in those 'trans-scientific' issues, to which we have already referred, which are in principle resoluble through systematic investigation of hard data but where such experiments cannot in fact be done because of time, resource or legal/moral limits.

It is on the basis of such arguments that Majone (1989), who developed his analysis from an initial research interest in Bayesian statistics, puts the case for a process-based regulatory approach through devising fora in which competing claims can be advanced in a manner which deters the 'capture' of public policy by a particular scientific school without effective challenge and to allow well-informed decisions to be taken in circumstances where scientific certainty cannot be attained. However, the development of an organization-process approach to risk management is not necessarily incompatible with a structural-design approach, and the former is often laid on top of the latter.

6.3.3 OVERVIEW: 'HOMEOSTATIC' AND 'COLLIBRATIONAL' APPROACHES TO RISK MANAGEMENT

Each of the seven generic areas of debate reviewed in section 6.3.2 raises serious issues for risk management which recur across different specialisms and areas of policy, albeit with different precise terminology and emphases. It is not claimed that the seven opposing positions are either necessarily mutually exclusive or jointly exhaustive. But they do cover many areas of the contemporary debate over risk management; and it seems likely that in many areas of risk management an approach that leaves any of the positions out of account is likely to be inadequate.

Many of the seven sets of 'doctrines' are in principle independent of one another. For example, one can combine an emphasis on process-based regulation with either a 'broad' or 'narrow' position on participation in risk management decisions. And both can be combined with either a 'complementarist' or 'trade-off' position. Hence there is a large array of possible combinations of positions even on these seven dimensions. But in practice some positions in these debates do tend to go with others. For example, those who favour anticipation are unlikely to be 'agnostics' over the possibility of institutional design (although those who would place the emphasis on 'resilience' may well be advocates of institutional design too). Those in favour of broad participation are unlikely to be pure 'quantificationists'. It may well be that the seven areas of debate could ultimately be reduced to some more basic set of distinctions, such as the well-known quadrants of the cultural theorists, discussed in the last chapter.

Moreover, another broad thread can be distinguished as running through many of these debates. Applied control-theory distinguishes between what Dunsire (1990) terms *homeostatic* and *collibrationist* regulation processes. A 'homeostatic' form of control uses feedback processes to achieve pre-set goals, whereas collibration has no such agreed goal, but works by 'making extremes meet' through 'opposed maximisers' set up to pull a system in different directions at once, such that the system's state at any one time is a product of the interactions among the various forces that are held in opposed tension, like the springs in a desk lamp (Dunsire 1978, 181, 207–8, 1986).

In risk management, what might be termed the 'homeostatic' approach places emphasis on institutional capacity to set determinate goals (for example, for aggregate social-risk tolerance) in advance and to convert those goals into quantified decision rules which experts can apply to particular cases, and organizations can incorporate into their standard operating procedures. Hence such an approach will tend to favour anticipation, quantification and the specification of outputs.

The alternative 'collibratory' view holds that ineradicable scientific uncertainties limit the capacity for reliable forecasting in many crucial areas (particularly in respect of slow-onset hazards like global warming), and that cultural variety and dynamics limit the capacity for robust aggregate goal-setting to be elaborated into precise technocratic decision rules. The implication is that the process of managing risk requires the design of institutions (both at corporate and public-management level) on the principle of the desk lamp rather than the thermostat, by explicitly juxtaposing rival viewpoints in a constant process of dynamic tension with no pre-set equilibrium (see Schwarz & Thompson 1990). Hence the collibrationists' position will tend to favour 'resilience', specification of process and qualitative debates over uncertainties more than the homeostatic view. In a broader sense, perhaps, the collibrationist position might even suggest that the seven areas of debate identified in section 6.3.2 need not be finally resolved in one way or another, but institutionalized in the process of risk management in a way that keeps the rival positions in opposed tension.

It would probably be fair to describe the homeostatic view as the current orthodoxy of risk management in the scientific and practitioner community, and the collibrationist view as much less widely accepted. Nevertheless, it must be recognized that the orthodox position has come under increasing challenge over the decade since the first Royal Society report was written; and collibrationists argue that their vision of control more accurately describes the underlying processes involved. It remains to be seen whether collibrationists can develop their position into a better-specified, more coherent and more widely accepted paradigm of risk management.

6.4 SELECTED EXAMPLES

In this section, we move from the generic level of discussion about principles of risk management to pick out six different areas of risk management and review the particular debates within them. The six areas are natural hazard management, public transport safety, the design of safety-critical software, the management of crowd-related hazards, the regulation of blood and 'sharps' and the decision advice issues involved in debates about global warming. The six areas are not intended to cover all of the many fields of risk management, or even to be a sample in any representative sense. Rather, they are intended to portray the variety of the contemporary debate which was discussed in summary form in section 6.3.

6.4.1 ENVIRONMENTAL AND NATURAL-HAZARD MANAGEMENT

Risks from the 'natural' environment are significant. Some indicative data for natural-disaster loss levels and US flood losses and deaths, are shown in figures 5 and 6. They display the characteristic year-on-year variability due to the chance interaction between human activity and hazard events that display magnitude–frequency variability over space and time, together with increasing absolute losses. As noted in section 6.1.1, it has been conventional to distinguish between 'natural' hazards – floods, high winds, earthquakes and erosion – and 'socio-technical' hazards. But from a risk-management perspective, this distinction is increasingly becoming blurred for three reasons. First, it is now known that extreme events are not inexplicably random 'acts of God' but the products of natural systems behaviour explicable in space and time. Consequently, the likelihood of hazard events can increasingly be spatially defined (hazard zones) and divided (micro-zonation) according to the varying levels of threat using extreme-event analysis which assesses past magnitude–frequency distributions to predict recurrence intervals (return periods) and probabilities of events of different size. Second, human activity has affected, to varying degrees, the behaviour of natural events systems in terms of the magnitude and frequency of extreme events, thereby causing the notion of 'natural hazard' to become increasingly replaced by terms such as 'quasi-natural hazards', 'hybrid hazards' and 'environmental hazards', as noted in 6.1.1. Third, as the terms 'hazard' and 'risk' are human-centred, the distinction between impact by environmental processes as against the effects of artificial hazards is

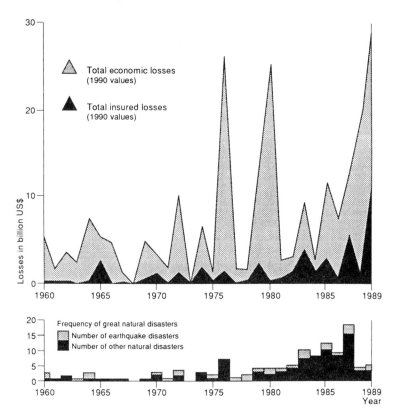

Figure 5. Natural disaster losses 1960–89 in constant 1990 dollars. (Source: Munich Reinsurance 1990.)

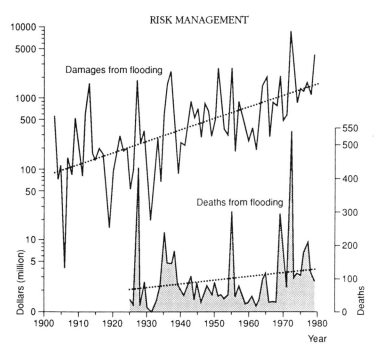

Figure 6. US Flood losses and deaths 1903–79. (Source: Arnell 1984, Fig 1.)

less marked in terms of management responses than was once thought.

Traditionally, natural-hazard management has been strongly compartmentalized according to the nature of damage causing events (such as earthquakes and floods) and dominated by studies of major events (disasters/catastrophes). Although a range of hazard loss-reduction adjustments are available (see table 2), there has been a tendency to focus on active or corrective measures employing technology and engineering to control the forces of nature (the so-called 'behavioural' approach; see Smith (1992)) rather than less conspicuous preventative measures that seek to reduce the vulnerability of society. Hazard management has often been a short-lived *ex post* response to events rather than a sustained programme because of general perceptions as to the uncertainty of future events which inevitably results in hazard management attaining diminished prominence in quiescent periods through a process that Freudenberg (1992) calls 'the Atrophy of Vigilance'. Thus emergency action and rehabilitation or reconstruction are often preferred to investment in anticipatory activities.

However, increased levels of scientific understanding across a broad range of 'natural hazards' has considerably improved predictive capacity, as described earlier, and in some instances forecasting ability (e.g. satellite monitoring of hurricane development and movement, automatic monitoring of rainfall and river discharge), thereby causing some switch in emphasis towards anticipatory measures. Both anticipationists and quantitativists have achieved increased prominence in the debate, because natural hazard events are predominantly repeated rather than random phenomena so that adjustments undertaken after one event can be interpreted as prior to a subsequent potential impact.

Natural hazard management is often a 'public good' and frequently involves public regulatory power. Many of those at risk from natural hazards refuse to acknowledge such events as naturally occurring phenomena, but instead see them as something that should have been tackled, preferably at no cost to themselves (Penning-Rowsell *et al.* 1986). Private and public organizations are often held to be responsible for the impacts of these hazards, and even for the hazards themselves, in the sense that 'something should have been done' to lessen the vulnerability of those at risk. If such regulatory activities are undertaken out of general-fund taxes or undifferentiated insurance premiums, 'moral hazard' or human risk homeostasis behaviour may counteract attempts to reduce overall risks. For example, coastal retirement colonies tend to be located in areas liable to flooding and erosion. Real-estate prices there are not depressed by this hazardousness because the market anticipates that publicly-funded protection will come as a result of interest-group pressures. And lobbying processes usually do bring about the expected protection, thus exacerbating the build-up of assets in vulnerable areas, which will then be used to justify yet more public investment in the future.

Location of primary responsibility is a key aspect of institutional design debates in this area. Natural hazards tend to be spatially delimited and impacts are often localized, but the resources and skill mix needed for their management is often only available to organizations with large jurisdictions and tax bases. Coastal hazards – flooding and erosion – are acknowledged to be poorly defined and tackled at a local level. Yet responsibilities often tend to be fragmented among a range of bodies and often located at the lowest territorial level of government, typically because of the influence of construction-related interest groups there. Inland flooding problems in major catchments are seen as a product of inadequate land use planning, such that urbanization creates more rapid runoff, thereby increasing the frequency and magnitude of high flows. At the same time, land-use control typically fails to protect floodplains from development, because of rent-seeking processes (that is, the tendency for the regulatory process to be captured by real-estate development interests).

Another key institutional design problem is how to organize hazard-protection services in the context of intensified legal and political blaming processes (Parker & Handmer 1992). For example, after the 1987 windstorm in the south of England and the 1989 Towyn floods in North Wales, much of the blame was laid on the alleged failings of the UK Meteorological Office to provide adequate forecasts and warnings, and some important legal cases have had the effect of increasing the legal liability on those responsible for issuing warnings. Inevitably (as those who favour a no-blame approach would expect when messengers are shot for the information they bring), the policy response is to limit liability, by refusing to delimit hazard zones, to offer generalized forecasts and warnings or even to refuse to issue any warnings at all. Similarly, defensive motives partly lie behind the attempt to define precisely the standards or levels of service that hazard warning or control agencies provide, in the context of flood-frequency estimates or probability of drought or slope failures. Because 'service' is difficult to frame with any confidence for floods or similar hazards that occur on average once in 100 years or more, and institutional memory tends to be destroyed by frequent reorganization, any reassurance that such standards of service give must be largely illusory and may even worsen the capacity to cope satisfactorily when unexpectedly severe hazards do strike (as 'resilienists' would argue). But such measures can serve as a way of limiting liability for the authority concerned in an increasingly litigious environment.

More generally, the contemporary natural-hazard management debate continues to be dominated by those who favour a quantificationist emphasis, allied with confidence about the scope for design and an emphasis on physical structures rather than decision processes. The traditional, and still dominant view, which is labelled the 'behaviourial paradigm', holds that geophysical extremes are the main cause of hazard impacts and that the problem is best resolved by the application of technology through engineering (Hewitt 1983, Smith 1992), provided that the technical problems can be defined carefully enough (with state-of-the-art technology) and that sufficient public funds are available for the necessary engineering works to reduce risks by designing out hazards. The idea of natural hazards as societal problems, and thus a product of human behavioural responses to factors such as land ownership, insurance-premium practices and tax-benefit régimes, less often comes into the orthodox policy frame of natural-hazard management. And the idea of modifications of human behaviour by changes in the incentive structure governing exposure to natural hazards rarely enters the normal conception of what 'risk management' means in this area.

However, in opposition to the orthodox behaviourial paradigm, social scientists with first-hand experience of Third World hazards have developed the so-called 'structuralist paradigm' (Susman *et al.* 1983, Waddell 1983). In this interpretation, natural disasters are seen to be the consequence of economic, social and political problems which are exposed or brought to a head by geophysical triggers, and hence, that action should be concentrated on social and management structures. Though the latter view remains a minority one, the cost-effectiveness of large-scale engineering schemes for natural hazard control is increasingly coming to be questioned. The growing expense of required defensive measures, the escalating costs of failure and the problems of the 'levée syndrome', where visible engineering works are perceived to bring absolute safety irrespective of the scale of such works, has lent weight to those who advocate placing rather more emphasis on non-structural approaches such as the use of insurance schemes and various aspects of anticipatory planning to minimize human vulnerability.

An interesting variant of the 'trade-off' debate in risk management is the safety–environment trade-off that arises in the natural-hazard field. The traditional engineering approach to natural-hazard management is to modify the environment to reduce risk. The ecological effects of such interventions may be significant. Flood-alleviation schemes affect valued river environments. Coastal protection can harm unique coastal ecosystems and may result in accelerated erosion elsewhere with adverse consequences. Drought-reduction policies often involve supply extension rather than water-demand management, and such policies can require new reservoirs in valued upland areas.

Yet increasingly influential 'green' pressures tend to portray the side-effects of the hazard reduction medicine as worse than the original disease. Part of the policy response has been an attempt to trade off the two values using a growing battery of environmental-economics techniques to provide a basis for decisions that can be claimed to be 'rational'. But that 'rationality' is rejected by 'egalitarian' cultural groups (in the high-group, low-grid quadrant of the cultural theorists' typology, as described in chapter 5), who argue that the natural hazard problem is essentially human-induced, and that the proper 'solution' is the inverse of the orthodox engineering approach to hazard management; that is, adjusting human behaviour to minimize potential environmental threat rather than changing or constraining the environment to suit human needs. It is interesting to note that these contrasting cultural views are encapsulated in the difference between the 'behavioural' and 'structural' paradigms of natural hazard management that were described above.

6.4.2 THE MANAGEMENT OF PUBLIC TRANSPORT RISKS

Though numbers of road deaths dwarf deaths arising from public transport accidents involving ships, trains and planes, much of the public debate over transport safety in the UK since the last Royal Society report has focused on the latter rather than the former. Why the apparently disproportionate public attention on the transport area with the lower kill rate? (Evans 1992). Sociologists can perhaps point to the extra opportunities that public transport accidents offer for blaming large corporations for their misdeeds. Lawyers can point to the special kind of 'trust' that may be implicit for passengers on public transport. Other social scientists can point to the special tendency of public transport accidents to create concentrated victim groups (because they tend to bring simultaneous disaster to many people at once rather than a more individualized pattern of harm), and thereby to produce action groups with a concentrated urge to blame.

Perhaps because of these features, much of the risk-management debate over UK public transport since the late 1980s has turned towards such issues as corporate liability, the institutional location of regulatory bodies (whether it is desirable to avoid conflicts of interest by separating regulatory and provision functions for transport), the capacity of the legal system to operate effective *ex post* scrutiny of major transport accidents, and the factors that make for system vulnerability as opposed to slips by individual operators (cf. Horlick-Jones 1990, Pheasant 1988, Wells 1992*b*).

The corporate liability issue reflects a debate on where the balance of blame should lie, between the operator whose slip is the proximate cause of the accident and those who are responsible for the overall context in which those individual operators work. In general, English law tends to focus the blame on individual operators rather than on those who set the context which affects the likelihood of operator failure and the vulnerability of the system to minor human slips. For example, after the 1987 King's Cross Underground fire in London, there

was an assumption that if the particular individual who carelessly dropped a match could not be identified by police inquiry, there was no criminal cause to pursue. (But there is of course a difference between legal and other forms of blaming: it should be noted that the chairmen both of London Transport and London Underground lost their jobs after the King's Cross fire.)

As noted in section 6.3, the case for the traditional emphasis on targeting blame on the individual who acts as the proximate cause of an accident is that it creates strong incentives for operators to take care, and in that sense parallels the case for traditional product-liability rules. But 'blamist' critics of the system argue, on strict liability lines, that there is no corresponding set of legal incentives operating at the managerial level. The issue has arisen most sharply in the context of the sinking of the car ferry *Herald of Free Enterprise* at Zeebrugge in 1987. The subsequent Sheen inquiry found that three members of the ship's company of the *Herald* had been seriously negligent, but also that the capsize was 'partly caused or contributed to by the fault of ... the Owners' (Department of Transport 1987, Decision of the Court) and that 'from top to bottom the body corporate was infected with the disease of sloppiness' (Department of Transport 1987, 14.1). But the Coroner ruled that a company could not be indicted for manslaughter and the subsequent attempt to prosecute P&O (the *Herald's* operating company) also failed. The *Herald* trial was interpreted by some as signalling a general failure of corporate liability principles, although others claim that the outcome is better explained as an isolated result arising from a particularly strict interpretation of the requirements of recklessness (Wells 1992*a*, chapter IV).

Debate about the capacity of the legal system to handle effective *ex post* investigation turns on issues about the rules of the game as identified earlier at section

6.2.3. A key 'scope rule' concerns the ability of inquests and official inquiries to apportion blame. Official inquiries are not always required to identify responsibility for accidents. For example, the Marine Accident Investigation Branch (MAIB) of the Department of Transport noted in its report on the *Marchioness* accident (the sinking of a pleasure boat in the river Thames in 1989 following a collision with a dredger) that the explicit statutory purpose of the official inquiry is safety improvement, not the apportionment of liability or the laying of blame 'except so far as is necessary to achieve the fundamental purpose' (Department of Transport 1991, 37). Debates about appropriate scope for imputing blame arise with particular force in relation to inquests, which involve a lay jury in English law, because lay juries may on occasion be more inclined than professionals to blame corporate bodies rather than individuals for disasters with a 'system' component. The juries in the inquests following the *Herald* sinking and the Clapham train crash of 1988 both returned a verdict of 'unlawful killing' (rather than 'accidental death'), but the jury in the inquest following the 1987 King's Cross escalator fire was instructed that such a verdict was not available to them.

A more general issue in the debate is the attempt to identify system characteristics leading to vulnerability to major accidents as against human error on the part of the 'proximate cause' individual(s). At issue here is not merely the question of scientific predictability, but also issues of 'justice' and blame. It could be argued that 'systems thinking' is beginning to become somewhat more widespread. Following the 1988 Clapham rail crash, recognition was accorded to the role of workers not present at the time of the crash, and of the organizational context in which the mistakes were made (Department of Transport 1989). The inquiry into the 1989 Purley rail crash also identified significant contextual factors (De-

partment of Transport 1990). In the case of both the *Herald* and the *Marchioness*, the inquiry criticized aspects of the operating organisation (Department of Transport 1987, 1991), and the *Marchioness* inquiry reported a 'malaise' affecting the Department of Transport and the entire marine community, emphasizing the effect of 'bad practices' that had grown up in the industry over many years (Department of Transport 1991, 43–44).

6.4.3 SAFETY-CRITICAL SOFTWARE DESIGN

Many organizations today are looking to the increasing use of IT as a way of dealing with the demands of risk management. But no mode of operation is hazard-free, and there are, of course, safety problems inherent in the use of computers themselves. Quite apart from the general problems of specifying the likely behaviour of increasingly complex computer programs and the precautions necessary to protect such software from the influence of computer viruses (Schulmeyer 1990) software is becoming a dominant component in many safety-critical systems, and this development poses special problems for risk management.

Some hazard-sensitive software applications are to be found in widely used equipment such as motor vehicles and medical electronic devices, where failures, even if serious, are likely to be relatively contained. But increasingly, applications are also being installed in systems where a single accident would be catastrophic, such as nuclear reactor protection systems and flying control systems for advanced aircraft like the A320. There is some technical concern underlying such applications, at the root of much of which is their general design complexity rather than software problems as such. But software often 'gets the blame' because there is a trend to increase the sophistication and complexity of technical systems by embedding additional control functions in software, and it is deceptively easy to produce complex software systems. Some have claimed that there is a need to develop clearer specifications of what is meant by 'safety' and 'security' in the context of software systems (see Burns *et al.* 1992).

Many of the safety-critical systems for which software control applications have been developed have extremely stringent failure-rate requirements, such as the oft-quoted 10^{-9} failures per hour standard for flying control systems in modern aircraft. Yet in software developments, in many cases it is not possible to evaluate the failure rate to that standard, before the system is deployed. In this context, there is an important debate between those who believe that software should not be deployed in systems with such stringent safety requirements (because its reliability cannot be measured to the appropriate standard in advance) and those in the opposite camp who believe that the absence of such measures is not an appropriate and sufficient reason for preventing deployment. At the root of this debate is a major philosophical question relating to the validity of statistical measures applied to design problems. Many would argue that it is not appropriate to treat the discovery and exposure of design errors in software (or any other medium) as a stochastic process.

Much of the design debate turns on whether the failure problem in software engineering is truly distinctive from that arising in the other engineering disciplines used in safety-critical applications. Conventional engineering approaches tend to place the emphasis on using well-tried practices to achieve high levels of design integrity, often without an attempt to put a precise figure on the likelihood of design failure. It is sometimes argued that such conventions are not appropriate for software because it behaves in a discontinuous way not encountered in other engineering disciplines. Against that is the argument that software is not distinctive as an engineering design problem (for example that many mechanical

and chemical systems operate close to limits and can also fail in a discontinuous and catastrophic way) and therefore that the design approach of the classical engineering disciplines is appropriate for dealing with safety-critical software also. But even if this argument is accepted in principle, real practical difficulties remain. Though it is developing, software engineering is a relatively immature discipline. As yet it has neither well-developed techniques for achieving high levels of integrity, nor well-established ways of improving design practice after serious mistakes.

The protagonists of the view that the appropriate route to the requisite quantifiable level of design integrity lies through formal mathematical methods of modelling and reasoning about software include the UK Ministry of Defence, which has recently incorporated such ideas in Interim Defence Standard 00/55. Following a clear analogy with other engineering disciplines, the argument here is that mathematical approaches provide the basis of a technological solution for the production of software of sufficiently high integrity for use in critical applications. This view is questioned by those who point to the problems of positively checking in advance the performance of software systems of even modest complexity.

Such emerging requirements that a mathematical proof of reliability should become mandatory for particularly key safety-critical software systems, raise questions about the form of proof that might be considered satisfactory for the testing of complex software (Mackenzie 1991, Wichmann 1992). In dealing with such issues, as there is no clearly agreed specification of what might constitute a proof, it seems inevitable that standards of operation will be socially negotiated rather than deduced or proven. Indeed, as such demonstrations or proof become legally required for some safety-critical systems, we may not only see informal negotiations over the issue of what constitutes an appropriate formal proof in the near future but also public litigation on the matter (Mackenzie 1991).

Quite apart from the difficulties in pinning down the residual complexities of some complex software systems, the human–computer interface is also at the heart of the debate about safety-critical systems. Several recent severe accidents, for example with nuclear reactor systems and commercial aircraft, have at least partially been caused by the failure of the human operators to understand the information presented to them through computerized interfaces. The normal 'blamist' reaction focuses on the errors of the operators or pilots. But investigation of accident reports suggests that the operators found it very difficult to assimilate the appropriate information from the system, and that the computerized systems are typically intolerant of errors made by humans in times of stress. From a broader perspective, the problem is therefore not to blame the operators but to devote more attention to developing systems and interfaces that facilitate human–computer communication and which are more tolerant of errors of human operators (cf. Harrison 1992).

It is clear that we should not expect the more widespread use of computers to usher in a risk-free society. Properly designed and applied systems have an enormous contribution to make to better risk management, but in crucial areas their design and assessment is also shifting some of the terms of the debate about risk and the manner in which we handle it. For their part, the software engineering community has only recently started to develop an understanding of the socio-technical aspects of the problem. What is really needed to put debates in the area on a sounder footing is a better understanding of the relations between the design and development process on the one hand, and the behaviour, including failure-mode behaviour, of the resultant software artefact and of the socio-technical system in which it is embedded.

6.4.4 THE MANAGEMENT OF CROWD-RELATED HAZARDS

Many of the generic areas of debate set out in section 6.3.2 appear in discussions of risk management involving human crowds, and some of the debates parallel issues that have already been raised in the three cases above. The physical, psychological and social aspects of major new engineering structures, like the Channel Tunnel, raise design complexity issues similar to those mentioned in section 6.4.3. Following crowding disasters, much attention is focused on issues of accountability and blame discussed in 6.4.2, and, as in the transport case, recent disaster inquiry reports have put increasing emphasis on organizational and management aspects (cf. Popplewell 1986, Fennell 1988, Taylor 1990).

Managers of venues or processes which involve the concentration of many people in a confined area often see their safety responsibilities in terms of 'crowd control' rather than 'crowd management'. The notion that being in a crowd is inherently hazardous, independent of the location and management of the crowd, typically characterizes reaction to crowd disasters after the event. There is a widespread assumption that crowd members put themselves at risk by their own choice, for example by deciding to attend a football match or pop concert, and this assumption is reflected in the frequent use of derogatory labels ('hooligans', 'mob') and attributions of 'panic' to those caught in a crowd crush. However, there is general agreement among disaster sociologists and psychologists that far from being irrational, flight behaviour in crowd disasters is almost invariably rational from the perspective of those caught in a crush (e.g. Sime 1990). Unfortunately, the expectation of panic is often self-fulfilling, as it leads to delays in warning which aggravate flight and injury.

The expectation of irrational behaviour characteristic of much analysis of crowd-related disasters encourages a 'narrow participationist' view of decision making, with the implication that responsibility for decisions should be kept closely in the hands of 'experts'. However, it has been argued that crowd management is more effective when the members of the crowd have sufficient access to information about the development of events and of the sources of possible hazards to allow individuals to decide on appropriate tactics. For example, research into evacuation of an underground railway station has indicated that the efficiency of crowd evacuation can be dramatically improved by using CCTV monitoring from a control room and then issuing clear information over the public address system, rather than relying on a general fire alarm or siren (Proulx & Sime 1991). The new technology of 'intelligent buildings' offers considerable potential as an aid to efficient management of crowd movement through the use of technically sophisticated communications systems.

Traditionally, crowd safety has been defined from an engineering perspective which models crowds as if they were physical structures and ignores the special dynamics of human communication. From this traditional viewpoint, the key elements of crowd safety are defined in terms of population sizes, movement flows and capacity of spaces and entry points. Though such an approach fits easily into a 'quantificationist' approach to the problem, designing for crowd safety on the assumption that crowds consist simply of physical objects in motion ignores the specifically human aspects of crowd behaviour (see Sime 1985). On the other hand, psychological research on crowd behaviour typically makes only limited reference to the physical environment in which behaviour takes place. There are some signs of a move to integrate the two approaches, focusing both on the physical environment and the information people need to act appropriate-ly in a crowd (ISE 1991), and towards building use and safety performance criteria in risk assessment and safety auditing (BSI 1991, section 8).

It has been argued that the relation between architectural or engineering design, information, management and buildings in use is of paramount importance to crowd safety (Cox 1992, Sime 1991, 1992). The indication of a shift towards increased use of feedback from research of buildings in use to inform new building suggests a greater emphasis on an anticipatory *ex ante* approach to crowd safety management (for example, the title of BS5588 has recently been changed from 'Fire precautions in the design and construction of buildings' to 'Fire precautions in the design, construction and use of buildings'). Understanding the way in which people use and comprehend buildings is directly related to effective design for safety. For example efficient circulation, ease of wayfinding and the provision of facilities such as seating in stadia may well have significant effects on public-safety levels (Taylor 1990), and developing better understanding of such social effects is a major issue for architectural research and education.

6.4.5 BLOOD HAZARDS AND SHARPS INJURIES

In all cultures, blood has a special symbolic character and the institutional arrangements for handling it, and the associated risks, have attracted attention from major figures in social science. In the 1970s, an important debate took place between Titmuss (1971), who claimed that the adoption of a market system for securing blood supplies led to a level of contamination of blood products which would not be achieved under a system of voluntary unpaid blood donation (the traditional UK system), and Culyer (1977), who argued that a market system could bring more economic efficiency to blood banking (see also Arrow 1972). The debate remains important (see McLean & Poulton 1988), and since the 1970s has had an added dimension because of the risk of transmission of HIV (through contact with blood or with other bodily fluids) as well as that of hepatitis B.

This new development has brought new risks into blood transfusions (notably for haemophiliacs), and much of the contemporary risk-management debate centres on the use of serological testing for HIV antibodies. As intimated in Chapter 4, the question of where and when to test raises major ethical, legal and political issues, particularly as current testing methods cannot conclusively determine current HIV status and as UK insurance companies can require applicants for life cover to report the results and even the fact of HIV testing. The new HIV hazard has also generated a battery of legislation, regulations and codes of practice in the UK applying to the handling of blood and to the use and disposal of sharps. These measures include the *Control of substances hazardous to health regulations,* 1988 (HSE 1988); the removal of Crown immunity from NHS hospitals in 1990; and the 1990 Environmental Protection Act which includes legislation concerning the disposal of clinical waste.

'Sharps', objects such as needles that are capable of puncturing the skin, clearly pose a potential threat to those whose work involves intimate contact with individuals who may be HIV positive, as well as involving risks to patients from infected health professionals (UK Health Departments 1990, Kiyosawa *et al.* 1991, Centers for Disease Control 1991, Heptonstall 1991). Although the latter issue has now come into the public and legal arena, the sharps regulatory debate began with concern about risks to health-care workers, because most health-care workers who acquire HIV and hepatitis B at work from infected patients do so through sharps injuries. Though the risk of HIV transmission during a sharps incident is approximately 100 times smaller

than the risk of transmission of hepatitis B (HBV, 30%; HIV, 0.3%), the new virus has made a dramatic impact on risk management in this area (see also RCP 1992). No doubt this impact can be explained in part because HIV is clearly a much more serious infection than hepatitis B. But issues such as dread risk, uncertainty and levels of social trust, discussed in Chapter 5, may well also help to explain this outcome.

The emphasis of much of the regulatory development has been laid on specification of products, with the emergence of new technical devices such as self-resheathing needles and protective clothing designed to make it less likely that the wearer will puncture skin unintentionally, or expose existing punctures to body fluids. Other devices, such as puncture-resistant sharps-disposal containers, are designed to reduce the risks resulting from disposal of sharps.

However, many technical issues remain unresolved, for example over the issue of how long immunization takes to give adequate protection or the value of zidovudine (ezidothymidine azt) prophylaxis after inoculation accidents (see Centers for Disease Control 1990, Jeffries 1991, Anon 1990, Brown *et al.* 1991, de Wind 1991, Ree 1991, Rhame & Russell 1991). But even if there were no major uncertainties about such topics, difficult issues of risk management remain. One is the risk–benefit calculus involved in the use of self-resheathing needles or the extension of precautions such as protective clothing or immunization beyond surgical workers to other groups of workers like domestics or porters who may also be exposed to risk from sharps (see Waldron 1985), and weighing the extra cost of such measures against the reduced risks of infection which result. 'Cost' itself may be closely linked with institutional behaviour and design (particularly for liability regimes), for example, how insurance premiums for medical negligence and related matters are set and

177

how public authorities decide to behave in the face of claims for compensation from the victims of medical mistake in public hospitals.

Moreover, though many of the new regulations have the effect of greatly increasing the formality of procedures which in the past were frequently unwritten and customary, in many cases they depend for their effect on how individual health-care workers choose to behave, not just in compliance with newly recommended and more stringent routines for handling sharps, but also in their personal responsibility for selecting the level of care to be taken. For instance, individuals must choose the appropriate level of protective clothing to put on after assessing the potential risk of exposure to blood or body fluids. Leaving such matters up to individual choice may limit legal liability (which is likely to be a consideration of key importance in the face of increasing threats of litigation), and avoids well-known problems associated with 'over-inclusive' framing of regulations, but such individual responses 'on the ground' may vary for several reasons (such as levels of training or legal knowledge) which deserve to be investigated.

More specifically, much of the UK regulatory debate about HIV transmission in health care has been between those who favour a 'universal' one-size-fits-all set of precautions against transmission to be applied uniformly and indiscriminately to all patients, and those who favour a more differentiated approach of identifying those high-risk patients who should be surrounded by additional precautions. The former approach derives broadly from the 'Universal Precautions' recommended by the US Public Health Service, published by the Centers for Disease Control in Atlanta (Centers for Disease Control 1987) and adapted for the UK in what is known as 'Universal Infection Control Precautions' (Wilson & Breedon 1990). The more differentiated approach is taken by the UK Health De-

partments Expert Advisory Group on AIDS (UK Health Departments 1990) and the UK Advisory Committee on Dangerous Pathogens (Advisory Committee on Dangerous Pathogens 1990), who argue for localized risk assessment based on epidemiological information from local public health departments or from genito-urinary physicians. The quality of the information base is itself a subject of major debate, and any collection of data is inherently controversial. Even within hospitals, there is some evidence to suggest that many sharps injuries are not reported (Piper 1990), perhaps because those responsible for or suffering from such injuries fear that they may be blamed and even stigmatized as a result of making a report.

Though many technical issues remain unresolved in the area, many of the more perplexing issues relating to the regulation of blood relate to human responses and behaviour. Proper investigation of such behaviour in the handling of blood requires giving attention to such basic issues as levels of fear and trust between health-care workers and patients. It also raises issues associated with risk compensation and the effect of alternative legal and economic incentive structures. Under pressure from increasing litigiousness and from changing financial régimes for health care, the way in which legal, economic and socio-medical factors interact in dealing with blood as a hazardous substance are central to the understanding of medical risk management.

6.4.6 DECISION ADVICE AND GLOBAL WARMING

Global warming is a particularly difficult area of risk management because of the diversity of causes, the complexity of mechanisms, the uncertainties that surround the nature, scale and timing of possible outcomes, and the international dimensions of the problem. Many scientists take a holistic view which considers the problem as due to the operation of a single, highly complex, global-scale system, but the managerial response is often essentially 'local'.

Global warming, otherwise known as the greenhouse effect or the heat trap, is widely claimed to form a significant component of global environmental change and is a central element in contemporary discussions on sustainable development. It is a classic example of an 'elusive hazard' (Kates 1985): cumulative, diffuse, slow-acting and insidious. The product of the long-term interaction between socio-technical systems and the natural environmental systems, it is seen by some as a symptom of the culminating phase of the 'great climacteric' (Burton & Kates 1986); an age of multiple crises which began with the Industrial Revolution and has witnessed transformed interrelations between human society and the natural environment, resulting in a 'risk transition' (Smith 1988) characterized by the gradual reduction in significance of some localized hazards, and their replacement by a new series of regional and then universal threats. These new 'first order' threats represent the products of highly complex interactions working at varying temporal and spatial scales and are sometimes referred to as 'problematics', 'syndromes' or 'concatenations' (Clark 1986).

The decision advice problem turns on the perceived urgency for positive action which cannot be based on scientific certainty. The uncertainty does not arise because global warming is new, or because the processes are not understood, but because of the scale and complexity of the problem. Climate is the great integrator and therefore reflects a huge range of influences, both natural and human-induced, working at varying spatial and temporal scales. There is not one but several greenhouse gases, produced through a multitude of natural and human activities, which work, together with other factors such as cloud cover, dust load and land use, through a com-

plex system involving both positive and negative feedback mechanisms.

Thus predicting change at global, regional and local levels, together with effects on sea level and the biosphere, is problematical and highly contentious, because of the shortness of the scientific record and fundamental inadequacies of knowledge regarding system parameters (such as ocean–atmosphere coupling, carbon fluxes and stores). Little wonder that analogues, scenarios and predictions are all contested (Agarwal & Sunita 1991), for the phenomenon of global warming is only detected as trends in a very noisy sequence of climatic data which are themselves only poorly understood. Thus the relation between greenhouse gases and climatic parameters (temperature, rainfall, wind, etc.) remains unclear.

Global warming is clearly an area where change is or can be equated with threat. Doomsday scenarios have focused on catastrophic outcomes, including coastal inundation and the possible extinction of some island sites, increasing extremes of weather and climate, biospheric destruction, the wholesale collapse of socio-agricultural systems and the creation of huge displaced populations (environmental refugees). As a consequence, the main impetus to public policy has focused on combating global warming through control of greenhouse-gas emissions. However, global warming could have beneficial effects which could, in some areas, outweigh its costs. Thus responses that focus on social adjustment to global warming (rather than affecting the cause) may prove more acceptable in terms of politics and economics.

Debate over the inconclusiveness of existing scientific results for policy decisions in global warming goes back many years (Maddox 1987, 1992). There is strong disagreement about the nature and timing of strategic decisions about industry, agriculture and resource use. The costs of errors in policy decisions could be enormous. Moreover, the control of the likely causes of global warming may well affect the developing and developed countries differently. Issues of fairness between regions as well as between generations are therefore involved (Rees 1991).

Discussion of the handling of potential hazards of global warming thus constitutes an arena in which the 'anticipationist–resilienist' debate is particularly sharp. The conflict between these two viewpoints focuses on six main disagreements (Krause *et al.* 1990): the extent to which global warming is scientifically established; the costs of prevention compared with adaptation; the distribution of 'winners' and 'losers'; the likelihood of catastrophic outcomes; whether or not adequate scientific data could be produced in time to allow preventative global action; and whether improved modelling would enable winners and losers to be reliably identified for the purposes of policy formulation.

Anticipationists argue that although neither the fact nor the possible causes of global warming have been conclusively demonstrated, the potential effects of such a phenomenon are so substantial as to make urgent precautions essential. Furthermore, they hold, to delay any measures until the scientific evidence is clearer is not a tenable option. Policies must be implemented now to control possible causative agents, and decisions must be taken about matters such as the resiting of coastal conurbations, and the siting or resiting of hazardous-waste dumps to areas well above sea level. Resilienists, on the other hand, argue that public policy should not be based on disputed scientific evidence, and that social resources should not be concentrated on responding to hazards whose basic existence is in doubt, but should be invested in scientific research focused on reducing uncertainties. Anticipationists attack this 'wait and see' policy as ignoring the

costs involved in incurring risks, as reflecting vested interests in the *status quo* and unbridled optimism in the efficacy of technology. As such, the two groupings tend to conform to the distinction drawn by O'Riordan (1981) between ecocentrism and technocentrism. The groupings are well illustrated by the current debate regarding coastal defence strategies in the context of accelerated future rise in global sea-levels, which essentially involve four main scenarios: defend/protect, retreat, adjust, abandon (House of Commons Environment Committee 1992 xl-xliii).

The scientific uncertainties involved in global warming also raise debates between 'narrow' and 'broad participationist' positions and between 'outcome' and 'process specificationism' (in the terms of table 4). The broad participationist case is that the lack of reliable scientific predictions is a reason for opening up the decision advice process to the kind of 'extended peer community' which was discussed in section 6.3.2. The case for narrow participationism, on the other hand, is that not all the phenomena associated with global warming are inherently unpredictable and 'trans-scientific', and that the inclusion of lay stakeholders in decision advice procedures could only result in slower and even less reliable results.

Global warming also brings out a debate between quantificationists and qualitativists, along the lines that were discussed in section 6.3.2. Quantificationists look for ways to develop quantitative techniques for presenting and understanding uncertainties, transforming them into 'usable knowledge' of high quality. One such system, which is intended to enable the analysis and communication of several different kinds of uncertainty (technical, methodological, epistemological and ethical) as well as relating uncertainty to quality, is the NUSAP system (Funtowicz & Ravetz 1991, Costanza, Funtowicz & Ravetz 1992). Others argue that the inherent uncertainties involved make the area a poor site for the application of QRA techniques. Colglazier (1991) argues that the arguments produced by both governments and pressure groups related to the management of this kind of risk tend to rest more on a value-loaded assignment of burden-of-proof than on a balanced interpretation of the contested scientific evidence; in such circumstances, qualitativists would argue, there is a danger either of producing misleading policy advice or undermining confidence in QRA, or both.

Finally, the renewed claims of a need for stronger institutional controls at a global level as originally advocated by Bruntland (1987) come at a time when the credibility of interventionist strategies has crumbled, command economies have declined and disintegrated, and when increasing numbers of ethnic groups are demanding freedom to decide their own future. The conflicts between 'globalism' and 'parochialism' have yet to be resolved, as was clearly testified in the outcomes of the 1992 Earth Summit in Rio de Janeiro.

6.5 CONCLUSIONS

6.5.1 SUMMARY AND OVERVIEW

Without attempting to cover all aspects of the diffuse field of risk management, this chapter has exposed some of the components of institutional design in this area and argued that risk management cannot ordinarily be conceived as a single-seated goal-setting process. The chapter went on to review some of the dimensions of the contemporary risk-management debate and argued that much of the debate can be seen as a contrast between an orthodox 'homeostatic' approach to risk management and an alternative, less developed and still-emerging 'collibratory' view. In the last section, it briefly outlined some of the different settings in which these debates are played out in practice. All of those areas involve detailed technical debates. Yet in every case there are also significant underlying issues of bringing together natural science expertise and knowledge about human behaviour and the operation of human institutions. Issues of how to constitute decision advice procedures, both of an *ex ante* and *ex post* kind, how to allocate blame and liability, how to organize effective regulatory structures, how to bring together different kinds of expertise into an effective

policy debate, arise in different ways in all of these cases and go to the heart of the institutional aspects of risk management.

6.5.2 AREAS FOR FURTHER RESEARCH

An area characterized by debates as important as those sketched in section 6.3.3 ought to be a fertile area for crucial experimentation. Yet the research map of risk management is a bit like the population map of Australia, with almost everything clustered round the edges and hardly anything in the central conceptual areas. And the 'edges' themselves are more like an archipelago of scattered specialisms isolated from one another than a single land mass (the notion of an 'archipelago' comes from Hewitt (1983)). Too much of the institutionally- oriented work on risk management is heavily descriptive or driven by restricted consultancy concerns. And too much of it is still essentially mono-cultural in its approach, implicitly embodying a single-optimum approach to institutional design (see Adams & Thompson 1991).

There are, of course, important and distinguished exceptions to this general characterization. But what is needed more research concentration on the central institutional issues and the design issues surrounding them, in a way that builds some bridges between the different islands in the risk-management-research archipelago. More systematic and theoretically informed assessment needs to be made of claims and possibilities surrounding the institutional design issues in risk management that were described earlier. At least three concentrated areas of research seem to be called for.

First, the important insights of the cultural theory school need to be pursued systematically by a methodical investigation of the strengths and weaknesses of different types of organization in risk management. As it is, we still know very little about what kinds of organization take or avoid what kinds of risk, why, and with what effects. Much of the discussion of safety-related behaviour is either aggregated at society-wide level or at a generalized corporate level. More disaggregation of organizational types, and more systematic comparisons of their risk-related behaviour, might help to clarify the areas of debate between 'broad participationists' and 'narrow participationists' as discussed above, and perhaps also between the 'blamists' and the those favouring a less blame-oriented approach.

Second, more systematic studies are needed to assess the rival claims of the 'trade-offists' and the 'complementarists', (and indeed of the other rival doctrines discussed in section 6.3.2) by developing data bases large enough to permit conclusions to be drawn more confidently than can be done from limited case-study evidence. The relation between levels of risk and economic loss or gain needs to be explored carefully across a range of organizations and a range of performance levels.

Third, we have very little systematic information about cross-national and cross-organizational variations in risk management in the public and private sectors. Only on the basis of systematic comparative work can we properly assess the claims of the 'blamists' versus the 'absolutionists', for example in assessing the effects of different liability and regulatory design structures (such as assertions about the effects of information openness, regulatory conflict of interest and the social composition of key players in the performance of public regulatory agencies). As it is, we know very little of why regulatory authorities take the risks that they do and what risks they do take (for example, reflecting the degree to which the regulators are themselves directly at risk from the relevant hazard and whether regulatory bodies of different types show systematic preferences between Type I and Type II errors, as referred to in section 6.2.1); how risk-regulating authorities interact with their environment; how risk-regulating authorities get resourced and how their resource structures shape their actions. There is both a rich body of general theory in this area and plenty of empirical material to be worked on; but the detailed work still needs to be done.

The institutional landscape of risk management has changed in many respects since the last Royal Society report on risk assessment, and to some extent the conceptual landscape has changed too, as this chapter has tried to show. Were there to be another such report a decade or so hence, it would be nice to think that there would be substantial further research progress to report in this area, producing much greater elucidation of the operation of institutional factors in risk management. There is more than intellectual enlightenment at stake.

REFERENCES

Ackoff, R.L. 1974 *Redesigning the future: a systems approach to societal problems.* New York: Wiley.

Adams, J.G.U. 1985 *Risk and freedom.* Cardiff: Transport Publishing Projects.

Adams, J.G.U. 1988 Risk homeostasis and the purpose of safety regulation. *Ergonomics* **31**(4), 407–428.

Adams, J.G.U. & Thompson, M. 1991 *Risk review: perception, varieties of uncertainty, sources of information.* ESRC end of award report.

Advisory Committee on Dangerous Pathogens 1990 *HIV – the causative agent of AIDS and related conditions: second revision of guidelines.* ACDP.

Agarwal, A. & Sunita, N. 1991 *Global warming in an unequal world: a case of environmental colonialism.* New Delhi: Centre for Science and Environment.

Akerlof, G.A. 1970 The market for lemons: qualitative uncertainty and the market mechanism. *Quarterly Journal of Economics* **84**, 488–500.

Anonymous 1990 Public health service statement on management of occupational exposure to Human Immunodeficiency Virus, including considerations regarding zidovudine postexposure use. *Canadian Diseases Weekly Report* **16**, supplement 2, 4–13.

Arnell, N.W. 1984 Flood hazard management in the United States and the National Flood Insurance Program. *Geoforum* **15**, 525–542.

Arrow, K. 1963 Uncertainty and the welfare economics of medical care. *American Economic Review* **53**, 941–973.

Arrow, K. 1972 Gifts and exchanges. *Philosophy and Public Affairs* **1**, 343–362.

Asch, P., Levy D.T., Shea, D. & Bodenhorn, H. 1991 Risk compensation and the effectiveness of safety belt use laws – a case study of New Jersey. *Policy Sciences* **24**(2), 181–197.

Baldissera, A. 1987 Some organizational determinants of technological accidents. *Quaderni di Sociologia* **33**(8), 49–73.

Baram, M. 1988 *Corporate risk management: industrial responsibility for risk communication in the European Community and the United States.* Ispra: CEC Joint Research Centre.

Bardach, E. & Kagan, R.A. 1982 *Going by the book: the problem of regulatory unreasonableness.* Philadelphia: Temple University Press.

Beder, S. 1991 The fallible engineer. *New Scient.* 2 November: 38–42.

Benedick, R.E. 1991 *Ozone diplomacy.* Cambridge, Massachusetts: Harvard University Press.

Black, D. 1958 *The theory of committees and elections.* London: Cambridge University Press.

Brennan, G. 1991 Civil disaster management: an economist's view. *Canberra Bulletin of Public Administration* **64** (May 1991), 30–33.

Brogan, A.J. 1991 'Safety case and/or rules: substitute or complementary? A vision of the future offshore safety regime'. Det Norske Veritas Classification. (Unpublished.)

Brown, E.M., Caul, E.O., Roome, A.P., Glover, S.C., Reeves, D.S. & Harling, C.C. 1991 Zidovudine after occupational exposure to HIV (letter). *British Medical Journal* **303**(6808), 990.

Brown, P. 1987 Popular epidemiology: community response to toxic waste-induced disease in Woburn, Massachusetts. *Science, Technology and Human Values* **12**, 78–85.

Bruntland, G.H. 1987 *Our common future: World Commission on Environment and Development.* Oxford University Press.

Bryant, E.A. 1991 *Natural hazards.* Cambridge University Press.

BSI 1991 *Fire precautions in the design, construction and use of buildings. Part 10, code of practice for shopping complexes BS5588.* British Standards Institution.

Burns, A., McDermid, J. & Dobson, J. 1992 On the meaning of safety and security. *The Computer Journal* **35**(1), 3–15.

Burton, I., Kates, R.W., & White, G.F. 1968 *The human ecology of extreme geophysical events.* Natural hazard research working paper no. 1. University of Chicago Press.

Burton, I., Kates, R.W. & White, G.F. 1978 *The environment as hazard.* Oxford University Press.

Burton, I. & Kates, R.W. 1986 The great climacteric, 1748–2048: the transition to a just and sustainable human environment. In: *Themes from the work of Gilbert F. White* (R.W. Kates & J. Burton, eds), pp. 339–360. University of Chicago Press.

CBI 1990 *Developing a safety culture: business for safety.* London: Confederation of British Industry.

Centers for Disease Control 1987 Recommendations for prevention of HIV transmission in health care settings. *Morbidity and Mortality Weekly Report* **36** Supplement 2, 28.

Centers for Disease Control 1990 Public Health Service statement on management of occupational exposure to Human Immunodeficiency Virus, including considerations regarding zidovudine postexposure use. *Morbidity and Mortality Weekly Report* **39**.

Centers for Disease Control 1991 Update: transmission of HIV infection during invasive procedures. *Morbidity and Mortality Weekly Report.*

Chemical Industries Association 1987 *A guide to hazard and operability studies.* Industry Safety and Health Council of the Chemical Industries Association Ltd.

Clark, W.C. 1986 Sustainable development of the biosphere: themes for a research program. In: *Sustainable development of the biosphere* (W.C.Clark & R.E.Munn, eds). Cambridge University Press.

Colglazier, E.W. 1991 Scientific uncertainties, public policy and global warming: how sure is sure enough? *Policy Studies Journal* **19**(2), 61–73.

Collingridge, D. 1980 *The social control of technology.* Milton Keynes: Open University Press.

Comfort, L.K. 1988 *Managing disaster.* Durham: Duke University Press.

Costanza, R., Funtowicz, S.O. & Ravetz, J.R. 1992 Assessing and communicating data quality in policy-relevant research. *Environmental Management* **16**, 121–131.

Couch, S.R. & Kroll-Smith, J.S. 1985 The chronic-technical disaster: towards a social scientific perspective. *Social Science Quarterly* **66**, 564–575.

Cox, S.J. 1992 *Risk assessment toolkit*. Centre for Extension Studies, Loughborough University of Technology.

Culyer, A.J. 1977 Blood and altruism: an economic review. In: *Blood policy: issues and alternatives* (D.B Johnson, ed.), pp. 39–58. Washington D.C.: American Enterprise Institute for Public Policy Research.

Cuny, F.C. 1983 *Disasters and development*. Oxford University Press.

Department of Transport 1987 *mv Herald of Free Enterprise. Report of the court No.8074. Formal investigation (The Sheen Inquiry)*. London: HMSO.

Department of Transport 1989 *Investigation into the Clapham Junction railway accident (The Hidden Inquiry)*. London: HMSO.

Department of Transport 1990 *Report on the collision that occurred on March 4th 1989 at Purley in the Southern Region of British Railways*. London: HMSO.

Department of Transport 1991 *Report of the Chief Investigator of Marine Accidents into the collision between the passenger launch Marchioness and mv Bowbelle with loss of life on the Thames on 20 August 1989 (The MAIB report)*. London: HMSO.

De Wind, C.M. 1991 Zidovudine after occupational exposure to HIV. *British Medical Journal* **303**, 1404.

Douglas, M. 1985 *Risk acceptability according to the social sciences*. London: Routledge & Kegan Paul.

Douglas, M. 1987 *How institutions think*. London: Routledge.

Douglas, M. 1990 Risk as a forensic resource. *Daedalus* **119**(4), 1–16.

Drabek, T.E. 1986 *Human systems response to disaster: an inventory of sociological findings*. New York: Springer-Verlag.

Drogaris, G. 1991 *Major Accident Reporting System: lessons learned from accidents notified*. Community Documentation Centre on Industrial Risk.

Dunsire, A. 1978 *Control in a bureaucracy: the execution process*, vol. 2. Oxford: Martin Robertson.

Dunsire, A. 1986 A cybernetic view of guidance, control and evaluation in the public sector. In: *Guidance, control and evaluation in the public sector*. (F-X. Kaufman, G. Majone & V. Ostrom, eds). Berlin: de Gruyter.

Dunsire, A. 1990 Holistic governance. *Public Policy and Administration* **5**(1), 4–19.

Echevarria, J.A., Norton, K.A. & Norton, R.D. 1986 The socio-economic consequences of earthquake prediction: a case study in Peru. *Earthquake Prediction Research* **4**, 175–193.

1991 *The European environmental yearbook*. London: DocTer International.

Evans, A. 1992 'Public transport and road safety'. Inaugural lecture as London Transport Professor of Transport Safety, University College, London.

Evans, W.N. & Graham J.D. 1991 Risk reduction or risk compensation – the case of mandatory safety-belt use laws. *Journal of Risk and Uncertainty* **4**(1), 61–73.

Fennell, D. 1988 *Investigation into the King's Cross Underground fire*. London: HMSO.

Field, S. & Jorg, N. 1991 Corporate liability and manslaughter — should we be going Dutch? *Criminal Law Review* March, 156–171.

Fife, I. & Machin, E.A. 1990 *Health and safety.* London: Butterworths.

Fisse, B. & Braithwaite, J. 1988 Accountability and the control of corporate crime. In: *Understanding crime and criminal justice* (M. Findlay & R. Hogg, eds). Sydney: The Law Book Co. Ltd.

Foster, H.D. 1979 *Disaster Planning.* New York: Springer-Verlag.

Freudenberg, W.R. 1992 Nothing recedes like success? Risk analysis and the organizational amplification of risks. *Risk – Issues in Health and Safety.* Winter 1992. (In the press.)

Funtowicz, S.O. & Ravetz, J.R. 1991 A new scientific methodology for global environmental issues. In: *Ecological economics* (R. Costanza, ed). New York: Columbia University Press.

Funtowicz, S.O. & Ravetz, J.R. 1992*a* Global risk, uncertainty and ignorance. In: *Global environmental risk* (J.X. Kasperson & R.E. Kasperson). United Nations University.

Funtowicz, S.O. & Ravetz, J.R. 1992*b* *Uncertainty and quality in science for policy.* Dordrecht: Kluwer Academic Press.

Gorz, A. 1989 *Critique of economic reason* (tr. G. Handyside & C. Turner). London: Verso.

Gribbin, N. 1988 *The Hole in the sky.* London: Corgi.

Haigh, N. 1989 *EEC environmental policy and Britain* (second edition). London: Longman.

Haigh, N. & Baldock, D. 1989 *Environmental policy and 1992.* London: HMSO.

Halpern, J.J. 1989 Cognitive factors influencing decision making in a highly reliable organization. *Industrial Crisis Quarterly* **3**(2), 143–158.

Handmer, J.W. 1990 *Flood insurance and relief in the US and Britain. Natural hazard research working paper No.68.* University of Colorado.

Handmer, J. & Penning-Rowsell, E.C. (eds) 1990 *Hazards and the communication of risk.* Aldershot: Gower Technical Press.

Handmer, J. 1992 Hazard management in Britain: another disastrous decade? *Area* **24**(2), 113–122.

Harrison, M. 1992 *Engineering human error tolerant software.* Department of Computer Science, University of York.

Heptonstall, J. 1991 Outbreaks of hepatitis B virus infection associated with infected surgical staff. *Communicable Diseases Report* **1**(8), R81–R85.

Hewitt, K. 1983 The idea of calamity in a technocratic age. In: *Interpretations of calamity* (K. Hewitt, ed.), pp. 3–32. London: Allen & Unwin.

Horlick-Jones, T. 1990 *Acts of God? An investigation into disasters.* London: EPICENTRE.

Horlick-Jones, T. 1991 The nature of disasters. In: *Emergency planning in the 90s* (A.Z. Keller & H.C. Wilson, eds). British Library/Technical Communications.

Horlick-Jones, T. & Peters, G. 1990 Measuring disaster trends part one: some observations on the Bradford Fatality Scale. *Disaster Management* **3**(3), 144–148.

Horlick-Jones, T., Fortune, J. & Peters, G. 1991 Measuring disaster trends part two: statistics and underlying processes. *Disaster Management* **4**(1), 41–48.

House of Commons Environment Committee 1992 *Coastal Zone Protection and Planning*. HC 17-1 Session 1991–92. London: HMSO.

HSC 1991 *Health and Safety Commission. Plan of work for 1991/2 and beyond*. London: HMSO.

HSE 1988 *The control of substances hazardous to health regulations*. London: HMSO.

HSE 1989 *Risk criteria for land-use planning in the vicinity of major industrial hazards*. London: HMSO.

HSE 1990 *Human error in risk assessment*. AEA Safety and Reliability Directorate/HSE.

HSE 1991 'Guide to health, safety and welfare at pop concerts and other similar events. HSE and Home Office, draft document.

ISE 1991 *Appraisal of sports grounds*. London: Institution of Structural Engineers.

Janssen, W. & Tenkink, E. 1988 Risk homeostasis theory and its critics: time for an agreement. *Ergonomics* **31**(4), 429–434.

Jeffries, D.J. 1991 Zidovudine after occupational exposure to HIV. *British Medical Journal* **302**, 1349–1351.

Jones-Lee, M.W. 1990 The value of transport safety. *The Oxford Review of Economic Policy* **6**(2), 39–60.

Kates, R.W. 1978 *Risk assessment of environmental hazard*. New York: SCOPE report no.8.

Kates, R.W. 1985 Success, strain and surprise. *Issues in Science and Technology* **2**(1), 46–58.

Kates, R.W. & Burton, I. 1986 *Geography, resources and environment: volume 2. Themes from the work of Gilbert White*. University of Chicago Press.

Katzman, M.T. 1988 Pollution liability insurance and catastrophic environmental risk. *The Journal of Risk and Insurance* **55**, 75–100.

Keller, A.Z. *et al.* 1990 The Bradford Disaster Scale. *Disaster Management* **2**(4).

Kletz, T.A. 1986 *Hazop and Hazan notes on the identification and assessment of hazards*. London: Institution of Chemical Engineers.

Kirby, A.M. 1988 High level nuclear waste transportation: political implications of the weakest link in the nuclear fuel cycle. *Government and Policy; Environment and Planning C* 311–322.

Kiyosawa, K., Soideyama, T., Tanaka, E. *et al.* 1991 Hepatitis C in hospital employees with needlestick injuries. *Annals of Internal Medicine* **115**(5), 367–369.

Kloman, H.F. 1990 Risk management Agonistes. *Risk Analysis* **10**(2), 201–205.

Krause, F., Bach, W. & Koomey, J. 1990 *Energy policy in the greenhouse*. Earthscan.

Kunreuther, H. 1989 The role of actuaries and underwriters in insuring ambiguous risks. *Risk Analysis* **9**(3), 319–328.

Laporte, T. 1982 On the design and management of nearly error-free organizational control systems. In *Accident at Three Mile Island: the human dimensions* (D. Sills, ed). Boulder, Colorado: Westview Press.

Latour, B. 1987 *Science in action.* Milton Keynes: Open University Press.

Lave, L.B. & Malès, E.H. 1989 At risk: the framework for regulating toxic substances. *Environmental Science and Technology* **23**, 386–391.

Lomas, O. 1990 Environmental protection bill impact on the utilities. *Utilities Law Review*, Summer, 60–67.

Lowrence, W.W. 1976 *Of acceptable risk: science and the determination of public safety.* Los Altos: William Kaufman.

Mackenzie, D. 1990 *Inventing accuracy.* Cambridge Massachusettes: MIT Press.

Mackenzie, D. 1991 *Negotiating arithmetic, constructing proof: the sociology of mathematics and information technology.* Programme on Information and Communication Technologies, University of Edinburgh.

McLean, I. & Poulton, J. 1988 Good blood, bad blood and the market: the gift relationship revisited. *Journal of Public Policy* **6**, 431–445.

Maddox, J. 1987 Half-truths make sense (almost). *Nature, Lond.* **236**, 637.

Maddox, J. 1992 Dangers of disappointment at Rio. *Nature, Lond.* **357**, 265–266.

Majone, G. 1989 *Evidence, argument and persuasion in the policy process.* New Haven: Yale University Press.

March, J.G. & Olsen, J.P. 1989 *Rediscovering institutions: the organizational basis of politics.* New York: Free Press.

Mitchell, J.K. 1990 Human dimensions of environmental hazards. In *Nothing to fear* (A.Kirby, ed.). Tucson: University of Arizona Press.

Molina, M.J. & Rowland, F.S. 1974 Stratospheric sink for chlorofluoromethanes: chlorine atom-catalysed destruction of ozone. *Nature, Lond.* **249**, 207–210.

National Research Council 1983 *Risk assessment in the Federal Government: managing the process.* Washington D.C.: National Academy Press.

Neilsen, R. & Szyszczak, E. 1991 *The social dimension of the European Community.* Handelshjskolens Forlag.

New Zealand State Services Commission 1991 *Review of state sector reforms.* Wellington, New Zealand.

Neyman, J. & Pearson, E.S. 1967 On the use and interpretation of certain test criteria for purposes of statistical inference. In: *The joint statistical papers of J. Neyman & E.S. Pearson.* Cambridge University Press.

O'Riordan, T. 1971 *The New Zealand Earthquake and War Damage Commission.* Natural hazard research working paper no. 22. University of Colorado.

O'Riordan, T. 1981 *Environmentalism.* London: Pion.

Ostrom, E. 1986 A method of institutional analysis. In: (F.-X. Kaufman, G. Majone & V. Ostrom, eds), *Guidance, control and evaluation in the public sector, chapter 22.* Berlin: de Gruyter.

Parker, D.J. & Handmer, J. (eds) 1992 *Hazard management and emergency planning: perspectives on Britain.* London: James & James.

Penning-Rowsell, E.C. *et al.* 1978 *The effect of flood warnings on damage reduction.* Flood Hazard Research Centre, Middlesex Polytechnic.

Penning-Rowsell, E.C., Parker, D.J. & Harding, D.M. 1986 *Floods and drainage: British policies for hazard reduction, agricultural improvement and wetland conservation.* London: Allen & Unwin.

Perrow, C. 1984 *Normal accidents: living with high risk technology.* New York: Basic Books.

Pheasant, S. 1988 The Zeebrugge–Harrisburg syndrome. *New Scientist.*, 21 January.

Pidgeon, N.F. 1988 Risk assessment and accidents analysis. *Acta Psychologia* **68**, 355–368.

Piper, J. 1990 One third of needlesticks go unreported at hospital. *Hospital Infection Control*, August, 107.

Popplewell, O. 1986 *Committee of Inquiry into Safety and Control at Sportsgrounds. Final report.* London: HMSO.

Posner, R.A. 1986 *Economic analysis of law.* (3rd edition.) Boston: Little Brown.

Proulx, G. & Sime, J.D. 1991 To prevent 'Panic' in an underground emergency: why not tell people the truth?' In: *Fire safety science proceedings of the third international symposium.* (G. Cox & B. Langford, eds). Elsevier Applied Science.

Quarantelli, E.L., Dynes, R.R. & Wenger, D.E. 1986 *The Disaster Research Center: its history and activities,* Disaster Research Center miscellaneous report 35. Newark: University of Delaware.

Raiffa, H. 1968 *Decision analysis.* Reading, Massachusetts: Addison-Wesley.

Rayner, S. & Cantor, R. 1987 How fair is safe enough? The cultural approach to societal technology choice. *Risk Analysis* **7**(1), 39.

RCP 1992 *HIV infection: hazards of transmission to patients and health care workers during invasive procedures.* Report of a Working Group of the Royal College of Pathologists.

RCEP 1988 *Best practicable environmental option.* Royal Commission on Environmental Pollution, twelfth report. London: HMSO.

RCEP 1989 *The release of genetically engineered organisms to the environment.* Royal Commission on Environmental Pollution, thirteenth report. London: HMSO.

RCEP 1991 *GENHAZ. A system for the critical appraisal of proposals to release genetically modified organisms into the environment.* Royal Commission on Environmental Pollution, fourteenth report. London: HMSO.

Reason, J. 1990 *Human error.* New York: Cambridge University Press.

Ree, H. 1991 Zidovudine after exposure to HIV. (letter). *British Medical Journal* **303**, 783–784.

Rees, J.A. 1991 Equity and environmental policy. *Geography* **76**(4), 292–303.

Reinhardtrutland, A.H. 1991 Note on risk homeostasis and nighttime pedestrian casualties. *Perceptual and Motor Skills* **73**(1), 50.

Reuter, J. 1988 *The economic consequences of expanded corporate liability: an exploratory study.* Santa Monica: Rand.

Rhame, F.S. & Russell, A.L. 1991 Zidovudine after occupational exposure to the human immunodeficiency virus. *New England Journal of Medicine* **324**(4), 266–267.

Roan, S. 1989 *Ozone crisis: the 15-year evolution of a sudden global emergency.* London: Wiley and Son.

Roberts, K.H. 1989 New challenges in organizational research: high reliability organizations. *Industrial Crisis Quarterly* **3**(2), 111–125.

Roberts, K.H. & Gargano, G. 1989 Managing a high reliability organization: a case for interdependence. In: *Managing complexity in high technology organizations: systems and people.* New York: Oxford University Press.

Rochlin, G.I. 1989 Informal organizational networking as a crisis-avoidance strategy: US naval flight operations as a case study. *Industrial Crisis Quarterly* **3**(2), 159–176.

Schulmeyer, C.G. 1990 *Zero defect software.* New York: McGraw Hill.

Schwarz, M. & Thompson, M. 1990 *Divided we stand. Redefining politics, technology and social choice.* Hemel Hempsted: Harvester Wheatsheaf.

Shell International 1988 *Shell safety management program.* The Hague: Shell International.

Sime, J.D. 1985 Designing for people or ball-bearings. *Design Studies* **6**(3), 163–168.

Sime, J.D. 1990 The concept of panic. In: *Fires and human behaviour.* London: David Fulton.

Sime, J.D. 1991*a* Accidents and disasters: vulnerability in the built environment. *Safety Science* **14**(2), 109–124.

Sime, J.D. 1991*b* Crowd safety and disasters in complex settings. In: *The changing face of Europe: disasters, pollution and the environment,* Conference Proceedings (draft papers). University of Bradford Disaster Prevention and Limitation Unit.

Sime, J.D. 1992*a* Crowd safety design, communications and management: the psychology of escape behaviour. Paper presented to Lessons Learned from Crowd Related Disasters conference, Emergency Planning Centre (Home Office).

Sime, J.D. 1992*b* Crowd safety and security in complex building settings: environmental design and management. In: *Accountable public architecture: designing and managing public buildings* (M. Conan & C. Zimring, eds). Butterworth Architecture. (In the press.)

Smith, D. 1991 Beyond the boundary fence: decision-making and chemical hazards. In: *Energy, resources and the environment* (J. Blunden & A. Reddish, eds). London: Hodder & Stoughton.

Smith, K. 1988 *The risk transition.* Environment and Policy Institute working paper. Honolulu: East-West Centre.

Smith, K. 1992 *Environmental hazards.* London: Routledge.

Stigler, G. 1988 The theory of economic regulation. In: *Chicago Studies in Political Economy* (G. Stigler, ed.). Chicago University Press.

Susman, P., O'Keefe, P. & Wisner, B. 1983 Global disasters, a radical interpretation. In: *Interpretations of calamity* (K. Hewitt, ed.). London: Allen & Unwin.

Tait, E.J. & Levidov, L. 1992 Proactive and reactive approaches to risk regulation: the case of biotechnology. *Futures*, April, 219–231.

Taylor, P. 1990 *The Hillsborough Stadium disaster, 15 April 1989. Final report.* Inquiry by the Rt. Hon. Lord Justice Taylor. London: HMSO.

Titmuss, R.M. 1971 *The gift relationship: from human blood to social policy.* London: Allen & Unwin.

Toft, B. 1990 'The failure of hindsight'. Ph. D. thesis, University of Exeter, Department of Sociology.

Turner, B.A. 1978 *Man-made disasters.* London: Wykeham Press.

Turner, B.A. 1989 How can we design a safe organisation? Paper presented to The Second International Conference on Industrial and Organisational Crisis Management, New York.

Turner, B.A. 1991 The development of a safety culture. *Chemistry and Industry* April, 241–243.

Turner, B.A., Pidgeon, N.F., Blockley, D.I. & Toft, B. 1989 Safety culture: its importance in future risk management. Position paper for The Second World Bank Workshop on Safety Control and Risk Management, Karlstad, Sweden.

UK Health Departments 1990 *Guidance for clinical health care workers: protection against infection with HIV and hepatitis viruses: recommendations of the Expert Advisory Group on AIDS.* London: HMSO.

Waddell, E. 1983 Coping with frosts, governments and disaster experts: some reflections based on a New Guinea experience and perusal of the relevant literature. In: *Interpretations of Calamity* (K. Hewitt, ed.), pp. 33–43. London: Allen & Unwin.

Waldron, H.A. 1985 Needlestick injuries in hospital staff. *British Medical Journal* **290**, 1285.

Ward, S.C., Chapman, C.B. & Curtis, B. 1991 On the allocation of risk in construction projects. *International Journal of Project Management* **9**(3), 140–147.

Watson, S.R. 1981 On risks and acceptability. *Journal of the Society of Radiological Protection* **1**(4).

Weick, K. 1989 Mental models of high reliability systems. *Industrial Crisis Quarterly* **3**(2), 127–142.

Weinberg, A.M. 1972 Science and trans-science. *Minerva* **10**, 209–222.

Wells, C. 1988 The decline and rise of English murder: corporate crime and individual responsibility. *Criminal Law Review* December, 788–801.

Wells, C. 1991 Inquests, inquiries and indictments: the official reception of death by disaster. *Legal Studies* **11**(1), 71–84.

Wells, C. 1992a *Corporations and criminal responsibility.* Oxford University Press.

Wells, C. 1992b Disasters: the role of institutional responses in shaping public perceptions of death. In: *Death duties* (D. Morgan & R. Lee, eds). London: Routledge & Kegan Paul.

Wheeler, D. 1987 Water pollution and public health: a time to act. *Environmental Health* **94**(8), 201–203.

White, G.F. (ed.) 1974 *Natural hazards*. Oxford University Press.

Wichmann, B.A. 1992 A note on the use of floating point in critical systems. *The Computer Journal* **35**(1), 41–44.

Wijkman, A. & Timberlake, L. 1984 *Natural disasters: acts of God or acts of man?* London: Earthscan.

Wildavsky, A. 1985 *Trial without error: anticipation vs resilience as strategies for risk reduction*. Sydney, Centre for Independent Studies.

Wildavsky, A. 1988 *Searching for safety*. New Brunswick: Transaction Books.

Wilde, G.J.S. 1976 The risk compensation theory of accident causation and its practical consequences for accident prevention. Paper presented at the annual meeting of the Oesterreichische Gesellschaft fur Unfallchirugie, Salzburg.

Wilde, G.J.S. 1982 The theory of risk homeostasis: implications for safety and health. *Risk Analysis* **2**(4), 209–225.

Wilde, G.J.S. 1988 Risk homeostasis theory and traffic accidents: propositions, deductions and discussions of dissension in recent reactions. *Ergonomics* **31**(4), 441–468.

Wilpert, B. 1991 'System safety and safety culture'. Paper presented to the Joint IAEA/IIASA meeting The Influence of Organization and Management on the Safety of NPPs and other Industrial Systems.

Wilson, J.Q. (ed.) 1980 *The politics of regulation*. New York: Basic Books.

Wilson, J. & Breedon, P. 1990 Universal precautions. *Nursing Times* **86**(37), 67–70.

Wynne, B. 1992 Public understanding of science: new horizons or hall of mirrors? *Public Understanding of Science* **1**, 37–43.

Yalow, R.S. 1985 Radioactivity in the service of humanity. *Thought* (Fordham University quarterly) **60** no. 236, 517.

Zimmerman, R. 1990 *Governmental management of chemical risk*. Lewis Publishers Inc.

APPENDIX: COST AND BENEFITS OF RISK REDUCTION

by Alan Marin

1. THE NEED FOR VALUATION

In making decisions at a societal level about how safety standards should be set, a balance is required between the benefits of safety and the costs of achieving it. Obviously if a costless way of reducing risks is available it should be adopted. In general it will be possible to reduce risks further at some cost, but if the cost is immense and the benefit trivial, the extra reduction is not worthwhile. The optimum level of safety will be when risks have been reduced up to the point where the cost of any extra reduction just equals its benefits, but to go no further. In economists' terminology, risks should be reduced until the 'marginal cost equals the marginal benefit'.

The above principle would apply to all kinds of decision, whether those of government in its own projects (e.g. deciding which stretches of motorways should be lit) or in imposing safety standards on private bodies and individuals (e.g. standards for lorries transporting explosive and/or inflammable materials). It will nearly always be possible to take measures that would reduce risks further (e.g. lighting every rarely used country lane), but the costs would outweigh the expected benefits.

The desirability of equating marginal costs and benefits, rather than insisting on the lowest risk that is technically achievable, has long been recognized in UK approaches such as ALARP (that risks should be As Low As Reasonably Practicable). The phrase 'reasonably practicable' implies a balancing of costs and benefits. Similarly in pollution control, the UK now describes its aim as BAT-NEEC (Best Available Technology Not Entailing Excessive Costs).

Whether or not it is officially recognized in statements of policy aims, in practice no country is prepared to reduce its citizens' living standards to just above subsistence by taking away all their surplus income to spend it on improving health and safety. There is always a trade-off to be made.

Policy thus entails a kind of cost–benefit analysis of projects and standards. However, very often the cost–benefit is implicit, relying on the intuitive judgement of the regulators as to what safety standards are reasonable. So as to achieve consistency and also to make it possible to check back on past decisions and see if they were sensible, or if the procedures could be improved, it is desirable explicitly to quantify the costs and benefits as far as possible. Furthermore, the quantification should allow us to *compare* the costs and benefits, so that we can find the point at which the marginal benefits of further improvements in safety will be outweighed by their extra costs. To weigh costs and benefits explicitly requires measuring them in common units and, so far, the only common unit suggested has been monetary value.

It is clear that in the absence of explicit cost–benefit, different decisions have implied very different amounts spent to save life at the margin (Mooney 1977, Marin 1986). One implication is that shifting the spending on safety between different areas could lead to saving more lives for the same aggregate spending. This would be achieved by reducing the amount spent where the extra safety per pound sterling spent is currently low and shifting it to areas where it is high. The number of lives expected to be lost where spending has been reduced would be more than outweighed by the extra lives expected to be saved where spending has been increased.

If the total to be spent on reducing risks to life were fixed, then avoiding the sort of inefficiency outlined in the previous paragraph would simply require that at the margin, the same amount of money is spent per life saved in all projects affecting safety. This is the requirement for cost-effectiveness. For example, if in deciding on road building projects in the UK, a fixed budget were allocated to safety improvements, then cost-effectiveness would only need to consider the different ways of affecting safety within this programme and ensure that the combination of methods chosen saved the most lives. This choice would require technical expertise, but is no different in principle to any engineering or other choices made in deciding on least cost production.

However, if the total to be spent on safety is not fixed arbitrarily, but it is possible to switch spending between different aims, then it also becomes necessary to decide on the value of reducing risks. If this is not done, then the amount allocated to risk reduction as compared to the achievement of other aims will be wrong. Altering risk will imply that more lives are expected to be saved or lost, so putting a monetary value on reducing risk involves putting a monetary value on the saving of life.

There are often objections to 'putting a price on life', also sometimes expressed as 'life is priceless'. There are various interpretations of these objections (some are discussed in Marin 1983), which often seem to be based on the view that by putting a monetary value on something it is brought within the purview of the market and as a result people will no longer treat human life as something special (see Kelman 1981, for a discussion of similar views in a different context). Nevertheless it is clear that neither as a society nor as individuals do we treat life as priceless and having an infinite worth: even those who know that cars are more dangerous than public transport often still travel by car when it is cheaper or more convenient.

Because of the widespread feeling that 'putting a price on life' cheapens it in some underlying non-financial, but ethical, sense of value, and because some people find it distressing to think about distasteful decisions involving the choice of life or death, it is tempting to leave them to a 'priesthood' who will take them on our behalf. They will relieve the rest of us of the burden of thinking seriously about such choices. Similarly those who feel that the choices are too complicated ever to be based on explicit criteria tend to advocate leaving the decisions to those who we hope will be 'sensitive and humanitarian decision-makers who will face up to the full difficulty of life-and-death decisions' (Broome, 1985).

But leaving decisions to special groups does not solve the problem of how these special groups themselves should decide. As argued above, relying on their individual, unexplained, intuition is likely to result in an unsatisfactory allocation of resources to the saving of life and avoidance of injury. In the absence of any superior criterion to deal with these problems, putting a monetary value on risk reduction seems the best way currently available. As discussed in Jones-Lee (1989), the other possible approaches to explicit decision making on risk reduction have their own difficulties as bases for dealing with the question of how to set standards and allocate resources. Therefore it seems that even if many people would have no wish to be involved with the decisions, sensible decisions will involve monetary evaluations.

2. METHODS OF VALUING SAFETY

If explicit monetary valuations of the benefits of reduced risk are to be used in cost–benefit approaches to social decisions, a method of calculating the required numbers is necessary. Initially we consider valuation of mortality and shall then mention more briefly the risks of non-fatal injury or morbidity.

For some time the most commonly used basis of valuation was the 'human capital' or 'foregone earnings' approach. This approach considers a person's earnings and treats the present value of those earnings (i.e. the capital sum which invested at a reasonable rate of interest would produce that level of earnings annually) as the economic value of the person concerned. Thus the present value of earnings foregone due to premature death would be the cost of each death expected as a result of a higher level of risk. One implication is that there is a zero value of those who do not work; whether because of age, health, unemployment or because they do housework, and housework is mistakenly omitted from 'earnings'.

Some decision makers, in an apparent attempt to avoid this implication, added an arbitrary allowance for 'pain and suffering' to the cost calculated from foregone earnings (examples are given in Marin 1986).

The human capital approach, with its basis that risk is to be evaluated by treating people as equivalent to capital equipment, is not only morally repugnant to some, but is also at variance with the usual approach to cost–benefit studies.

For these, valuations are based on what the goods or services are worth to those affected directly or indirectly by the project (e.g. part of the benefit of an irrigation scheme is valued by how much people will pay for the extra crops produced). At first sight it might seem that the standard cost–benefit procedure would be inapplicable to projects and regulations affecting mortality: the equivalent question would seem to be how much those whose lives lost would pay to continue living, or equivalently how much compensation they would accept to allow their lives to be lost. The problem with using such questions is that it is likely that most people would pay all that they could raise to save their own or close relatives' lives, and that some would require infinite compensation for its loss. Even if some would accept very large but finite sums to leave to their heirs, even a single answer of 'infinity' would be enough to throw out a project involving extra fatalities, or to reject any loosening at all of any safety standards whatsoever.

However, in practice these questions are not the relevant ones for the assessment of changing risks. In most projects and safety decisions, at the time the decisions are made, it is not the case that we know which particular person will live or die as a result of any variation in the level of risk. Instead there are typically very many people who will each have a slightly higher or lower risk of dying. In this context the relevant question is how much people will pay for a very slight reduction in their chance of premature death or how much compensation they would require to accept slightly higher risk; when the probability of death is still very far below one.

For such changes in risk, honest answers of 'infinity' are virtually inconceivable. In the example above, people who know that there is a higher risk still do travel by car. Thus by concentrating on the total sum that all those who might be af-

fected would be willing to pay to reduce their risk, it is possible to value the benefit of a change in risk which only alters each individual's risk by a small amount. It is now widely accepted this is the correct way to value risks (for some objections see Broome 1978, and the articles in Part II of Jones-Lee, ed. 1982).

A useful way to summarize the value of risk for decisions, but one that can be misleading if used without thought, is to express it as the 'value of a statistical life' often shortened to 'value of life'. There are various routes to this summary value.

One route uses the theory of expected utility maximization, but given the problems with that theory (see, for example, Machina 1987) there is some attraction in the argument of Mishan (in Jones–Lee, ed. 1982) that answers to the right questions are directly usable in cost-benefit analyses without relying on the assertion that the hypothesis of expected utility maximization is either descriptively or prescriptively valid.

A simpler way is to note that if people will each pay an average of £n to reduce their probability of death by x^{-1} per year (where x^{-1} is very small), then a group of x such people would average one death less per year, so they would together be willing to pay £x. n to avoid one expected death. Hence £x. n is the 'value of a statistical life'. Although common, and a useful way to summarise different studies, as well as being a convenient form of the input into cost–benefit studies, the term 'value of life' in this context can be misleading. It does not require anybody to say that the value of their own life, or of any other particular person, is equal to a certain sum of money. It is simply the summation of many of the small sums of money to compensate for small increases in the probability of earlier death.

3. EMPIRICAL RESULTS

There are by now many studies using different procedures actually to estimate the compensation people want for small increases in risk or are prepared to pay for small reductions in risk. Useful recent summaries are Jones-Lee (1989) and Fisher *et al.* (1989). The most widely used procedures are either to ask questions about hypothetical choices or to look at situations where people can choose different levels of risk. Examples of the former are questions about the willingness to pay for travel or safer airlines. In the latter, the most analysed situation is the labour market, where different jobs have different risks. Although clearly many of the highest paid occupations have virtually no job associated risks, the hypothesis is that once the other factors governing earnings have been allowed for (e.g. educational requirements) then extra risk is associated with higher earnings. Statistical analysis supports this hypothesis, and allows the calculation of the increased earnings associated with a unit increase in risk.

Although there are major differences in the estimates from different studies, many of these are explicable. The results typically give values of statistical life much higher than given by the human capital calculations. For example in the UK, in 1990 earnings, the human capital approach would give about £235 000. The two most widely quoted UK studies are Marin & Psacharopoulos (1982) which used fatal accident rates at work across the whole range of occupations, and Jones-Lee *et al.* (1985) which used a questionnaire on willingness-to-pay for improved safety (among other questions). These two studies gave surprisingly similar results, given their completely different procedures. In 1990 earnings (incomes, rather than prices, should be used to update willingness-to-pay for risk studies) their values of statistical life would be about £3 million.

The two recent surveys mentioned give their own summaries. Fisher, *et al.* (1989) say: 'the most defensible empirical results indicate a range for the value-per-statistical-life estimates of $1.6 million to $8.5 million (in 1986 dollars)'. Following further discussion they add 'the lower bound estimate of $1.6 is unlikely to be higher than the true value for policy decisions'.

Jones-Lee (1989) finishes his survey chapter by focusing on a set of studies he argues are the '... more reliable estimates ... Focusing on these estimates, their mean and median are, respectively, £2 230 000 and £1 890 000' (in 1987 prices). 'Finally, if one is to attempt to identify a subset of the *most* reliable estimates, then ... the mean and median ... are respectively £2 830 000 and £2 470 000'. He continues 'it is very difficult to resist the conclusions that (a) the value of statistical life for more commonplace risks almost certainly exceeds £250 000, (b) it is highly probable that the value is at least £500 000. The last of these conclusions seems all the more persuasive when one bears in mind that the two most recent and comprehensive empirical estimates for the UK (namely those of Marin & Psacharopoulos 1982 and Jones-Lee *et al.* 1985) both produce estimates in the region of £1 900 000 in 1987 prices.'

Some wage-based studies published too recently to be included in these two surveys, and which used more sophisticated statistical techniques imply higher values (Siebert & Wei 1991, Garen 1988). Although estimates of the value of life of over £2 million may seem very high, it should be remembered that they come from estimates of willingness-to-pay for small changes in risk. The £2 million is perhaps more acceptable and more accurately stated, when expressed as saying, for example, that given current UK road-accident deaths (a risk of about 10^{-4} per annum for motorists), drivers would be prepared to pay £20 per year for a 10% reduction in their risk of a fatal accident.

4. OTHER ASPECTS OF VALUING CHANGES IN MORTALITY

A. TYPES OF DEATH

From formal studies and more casual evidence, it is clear that people view the chance of some sorts of death more seriously than others. For example, in the Jones-Lee *et al.* (1985) study, when respondents were given a choice of three possible causes of death and asked which they would most like to be reduced, 11% said motor accidents, 13% heart disease, and 76% cancer. Furthermore, the sums that those who gave priority to cancer risk were prepared to pay were much greater than the others were prepared to pay. The excess amount these people were prepared to pay to reduce the risk from cancer was even greater if compared to the overall value put on the risk of death from road accidents (mentioned above).

The higher value put on this risk may reflect the pain and suffering involved, even in non-fatal cases. Clearly valuation of risks should allow for both the pain and the aversion to particular forms of death, though currently evidence is sparse.

Other categories of fatality where it has been suggested that there is particular aversion, and therefore larger values should be placed on avoiding risk, would include cases where individuals cannot perceive the incident which triggers the death and therefore feel powerless to take avoiding action. Examples would include nuclear radiation and asbestos dust. This aspect may itself be part of the reason for the greater willingness to pay for cancer reduction. Consideration of differing apparent attitudes to public transport and car accidents has suggested that even where the cause is apparent, people are still more worried about potential causes of death where

they feel helpless to influence their own fate than about those where they feel (however illusory in reality) that they can do something themselves. (A brief discussion, and references, is in Slovic *et al.* 1984).

Insofar as the monetary values of risk reduction quoted above are based primarily on studies considering fatal accidents at work and for drivers, they would be very much a lower bound for risks involving these other factors.

B. VERY SMALL CHANGES IN RISK

Some regulators have worked on the assumption that there are levels of risk to each individual that are so small that they can be completely ignored (HSE 1988 proposed 10^{-6} per annum). This would imply that one can ignore any increases in risk from a particular project that still leave each individual affected by it below the threshold. Conversely it is not necessary to try to reduce risks any further once the effect on any individual is below the threshold. However, because very many people may be affected by any one source of risks, in aggregate there may still be an expectation that on average lives will be lost because of this source.

Actually, the basic premise is mistaken. Even though an individual's change in risk is tiny, it does not follow that the individual would not be prepared to pay a tiny sum to avoid it. However, if each individual is prepared to pay a very small amount to avoid such a risk then, if there are very many affected, a non-trivial amount would represent the aggregate willingness-to-pay (HSC 1988).

It can also be shown, using the theory of expected utility, that given the standard assumptions of the theory, the value of statistical life can be viewed as the limit derived from individual willingness-to-pay as the change in risk tends to zero.

Thus, even if each person's risk is already low, the benefit of further reductions in risk should still be valued in the same way as before and compared to the cost of achieving the further reduction. (For a summary of the objections to the notion of acceptably small risk more generally, see Slovic *et al.* 1984.)

C. VERY LARGE CHANGES IN RISK

In explaining the willingness-to-pay approach to the valuation of changes in risk, it was stressed that the approach is relevant to situations where the risk involved is well under certainty. There are reasons to expect that as the risk gets much larger, then the compensation an individual would require will grow more than proportionately (see Jones-Lee 1989). There is likely to be some limiting level of risk that is the maximum an individual would ever voluntarily accept under normal circumstances. Using expected utility theory it is possible to link this maximum risk to other features of individuals' behaviour and check for a plausible consistency between the monetary value of life and the maximum risk level in any set of decisions. At present there is probably not enough evidence to be categorical about suitable maximum risk levels.

For most policies this is not very important, but for a few areas further evidence would be desirable. An example is the question of exposing a few workers to relatively high levels of radiation in nuclear power stations, or many to low levels.

D. AGE

The figures given for the valuation of risk are mainly based on studies looking at adults – perhaps averaging mid-40s – and the valuations are suitable for risks likely to affect a fairly random sample of the population. As people get older, and there is an increase in their chances of mortality from causes other than the source of the risk being valued, the willingness-to-pay for this risk would be ex-

pected to decrease. There is some evidence to support this decline after middle-age. Thus if valuation is applied to decisions that will affect mainly the elderly, a somewhat lower value of statistical life would be appropriate.

E. PAYMENT FOR OTHERS

So far we have considered the willingness of people to pay for their own safety, or to accept compensation for an increase in their own risk. The estimates quoted above were for this. In addition, many people may be willing to pay for reductions in other people's risk. Evidence has primarily focused on willingness-to-pay for relatives' safety. Studies by Needleman (1976) and Jones-Lee *et al.* (1985) suggest about 25–50% should be added on to individuals' willingness-to-pay for reduction in their own risks, to allow for the amount others would be prepared to pay. One study, Viscusi *et al.* (1988), looked at non-fatal risks (illness from inhaling pesticides) and found that willingness-to-pay for reducing others' risks actually aggregated to more than own valuations. Essentially this is because of the many other people involved once general social risks are considered.

However, it is not clear that other people's willingness-to-pay for the reduction in risk should be fully added on the own willingness-to-pay (see Jones-Lee, 1992). It depends on motivation. For example, if the motivation is pure altruism in the special sense of one person reflecting what the other person would want for themselves, then the amount they would pay for the other's safety should not be included. It would be double counting to add this onto the person's own valuation. Adding-on also ignores the choice between spending money on another's safety and on other items that give them benefit. Conversely, if the motivation is because one relative or friend would miss the other's company in the event of death because of exposure to risk, then relatives' and friends' willingness-to-pay should be added on.

The issue is too new for evidence yet, but if nothing at all is added on to the value of statistical life derived from the payment for people's own reduction in risk, at the very least it strengthens the case for not using too low a valuation.

F. OTHER COSTS

There are extra costs to society in many cases, when higher risk leads to more deaths. For example, police and health services costs in road crashes involving fatalities. These should be added onto the value of statistical life derived from willingness-to-pay for risk changes. For example, in 1985 prices the Department of Transport estimated these costs as £1 470 per fatal road accident; equal to just under £2 000 in 1990 prices. To the extent that potential damage to property is not taken into account in people's willingness-to-pay to reduce risk, these should be added on also. For fatal road accidents these would add another £2 500. Both are very small as compared to the value of statistical life.

G. NON-FATAL RISK

Most of the empirical work has been on payment for changes in the probability of death. The data on non-fatal risks has not been good enough for separate inclusion in many of the wage-based studies. Furthermore, there is a range of disabilities and illnesses each of which is likely to be viewed differently. If, as is likely, non-fatal injuries in general are positively correlated across occupations and industries with fatalities, then estimates of willingness-to-pay calculated from the relation between variations in wages and variations in mortality rates will be picking up the premia for non-fatal accidents as well. Thus there should not be any extra added for the risk of non-fatal accidents in deciding on safety standards, and, strictly speaking, the estimates from such studies should only be used for decisions where the ratios of fatal to non-fatal risks are likely to be similar to those of work-related risks (e.g. in road safety).

The questionnaire-based studies are not subject to this limitation, as long as the questions are specific enough to ensure that respondents do not include non-fatal risks in the hypothetical situations about which they are being questioned.

Some US studies have used data on non-fatal injuries and illnesses either in addition to fatal accidents or on their own. An example of the former is Moore & Viscusi (1988) who found a willingness-to-pay which gave a value per statistical injury of $20,000–$30,000. This was in a study that had a value of statistical life of $6 million. Thus, from this study the value to be allowed for non-fatal injuries (which were severe enough to involve days off work) was less than 0.5% of the value per fatal injury. Other US studies have typically found similar orders of magnitude of 1% or less for non-fatal as compared to fatal injuries.

As with risks of death, the valuation of non-fatal risks should include the more direct resource costs due to an injury. For example in the UK, the Department of Transport estimated the resource costs of all road accidents resulting in serious non-fatal injuries as £5 570 in 1985 prices.

One UK questionnaire study which is at a preliminary stage is currently suggesting a value per statistical injury similar to the Moore & Viscusi figure quoted above.

5. CONCLUSIONS

Despite some of the remaining uncertainties indicated, it seems clear that it is possible to value the benefits of reductions in risk. The results are firmest for cases involving deaths from accidental injuries across a wide range of the population. In such cases there are strong reasons to suggest that a value of £200–£300 for each change in the risk of mortality of 1/10 000 would be a sensible minimum value. Expressing the same value in the conventional and more convenient way (although misleading if used carelessly), the value of statistical life to be used in the cost–benefit of risk changes would be £2–3 million.

REFERENCES

Broome, J. 1978 Trying to value a human life. *Journal of Public Economics*, **9**(1), 81–100; discussion in **12**(2), 1979, same journal.

Broome, J. 1985 The economic value of life. *Economica* **52**(207), 281–294.

Fisher, A., Chestnut, L.G. & Violette, D.M. 1989 The value of reducing risks of death: a note of new evidence. *Journal of Policy Analysis and Management* **8**(1), 88–100.

Garen, J. 1988 Compensating wage differentials and the endogeneity of job riskiness. *Review of Economics and Statistics* **70**(1), 9–16.

Health and Safety Executive 1988 *The tolerability of risks from nuclear power stations.* London: HMSO.

Health and Safety Commission 1988 *Comments received on the tolerability of risks from nuclear power stations.* London: HMSO.

Jones-Lee, M.W. (ed.) 1982 *The value of safety.* Amsterdam: North-Holland.

Jones-Lee, M.W. 1989 *The economics of safety and physical risk.* Oxford: Blackwell.

Jones-Lee, M.W. 1992 Paternalistic altruism and the value of statistical life. *Economic Journal* **102**(410), 80–90.

Jones-Lee, M.W., Hammerton, M. & Philips, P.R. 1985 The value of safety: results of a national survey. *Economic Journal* **95**(377), 49–72.

Kahneman, D., Slovic, P. & Tversky, A. 1982 *Judgement under uncertainty: heuristics and biases.* Cambridge University Press.

Kelman, S. 1981 *What price incentives?* Boston: Auburn House.

Machina, M.J. 1987 Choice under uncertainty: problems solved and unsolved. *Journal of economic Perspectives* **1**(1), 121–154.

Marin, A. 1983 Your money or your life, *The Three Banks Review* **138**, 20–37.

Marin, A. 1986 Evaluating the nation's risk assessors: nuclear power and the value of life. *Public Money* **6**(1), 41–45.

Marin, A. & Psacharopoulos, G. 1982 The reward for risk in the UK labor market: evidence from the UK and a reconciliation with other studies. *Journal of Political Economy* **90**(4), 827–853.

Mooney, G.M. 1977 *The value of human life.* London: Macmillan.

Moore, M.J. & Viscusi, W.K. 1988 The quantity-adjusted value of life. *Economic Inquiry* **XXVI**, 369–388.

Needleman, L. 1976 Valuing other people's lives. *Manchester School of Economics and Social Studies* **44**, 309–342.

Siebert, W.S. & Wei, X. 1991 'Testing wage differentials for job hazards in the UK with a simultaneous equation model' University of Birmingham, Department of Commerce. (Unpublished.)

Slovic, P. *et al.* 1984 Behavioral decision theory perspectives on risk and safety. In (K. Borcherding, ed.). *Research perspectives on decision making under uncertainty.* Amsterdam: North-Holland.

Viscusi, V.K., Magat, W.A. & Forrest, A. 1988 Altruistic and private valuations of risk reduction. *Journal of Policy Analysis and Management,* **7**(2), 227–245.